# *I* SURRENDER *All*

DAVE SPIERING

Quantum Discovery
A LITERARY AGENCY

I Surrender All

First Edition
Copyright © 2013 by Dave Spiering
ISBN 978-1622950584

Second edition
Copyright © 2023 Dave Spiering

ISBN
978-1-960197-75-7 (Paperback)
978-1-960197-76-4 (eBook)

# I
# SURRENDER
# All

# TABLE OF CONTENTS

Acknowledgments ......................................................................... vii

"What is Truth?" ............................................................................ 1
"Is the Bible Alone Truth?" ........................................................ 14
"Is Jesus the Only Way to God?" ............................................... 28
Christ or Caesar? ......................................................................... 42
Nothing is Worth Dying for ....................................................... 56
He Who Loves Family More than Me ......................................... 70
The Lust of the Flesh ................................................................... 83
Choked by Riches ........................................................................ 98
Ashamed before Men .................................................................. 111
Proxy Christianity ...................................................................... 125
Forsaking the Body .................................................................... 138
Seeking Peace ............................................................................ 152
God Owes Me.............................................................................. 164
I Did it My Way........................................................................... 176
God Will Make an Exception For Me .......................................... 189
Why Me? ..................................................................................... 201

# Acknowledgments

What value does each of us have as a person? Those who ever saw the 1946 movie "It's a Wonderful Life" would remember the observations of the angel Clarence. He pointed out to George, the main character, how each life touches and influences the lives of those around, some-times in critical ways, enabling others to do the great or meaningful deeds that they were able to accomplish. I can testify that in writing this book, I am a debtor to people like Lee Howard and Donna Lawrence, both of Lamar, who helped save me from my own atrocious penmanship.

But there are two others who must be remembered as well. Back in the 1990's there were two special girls in the Junior Church Class that I was leading. On several occasions, they accompanied Jack Stahl and myself to our nursing home services. Their favorite song was "I Surrender All." In their simple childhood devotion, they were doing just that. One of them, Amanda Wood, has since grown up to be a devoted servant of the Lord in our congregation at Milford. The other one, Rebecca Hazard, has gone on to meet the Lord. The Faith and zeal of these children proved to be an encouragement and inspiration to me.

We may never know this side of heaven whose life we will touch, or when. But even what might be called a small deed of faithfulness might be the spark triggering great things to happen in the cause of Jesus. As with the testimony of Abel, (Hebrews 11:4), it will speak long after our deaths. Rebecca still lives, both in her presence with Jesus and her witness while she was here. And I am a debtor to those like her and Amanda, in the original thought behind this book. My prayer is that it may lead you, the reader, as well, to follow in their zeal for service and walk of faith. None of us are in it alone, and each of us has our own legacy to fulfill. Who knows what lives you may touch in your faith for Jesus as well.

# I

# "WHAT IS TRUTH?"

*"Pilate said to him (Jesus), 'What is truth?'"*

—John 18:38

When I was ten years old and growing up in northeast Iowa, I attended a mainline denomination Protestant church most Sundays. I had never been baptized and was aware of it. Now, I was a questioning preteen who, at least on the verge of spiritual accountability, felt the need to be baptized. By then, I was definitely grappling with sin and a desire to please God. I also worried that if I died right then, I wasn't sure about going to heaven. Over the course of the next several weeks I discussed this with my preacher and other leaders in the church. During these talks, we examined both the mode of and reason for baptism. All of us basically agreed, or I was taught, that in the olden days, baptism was done by immersion. But that was then and this is now. In this modern and enlightened age, most denominations had improved on this system and believed that sprinkling was every bit as good as immersion. No modern church of that denomination, in America anyway, even had a functioning baptistery, and people would think it odd for me to go against church teachings. As a result of all this, a few weeks later, my parents sent me forward one Sunday morning, and I was baptized by sprinkling. I was now considered a Christian in the eyes of all those involved.

1

I was too young to know about all the historical debates over the issue of sprinkling versus immersion. The mode and the purpose of baptism had been exhaustively argued over the centuries and so had the standards of who would or would not benefit from it. All I knew, though, was that I had a spiritual need in my heart. I had no clue what "modernism" was. It was beyond me that old standards of belief in right and wrong were now being abandoned in an almost universal quest by spiritual leaders for relativity, relevancy, and rationalism. This new reality, accepted by so many theologians, was something beyond my young brain. I only knew one thing: the sprinkling of water on my head in the name of the Father, Son, and Holy Spirit had failed to bring the peace for which I was seeking, so I kept on searching.

Over the next few years, I got my first real taste of what relativism, relevancy, and rationalism were all about. It was in 1965 that the "Now" Generation, or the Baby Boomers, stormed onto the scene. I was twelve, in junior high school, and experiencing a taste of freedom that comes with maturity. The "Now" Generation began to reject the very pinions of social order, as personal integrity, sexual morality, and Christian values, and were replacing it with what appeared to be chaos. These cataclysmic changes threatened the accepted institutions of American society and challenged, my personal mental picture of what our country was supposed to stand for. It now became all too clear to me that liberty and responsibility had to go hand in hand. In a positive way, this forced me to broaden my intellectual horizons to try to understand this new way of thinking. Intellectual honesty became critical in my way of thinking.

I was also now aware of the American Civil Liberties Union (ACLU) and the Earl Warren (Supreme) Court. Things seemed to be adrift, both in the streets and in the legal chambers. I was becoming aware of not just the premise that all truth is relative but in how this affected society. I began to seek answers and search for intellectual integrity, or honesty. This quest lasted years. The initial part, seeking peace with God, alone took nearly a decade. During this time, I questioned all absolutes as well, and thought through what the absence of them meant to both the individual person and the world. What soon became clear was the existence of a universal law of reason, or a basic intellectual integrity, and a designed order to all things. This led me to see several absolutes as foundational to both my spiritual and intellectual needs. I came to believe that deep down, the majority of people in our world were also seeking the same answers in their quest for meaning in life. I was also deeply troubled in wondering if the Church was ready or capable to answer them. However, I did find some comfort in a study of ancient history.

Seeking truth did not begin in our modernist age. Its origin was when Adam, or Eve, asked directly either God or Satan about it. The quest came in many different ways, as is seen later, when Pontius Pilate asked it of the one who claimed to be truth. He wasn't interested in a theological or philosophical argument or in the meaning of life. He was very honestly and pragmatically wondering at that moment if truth really did exist, or at least in Palestine. The Jews, at that time, angrily demanded the crucifixion of their own promised king and, in doing so, even allied themselves with archenemy Rome. All of this would probably lead any sane observer to question truth as well. The questioning of God, or for a god, that began with Adam didn't end with Pilate either. The quest for truth, to a large degree, reflects on our human condition, and a look at world beliefs shows this. Solomon said as much in this generic statement a millennia before the birth of Christ: "That which has been is that which will be, and that which has been done is that which will be done; and there is nothing new under the sun." (Ecclesiastes 1:9). Even in Solomon's day, philosophers and teachers probed for reality. Some, like the proponents of New Age rationalistic supposition, argued over whether truth can even exist outside of our five senses or personal experiences.

In the fifth-century BC, Protagoras (481-411) a Greek philosopher proposed that no absolute truth could be found, at least outside of man.[1] All reality was to be measured or seen only through our senses. As such, he ruled out any revelation of supernatural knowledge. This belief system is called "materialism", which states that physical things alone, without spiritual interference, determine the existence and interaction of all things physical.

Gautama (563-483 BC), the Great Buddha, also emphasized that true knowledge came through inner focus and from experience. One sect of Buddhism, the Zen, believes, "You find truth only in your experience, not in thinking about it (too much) or listening to someone talk about his

[1]   Paul Herrick, "Is Truth Relative." Seattle Critical Review, http://wwwseattlecritivalreview. com/Volume2,/truthrelative.html (accessed August 20, 2012).

experience." Such truth doesn't even include someone else's experience or writings, "Life was also meant to be lived, and not wasted trying to think up theories about it."[2] This belief system is called Existentialism.

Reasoning, or living, by experience alone can create a lot of difficulties in life. For the purist, one of them is placing any faith in observations made by other reasonably intelligent people. This viewpoint makes it impossible to accept any historic, scientific, or other observations without being intellectually dishonest. To honestly follow any such belief, they would have to test for themselves every experiment, technological advance, or business theory before they could trust or apply them. Even without copyright issues, they would ultimately have to recreate the universe if they take their belief to its logical conclusion. Maybe that's why they're told not to think too much. But in so doing, existentialists "cop out", or accept blindly, such knowledge and commit intellectual dishonesty. To do otherwise would render them unable to run water from a faucet until they had proven the existence of water and taken it every step from ocean, to rain, to reservoir, to water tower, to faucet, and then do this every time they wanted a drink. After all, reality might have changed in the meantime.

This also brings up a problem when there are conflicting observations. These can play havoc with the existential mindset. Since no one is capable of observing, processing, and remembering everything from every direction, personal perspectives will vary. A good analogy is in the story of the blind men and the elephant. Four blind men were given an opportunity to tell what they believed an elephant was like. For the one holding its tail, the elephant was a rope. Another, holding a leg, believed it to be a tree. The trunk reminded the third of a snake. Feeling an ear or tusk only provides more conflicting data. Throw in a little ego and stubborn zeal and a full-fledged religious war can result.

Basing truth on observation alone, combined with a refusal to acknowledge certain sources of reality, will skew the outcome and cripple us both intellectually and spiritually. Most modem existentialists do accept the observations of others, but maintain a total rejection of a supernatural realm. This is intellectual dishonesty. Oddly, though, this is what many call rationalism. Truth or reality is what they say it is. And included in this

---

[2]     Floyd H. Ross, and Tynette Hills, *The Great Religions By Which Men Live*, (Fawcett Pub., 1956).

is their presupposition of no spiritual accountability. In their minds, either there is no spirit world, or if it does exist, it poses little threat or benefit, and its influence is severely limited. Most humanists would argue, since no one's ever scientifically observed a soul leaving a body, it either doesn't exist or has limited importance. What is lost in this argument is intellectual integrity. Also, the influence of a whole realm of reality is denied out of existence. A genuine knowledge of truth can't happen if key ingredients are excluded from one's thought process.

In all fairness, there are some existentialists and humanists who do accept, and even embrace the spirit world. The (English) Royal Academy of Science has confirmed the existence of the supernatural realm. But these people's views rarely line up with the Biblical models as most of their documented spiritual encounters are with demons. These spirits are not God's friends, and their goal is to lead people away from God. But most humanists find this acceptable as they don't really like His standards either, and have an appreciation for these demonic alternatives. Once again, reality and truth are skewed by a denial or suppression of reality.

How this applies in our society can be observed in many ways. One is in our modern history books. Most of today's American texts focus on current social issues, such as women's rights, the environment, gay rights, etc. People from the past who were advocates for these issues are thought about as being heroes, while their opponents are painted with the brush of bigotry. Religious and moral areas are either ignored or mocked. Allusions to our founders as being primarily Christian have been rewritten. Alexis de Tocqueville's 1830's observations of ours being a Christian nation of property owners have been covered over by most of our intellectual elite, as is almost all of our religious past. If truth is what they say it is, so is history. If history doesn't suit the modern mind, it is rewritten until it does. And since our past provided the launching pad for America's greatness in the world, this helps explain the existential left wing's hatred of it and apologies for it.

To them, individual initiative, liberty, religious values, and moral absolutes all carry a modern stigma of "hypocrisy." American "Exceptionalism", that is, our preeminence among nations, has become a burden and something President Barack Obama has often apologized for. Granted, not everything in our nation's past is good, the mistreatment of non-Whites is a prime example, but by denying the existence of certain truths to the debate over what is good makes everyone a loser.

A belief system based only on what one chooses to observe, or feel could exist, is illogical. For example, no one has ever seen a purple unicorn, but to say such an animal could not be, based solely on observation alone, is ludicrous. In 1491, the same claim of logic denied that the earth was round, to most people, anyway. Any existence of a new world was viewed on the same level of acceptable truth as that of fairy tales. If the government of Spain had taken a vote of all the scholars in the country, or if they had a Supreme Court that ruled any official government policy acknowledging the possibility of a new route to Asia as unconstitutional, Columbus would never have sailed in 1492.

Yet this is just the standard of reality, or truth, used today from the courts to the schoolroom to the media. Simply because something has not been postulated, demonstrated, or observed, does not mean it cannot exist. It also shows that the enlightened modernist has the same heart and prejudice as his fifteenth-century counterparts. Ignorance and bigotry are not positions, they are attitudes. Also, cause and effect are universal to all. As the intentionally ignorant stood in the way of progress then, so they are also doing today, only their costumes have changed.

Self-imposed ignorance in observation can lead to some very illogical and unscientific conclusions. For example, in past years, and especially before embalming, it was quite common to bury someone who was not dead.[3] A person could be declared dead only to revive after burial. The internal claw marks in the coffins of a number of exhumed remains confirm this reality. In such a case of pre-death burial, it is only logical for the living among the dead to cry out for help. From beneath the ground these cries would be muffled and be realistically undistinguishable. A passerby hearing these cries would have the knowledge that dead people don't moan and groan or scratch in the ground. Since, by their logic, it couldn't be a living person, it must be a ghost or demon making that noise, or maybe it is an ancestor displeased with his descendants and in need of appeasement or food. How much ancestor worship or cemeteries being labeled as haunted has resulted because no one thought about exhuming a recent burial to see if that person was still alive? So today, many scientific

[3]    Barbara Mikkelson, "Snopes.com." Last modifies 2006. Accessed July 11, 2011.

observations are skewed, and some scientific truth can't even be explained because of a denial of God.

There is also a problem in going by "observation alone," as seen in the theory of relativity. Albert Einstein (1879-1955) established that observation of any event would be affected by one's location. A ball dropped on a moving train has but one trajectory. To the one dropping it, that is straight down, but an observer on a platform by the train will see it fall at an angle. Someone on another train, depending on direction and speed will see some-thing quite different.

Another example is the position "up", the point directly above a person or zenith. Two people in two different places on our planet will have very different views of what "up" points to. But, while observations vary, the same laws of physics apply.

This gets more complicated. As our earth spins on its axis, it revolves around the sun. The sun also rotates in the Milky Way galaxy, which, in turn, is itself moving in relation to an ever-changing universe. Theoretically, there may also be other masses the size of our known universe. Our observation of even what is directly above us in space now will never, by us anyway, be seen in exactly the same way again. All of creation around us is in a constant flux of change. The ancient Greek Heracleitus (540-480 BC) argued, "You cannot step twice in the same (exact) river, for the waters are ever flowing on you."[4] In reality, even the laws of gravity, motion, speed and direction of light, as well as other absolutes of physics are subject to altering and warping based on our location in the fabric of space. Yet our bodies are designed to live only with these laws as we know them.

When God is left out of the equation, man tries to grapple with this concept in his own way. Protagoras comforted himself with the belief, "Man is the measure of all things" at least in things pertaining to himself.[5] He didn't claim to know whether or not any gods existed. It fell to man to adapt and make his own destiny. Others struggle with the very concept of reality itself. The Buddhist believes that except for man, there are no absolutes.[6] This dovetails into man, above all, taking this one step further. As the universe is but a fleeting illusion, only man, who thinks, can lay

---

[4]    Will Durant, Thee Life of Greece, (New York City: Simon And Schuster, 1939), 145.
[5]    Ibid,362.
[6]    Illustrated Book Of All Religions, (Star Publishing Co.: 1895), 88.

claim to real existence. Rene Descartes (1596-1650), added to the debate, "I think, therefore I am."[7] He saw the human mind as above and separate from natural function. He did, though, acknowledge the superiority of the human mind in any quest for truth. We are reasoning, rational beings. What reason should show us, he believed, is that we are mere observers in a process that began long before our birth, and will continue long after our departure. He did, however, acknowledge the reality of something greater than us is at work. At some point, there had to be a cause or an origin. The often postulated big bang, which would have violated almost every law of physics known to man, requires more faith than belief in a god (God). Mankind has a place in this great existence and a purpose. "He (God) has made everything appropriate in its time. He has also set eternity into their heart, yet so that man will not find out the work which God has done from the beginning even to the end" (Ecclesiastes 3:11). In reality; we really have only clues, all pointing toward a Creator.

It would be something comparable to a sheltered Iowa farmer whose knowledge of the oceans was limited to only knowing that they exist. He gets a chance to visit one for the first time and begins observing it. Watching the tide rising, he calculates that at its present rate the highest mountains on earth will be covered in eight months. He makes an emergency phone call to his family back home and tells them to empty the savings account and buy the biggest ship they can find. When he returns to the beach a few hours later, the tide is going out. Again he calculates and concludes that the oceans will all dry up within ten months. He calls his family again and says sell the farm and invest in water. This is similar to observations the modernist has made regarding our world over the last few centuries, global warming, or climate change, comes to mind. In the 1970's, the world seemed headed into an ice age. Now, we are told, the world will perish in a man-made oven. If, and how much, man has affected the climate is subject to question, but we definitely must have a bigger picture before can we draw any real conclusions, and we need them from sources other than ones that have proven themselves to be intellectually dishonest.

Our world, and indeed the universe we live in, is undergoing constant change. The Psalmist saw this. "Even they (the heavens) will perish but

[7]    Colin Brown, Philosophy and the Christian Faith, (Downers Grove, IL: InterVarsity Press, 1969), 51.

Thou doest endure. And all of them will wear out like a garment... But Thou art the same, and Thy years will not come to an end" (Psalms 102:26, 27). Does this mean the universe is but a fleeting illusion, as many claim? Since man claims to be the measure of all things, let's make a comparison. People change, depending on the station of life they are in. If a person is observed at different ages, does this make them any more or less a person? Or are they more or less real? Does death erase the fact that they once lived? Even as their dimensions, organs, or thought patterns change, personhood does not, nor do the basic rules of their survival change. They also remain the same. The same is true with the universe. All is still real, even if our observations differ totally from those at another time or place. Our observations do not determine reality. And, indeed, if man is the measure of all things, who was it who created this "measure" and for what purpose? There is a God, an absolute reality, and a truth that exists around us, whether we recognize it or not.

This brings up another question. Based upon our changing cosmos, is this truth subjective, self-created, or is it objective in reality and beyond the control of anything in creation? When is truth relative, and when is it fixed? Some truth is definitely subjective, and economics is a perfect example of how subjective truth works. From 1634 to 1637 "Tulip-mania" swept the Netherlands. Over this period, speculation and greed bid up the price of tulip bulbs to as much as [inflation adjusted] twenty thousand dollars each.[8] Subjective truth created this value, or bubble, in direct contradiction to underlying market forces. This was much like the subprime mortgage bubble of our day. A subjective anticipation of gain often drives market and economic activity, such as what is fashionable and what is not, and whether it is a time of prosperity or a recession. In general, when people feel the economy is doing well, it will do well; if they do not, it won't. That is why consumer confidence is watched so closely.

Economics is also a perfect example of how objective truth works. Value is determined by supply and demand. These fixed rules set the underlying market fundamentals. Scarcity or abundance, purpose and need all play out in the market place. This exposes one of the dangers of our monetary policy: Our money is "fiat" or "let it find its own value by decree" money. It is not tied to gold, but its value is determined by

---

8    "Facts And Fallacies." "Readers Digest," 1988, 38-40.

how much of it there is in relation to demand for it. If a government puts its money printing presses into overdrive, creating a vast volume of this medium of exchange, as money is called, supply exceeds demand. Unless it does this in one of those rare moments when people are stuffing their mattresses with it, inflation will happen, regardless of the state of the economy. Certain governmental policies, or the lack of them, will directly influence the economy. In being governed by definite economic laws, as well as by speculation, both subjective and objective truth play their parts.

When it comes to morality, most Americans believe truth is subjective and relative with observations or situations determining their perspective of reality and of life choices. The result is to detach truth from any superior being or intelligence. This is like little children making up the rules of the game as they go along to assure they will win. It is also like trying to run a factory without an outside source of electricity, where the workers are told to pedal exercise bikes and generate their own. The whole operation will fail on its own merits. There is no credible source to sustain it.

Also, regardless of whether truth is viewed as factual, fixed, subjective, or as an absolute, it arises from an intelligent mind. "The Lord possessed me (created wisdom) at the beginning of His way, before His works of old" (Proverbs 8:22). Again, in Proverbs 3:19, God "by wisdom founded the earth; by understanding He established the heavens." Both knowledge and wisdom are created, the product of an intelligent mind. People can create knowledge artificially but only because of their intelligent minds, which were created by *the* intelligent mind. Any standards or values man has can only reflect on the absolutes as given by God or the lies of a lesser source. In addition, truth is truth whether we recognize it or not. Remember Columbus?

Granted, the farther down the scale that the origin of truth or knowledge goes, the less encompassing it is. God's truth is universal; it applies to all times, all places, and all circumstances. Man's truth, as in governments, an economy, or a factory, generally applies only to those within it. In a global economy or culture, there will be some overlap. Misuse of financial policy, or a wrongful valuation of a commodity in one nation, to a certain degree, affects others. A look at the recent Greek financial crisis shows how roughly eleven million people have crashed the world's financial markets, beginning in 2010. On the other hand, it may only affect a few. Any artificial intelligence or truth created by two teenage girls on cell phones will usually only affect them. Also, what one individual sees as beauty in the opposite sex, or what is truth to them, rarely affects more than a relatively small number of people. A totally subjective truth in our minds, like daydreaming, usually only affects us personally.

Not all of inner truth is subjective, though. Lao-tse (570-490 BC), the central figure of Daoism (Taoism) caught a glimpse of this. One of his teachings was, "The closer to its source, the clearer is the stream". Within our deep nature he saw that inside us is a source of peace, light, and truth. The Apostle Paul pointed to this concept in Romans 2:15, "In that they show the work of the law written in their hearts…" This is a reality that, for years I myself was not willing to see, though, looking back on myself at age ten, this is exactly what was stirring inside me. I had to overcome my own prejudices and presuppositions against subjective, or inner truth to see this. God created us with an innate knowledge of right and wrong, or an inner light.

God showed me this through my involvement with the Right to Life movement. Over the years, I've had opportunities to talk to well over a thousand children. Of them, only one preteen favored abortion. This compares with, depending on the poll, slightly over half of all adults claiming to be prolife. In this boy's case, his mother, having gone through at least one in her past, affected his perspective. This is, by no means, the only moral issue in which there appeared to be an innate inner-light. But it only makes sense, as we were created in God's image (Genesis 1:26), and Jesus said of the little children, "For the kingdom of God belongs to such as these" (Luke 18:16). It is when we stop listening to this light that we get into trouble. "And I was once alive apart from the law; but when the commandment came, sin came alive and I died" (Romans 7:9). Our problem is, we all sin and lose this light.

Why is it then that all of us try to hide from or explain away truth? Almost always, this is a matter of the will. While sometimes we just don't see it, usually we are not comfortable with the truth. The ancient Greek philosopher Plato (424-348 BC) sheds some light on this. He is known for, among other things, his allegory of the cave, or "Shadow Science." He envisioned all people as being bound in an allegorical cave facing away from the door. They are limited to seeing only shadows of the real world passing by on the outside of this door. Plato asked the question as to what would happen if these people somehow were freed from their chains. Nearing the door, they would be struck by the light. As their eyes adjusted, the objects that they once saw only in shadow form would become visible. These images would be greatly discomforting, leading many to return to the comforts and ignorance of their chains.

This analogy applies to all forms of truth, including that of physical form and substance, natural law, factual understanding, moral, and spiritual truth. The real world Plato speaks of included them all. Truth stands on its own merits; it is not limited to one source, by our ability to observe it, nor by our unwillingness to do so. Gravity existed long before Sir Isaac Newton (1642-1727) was bopped by an apple, and it would continue to exist even if the Supreme Court were to rule it unconstitutional. The world was round long before Columbus and other explorers proved it was. Eratosthenes (276-194 BC) even calculated its circumference to within two hundred miles. No flat-earth society will ever be able to deny it into flatness.

The existence of truth and the acceptance of it, however, are two different matters. There is a story of a man who was on an emergency room gurney. As an intern came up to him, the man said, "I am dead!" The intern tried every argument until he finally showed the man that a (dead) cadaver didn't bleed when it was cut, while a live person did. Then the intern cut the man's finger and blood began to flow. The amazed man responded, "This is remarkable, dead men do too bleed!" John said it well, "In Him was life and the life was the light of men. And the light shines in the darkness and the darkness did not comprehend it" (John 1:4, 5). But the world loves its cave. In 3:19, John adds, "The light has come into the world, and men loved the darkness rather than the light for their deeds were evil." Those of the world, the existentialist, humanist, and atheist, all love their cave, and many of these work hard to deny, suppress, or contradict any truth that exposes them for what they are.

The sad reality is that we, in the Church, are all too often just as guilty. We may claim to be of the truth, but time after time, we let the wisdom of the world determine our directions. Whether or not our deeds are evil, we fear the world and don't want confrontation. Also, very often we're not really quite sure what we ourselves believe. The Church fears man, and evidently, has lost its godly fear of the Lord.

"The fear of the Lord is the beginning of knowledge" (Proverbs 1:7). Too often, our fear of the world leads us to seek a different kind of wisdom, one of compromise or a more palatable belief system and a less abrasive truth. "But the Spirit explicitly says that in latter times some will fall away from the faith paying attention to deceitful spirits and doctrines of demons" (I Timothy 4:1). While this might make life easier here, it does us no good. It also provides a poor witness to the world. Do we honestly believe we can have it both ways, the world and the kingdom of God? "He who is not with Me is against Me, and he who does not gather with Me scatters" (Matthew 12:30). It is impossible to build a better tomorrow either for us, or for the lost, if we are not willing to work for it.

Repentance requires a heartfelt examination of where we are and where we need to be. It also calls us to not just look at our sin, but act upon it. "For if anyone is a hearer of the word and not a doer, he is like a man who looks at his natural face in a mirror; for once he has looked at himself and goes away he has immediately forgotten what kind of person he was" (James 1:23,24). God calls us to be doers. This is especially important as we confront the attacks of the world.

There are few in the Church who have not faced at least some of the arguments of the world. Relativism is a big destroyer that has found its way in and leads us to accept what is false. It may be simply because it appeals to our desire to please the flesh. Others accept it out of surrender, as they are made to feel it is them against everyone else. Timidity, or spiritual cowardice, may be our weakness; we don't want to antagonize anyone by taking an unpopular stand. On rare occasions, it is ignorance. But God provides us all the tools we need to be over-comers. The knowledge is out there, and prayerfully, this will provide some of that needed equipping. What is essential is our love for and commitment to the truth.

In my own quest, or spiritual pursuit, I did find the fulfillment I was seeking. On July 21, 1971, I was baptized into Christ and accepted Him as truth. But that didn't mean all trials and challenges were behind me. The world challenges all of us. The question is, will we stand up for Jesus and meet that challenge?

# II

# "IS THE BIBLE ALONE TRUTH?"

*"Sanctify them in the truth; Thy word is truth."*

—John 17:17

There are really multiple questions asked here in the guise of one. The first one is assumed. Is the Bible, in its entirety, really truth? This question leads to another one. Is there some sort of standard to determine if it is true? After all, just because someone claims something does not necessarily make it so. If it was, and the promises of every commercial were true, we would all be at our ideal weight, without wrinkles, and with a full head of non-gray hair. We would all be rich, drive the best cars on the planet, have trophy wives or showcase husbands, and so it goes. Also, there would be peace and a perfect economy; we all would live in harmony with no crime. But claims alone cannot establish legitimacy.

Evidence is essential to back up any claim. One line of reasoning is in what we can know about God by nature. "For since the creation of the world His invisible attributes, His eternal power and divine nature, have been clearly seen, being understood through what has been made, so that they are without excuse" (Romans 1:20). Psalms 19:1 adds, "The heavens are telling the glory of God: and their expanse is declaring the work of His hands." So much evidence points to a designer that even the atheist and humanist find it impossible to deny it all. One example is found in ordinary water, or H2O. Similar, but heavier, molecules show how freaky water is, with its unique hydrogen bonds. Carbon dioxide or CO2, for example, melts at -109 degrees F and boils at -70 degrees F. Ammonia NH3, about the same weight as water, melts at -108 degrees F, and boils at -70 degrees F. Realistically, water should melt and boil at similar temperatures, well below 0 degrees. But then, its universal solvency (so many things dissolve in it), and abundance, which make it so beneficial to life, would be unavailable to support it. There is no other natural molecule that could take its place.

One of the arguments that the materialist, one who leaves God or spiritual interaction out of the picture, or evolutionist, uses to meet this is, in essence, a statement of blind faith. Water, exists simply because it exists, and no explanation is needed. This sounds a little like the beliefs of Zen Buddhism. Using the same logic, someone could look at the Eiffel Tower and say it exists simply because it is, and no causator or explanation is necessary. This is very close to the incredulous claim that all reality itself is merely a mirage or it only becomes real when man wants there to be reality; but let's get real, if we really had the power to will things into or out of existence then why do we have the angst we now suffer with? Pardon the double talk on reality, but this concept of reality is presently accepted by millions of our fellow earthlings.

In 1994, while in Springfield, Missouri, I happened to be stopped at a red light behind a vehicle with an interesting bumper sticker. It read *question reality*, and the driver looked about college age. My first urge was to pull around and get in front of them when the light turned green, and hit my brakes. When they proceeded to go around me I would then yell out my window, "I'm not real!" Wisely, I resisted the temptation. It is amazing, though, how many of those who argue, "There is no reality," when it suits their purpose, will so quickly react and call the police or sue any "non-reality" when they cause them pain. Their actions are just another facet of intellectual dishonesty. This, alone, makes it very hard to even respect, much less accept their beliefs.

## Origins

Since it is only logical to assume there is a created order, the question becomes one of origin. Did God, or some intelligent forces create it or could everything arise from a natural process? The sixth-century-BC Greek Anaximander (611-547 BC) explained the cosmos along materialistic or evolutionary lines. In a primordial ooze, various forms developed into primitive organisms. Fish, animals, and even man evolved from these simpler forms. He did ascribe all things to a living eternal causator who was impersonal (detached from us), and without moral values. His was among the few materialistic creation accounts.

Other Greek accounts of our origins attribute it to deities of a more personable nature. The Greeks were not alone in contemplating our origins or looking to a creator. Across the globe, from Indonesia to America, from Africa to Asia, multiple creation accounts abound. Virtually all before 800 BC acknowledge a creator. While not all of these creators were kindly disposed to the human race, all were intelligent and powerful. Creation itself begs for an intelligent master designer just as the existence of a motor does to an inventor or builder.

Intelligent human minds recognize this as well; with these diverse creation accounts from other religions acknowledging just such a creator or grand architect. Since the ancients were closer to the source of creation, they would have had more evidence. The modem religion-philosophies of Atheism, Humanism, and Existentialism (or sects of them) still have an abundance, though, even without what was invariably lost over time. It wasn't until long after, as seen in religions such as Buddhism, that the focus of creation began to be altered to circumvent this. As earlier argued, modern existentialism, traces its roots back to Buddhism, and to a lesser degree Hinduism. Buddhism was an exception to the recognition that most ancients had of a god. In fact, oddly enough, Gautama, while affirming the devil and his daughters, since these tested him in his time of searching, never really acknowledged God or a god outside of man. He taught that the ultimate goal of man was to meritoriously attain his way to Nirvana. Since there was no god (God) to arrange salvation, man was his own god and had to work out his own salvation. He didn't attempt to explain beginnings or any origin of the laws by which man could be saved; these were not important. What is, is because it is, and this was all-important. All that matters is the here and now and the direction that one is going. The universe is in a constant state of life and death, decay and rebirth. Physical laws, the natures of elements, life, all are just there just because they are (like the Eiffel Tower?).

Ultimately, it takes more faith or blind faith, to believe in an origin without a cause or a creator than to accept any claim of the Bible. As mentioned before, a big bang, which scientists can't duplicate, would have defied physics. Since many scientists reject the Biblical account on the same principle, that it too, defied physics, this exposes another intellectual dishonesty on their part. They accept one in blind faith while rejecting another by labeling it as blind faith. But assume, for the sake of argument, somehow a big bang did happen as they claim. The gradual coalescence of matter would have to overcome such physical laws as Roche's Limit, where smaller objects arc fragmented by larger ones, and kinetics, where objects tend to fragment each other on collision. Assuming enough time passed for stars to form before their internal fires, and the resulting pressures, spewed their masses away, there is still a problem with biogenesis or the origin of life.

## Science

Amino acids, which are the building blocks of proteins, and thus, life, are molecularly polar. This helps them to suspend so well in water, which itself is molecularly polar and ionic. In natural formation, there is generally about a 50/50 breakdown between "left" and "right" handed ones. These can also form chains in nature, without the benefit of a living organism creating them, but in order for these chains to function, there must be functional compatibility. All chains of most of our proteins are made up entirely of left-handed amino acids. Any insert into a chain of an opposite poled amino acid would break the chain as far as function-ability is concerned. Genetic material, or DNA, is made up exclusively of right-handed amino acids. If any of those in a chain are wrongly poled, as a left-handed one in the right-handed chain, the protein can't function. This gets into a discussion of chirality, and how two molecules, identical except for polarity, are actually opposites. Another problem is with the twenty-two amino acids that are in the peptides (proteins) themselves. Certain alignments are essential for function and compatibility with other protein chains. For even the beginning stage of life to be possible, the odds are incredibly remote that this could happen by chance. One optimistic estimate put this at one in ten to the 518th power, or one followed by 518 zeros.

Let's try putting this in perspective. Assume that each atom in our universe of, by one estimate, ten to the eighty-sixth power atoms were to some how transform into its own universe, and every one of those atoms were some-how formed into amino acids. If all of this whole mass existed for a google of years, one followed by one hundred zeroes, the odds are still a better of an earth-star collision on any given day than of biogenesis by chance. This doesn't begin to address the odds against a genetic progression of life according to any evolutionary model or the advent of man. A good book on Creationism would greatly expand this point, and there are many on the market. Just a sampling would include *Darwin's Black Box*, 1998 by Michael J. Behe, *Darwin On Trial, 1993*, by Phillip E. Johnson, and *The Natural Sciences Know Nothing Of Evolution*, 1981 by A. E. Wilder-Smith.

There probably would not be an issue with creation if it weren't for an attitude of willful ignorance. There is a definite hatred of God and His moral truths by those who don't want to be judged by it. They realize they are under His wrath and prefer denial rather than change. They want to stay in their "caves" and rationalize away the existence of a doorway out. They seem to be trying for a head start on those hiding under the rocks and mountains to escape judgment (Revelation 6:16). "For the wrath of God is revealed from Heaven against all ungodliness and unrighteousness of men, who suppress the truth in unrighteousness" (Romans 1:18). And again in, (Romans 1:21, 22) "For even though they knew God, they did not honor Him as God Professing to be wise, they became fools."

Paul used the term "suppress the truth" for a reason. If the atheist and existentialist were dealing with the issue of "origins" with intellectual integrity, honesty, and in a fair and forthright manner, their position would at least merit respect. Granted, there are a few who do disbelieve in all sincerity. But all too many have willfully suppressed evidence, even attempting to destroy it. One example is from Texas. Along the Biloxi River near the hamlet of Grandville, is a rock outcropping. This outcropping had committed an unpardonable sin, it mingled Cretaceous era footprints, claimed to be in excess of sixty-five million years old, with twelve large human ones. One archeologist, Carl Baugh went so far as to remove a limestone ledge and reveal even more, dispelling any possibility of a hoax. On August 12, 1989, Dr. Don Patton presented photographic and other evidence to a creation conference in Dayton, Ohio. Within forty-eight hours, the best of the human-like footprints had mysteriously been destroyed. Other desecrations have since followed. Now, the best evidence is gone.

Meanwhile, at the Bernifal Cave near Les Eyzies, France, more evidence of a confluence of humans with dinosaurs has also been suppressed. According to Jack Cuozzo, *Buried Alive* 1998, carvings of dinosaurs commingle with those of mammoth and other mammal species. Around the world, such evidence abounds, but the so-called scientific community meets it with an almost universal rejection. Even world leaders are hard-pressed to acknowledge it. Look at what happened to 2012 presidential primary candidate Rick Perry when he dared to even mention Creationism as a possible alternate theory to evolution. In the seventeenth-century it was Pope Urban VIII who suppressed Galileo Galilei (1564-1642) when his views challenged the status quo. This only shows that while the prevailing religion, or perspective, of man might change, the heart does not. Jesus said, "Seeing they may not see, and hearing they may not understand" (Luke 8:10).

## Language

Language is one of those critical leaps that separate humans from the rest of the animal kingdom. This is not an attempt to address those claiming that animals have their own simple, or even complex, language, but there are well over six thousand different human languages in thirteen basic language families. If evolution was true, the more developed a culture or nation is, the more advanced or complex the language should be. The more simple a people, the less sophisticated should be their syntax, or structure, and the more Creole-like their language should be. In the real world, just the opposite is true. This patterns more of what would be expected if language had an original divine origin, and the advance of society combined with the commingling with others eroded the structure of language. "Therefore its name was called Babel because there the Lord confused the language of the whole earth; and from there the Lord scattered them abroad over the face of the whole earth" (Genesis 11:9). If God created the major language families, logically the 6,909 (by one count) languages, plus others that died out, would, over the last five to six millennia, have diverged from them.

The scientific community has, as a whole, rejected this Scripture as it has continued to lob attacks at other Biblical claims as well. They have also been joined by many a college archeological and history department in our modern age. Noah and his ark have been deluged with challenges. One of the most outspoken assaults is over the volume of water, or lack of it, on planet earth to sustain this flood. Challenges have also been made to Genesis 7:11, "All the fountains of the great deep burst open."

Interestingly enough, the pro-evolution science magazine *Discover*, October 1994, refuted both of these arguments. As the issue reported, there is, locked under central Europe, the Andes, and New England, enough water to more than double the volume of our present day oceans. Also, from time to time, this trapped water finds a way to vent to the surface.

Both science and history notables have attacked the Bible in regards to leprosy as well. They especially take issue with the sanctions in Leviticus 13. The Bible treats leprosy as if it was a highly contagious disease. Since modern leprosy is not virulent, the modernist assumes that it never was. Biblical sanctions, therefore, were unnecessary at best and genuinely quite cruel in the cost to family and relationships. Once again, the same issue of *Discover*, as well as multiple other sources, has come to the rescue. They now acknowledge an extremely aggressive form of the disease swept much of the known world between 600 BC and AD 600. It is also now assumed it was more virulent as well in the millennium before, in Moses's day.

## Archeology

Archeology has provided a great deal of evidence for the trustworthiness of the Bible as truth. It has been fascinating over the years to see just how many attacks on Biblical reliability the archeologist's shovels have dismissed. One huge one was the existence of Assyria. Then, in 1842, French archeologist Paul Emile Botta unearthed the remains of Nineveh. There has also been the discovery of Solomon's stables (II Chronicles 1:14), ivory from Ahab's house in Samaria (I Kings 22:39), and proof of both David's and Solomon's wealth. This is but the tip of the iceberg. It is now confirmed that Quirinius was governor over Syria at the time of the census tax (Luke 2:1), and Gallio was proconsul of Corinth (Acts 18:12) and Achaia. These and other so-called errors were long used to "discredit" the Bible.

But this evidence has not even phased skeptic attacks on the literal account of Adam and Eve, the flood, all the miracles, or a host of other Biblical claims. The miracles at the exodus are all explained away as natural events that just happened by chance when they did. But because Noah's Ark has not been found, or the location of the Garden of Eden hasn't been identified, does not mean these didn't exist. Whether every event in Exodus is proven to be an actual, bona fide miracle, or if in some cases, natural phenomenon that God timed to show His glory is immaterial. The fact that He caused them and communicated to Moses before they happened, and they were used to deliver His people, is proof enough. Whether or not Pharaoh's chariots are ever found at the bottom of the sea does not disprove Biblical claims. If Amelia Earhart's (1897-1937) plane is never found does that mean she never flew it? To an honest mind, any verdict must be based on all the evidence that is available. Hiding behind the little that has not been proven or disproven in the light of overwhelming evidence can't rightly be called rationalism. It is intellectual dishonesty, at best and smacks of a prejudicial bias.

The very Scriptures themselves have been attacked regarding their authenticity, authorship, and integrity. The most famous of these may well be *The Composition Of The Hexateuch*, 1876 by Julius Wellhausen (1844-1918). He asserted that writing did not come into existence in the ancient world until after Solomon's kingdom, (967-927 BC). In his documentary hypothesis, as he sets forth in his book, he claims that all knowledge at that time was in the form of oral tradition; the Israelites handed it down and enlarged upon it. Then, after Solomon and over almost the next millennia, a composition of unknown authors gradually edited and expanded it into the form of our Old Testament. Deuteronomy, he claimed, wasn't written in 1410 BC, it was largely compiled in the days of Josiah, about 621 BC. This was how Wellhausen interpreted II Chronicles 34:14 and the discovery of the missing book of the Law. He asserted, the Old Testament, minus a few church additions, was finally put in its present form at the Council of Jamnea, AD 90 (between AD 70 and AD 135).

While several of his premises were already seriously undermined, 1947 was a very bad year for his theory. A young Arab shepherd found a cave at Qumran where books of the Old Testament, some dating back at least two centuries before Christ, were stored. His theory of a steady revision of texts was critically damaged. Later evidence would further debunk it, such as the discovery of the Lachish letters dating to Jeremiah's day.

Since his time, it has been well documented that writing existed long before Abraham, and his 1876 BC call from Haran (Genesis 12:1). This definitely proves the ability of Moses to have written Genesis, Exodus, and Leviticus while at Mount Sinai, (1446-1445 BC). Later he would write Numbers and almost all of Deuteronomy, possibly by the hand of Eleazar. Through an abundance of evidence, from the documented temporary repentance of Nineveh to the proof of Shishak, Pharaoh of Egypt, who stole Solomon's wealth from his son, the writing of the Bible has been confirmed. The only real controversy is in the hearts of those who refuse to believe the evidence.

The Bible in its entirety is God's truth given to us. "All Scripture is inspired by God and is profitable for teaching, for reproof, for correction, for training in righteousness," (II Timothy 3:16). There is yet one more line of evidence, which will be looked at in greater detail in the next chapter. This is the resurrection of Jesus Christ. It is foundational to all we hold dear, as I Corinthians 15 shows. Verse 32 says, "If the dead are not raised, let us eat and drink, for tomorrow we die," and again, in verse 17, it says, "And if Christ has not been raised, your faith is worthless; you are still in your sins." If indeed He was raised, He is Lord, and since He affirmed that the Old Testament was Scripture, this makes it so.

## The Bible as Science

The Bible is true, but is there other truth outside the Bible? There have been those over the years who have felt that it's the ultimate source of even scientific truth. When George Washington Carver (1864-1943) went into his laboratory, he took one, and only one, book: his Bible. Some regard him as the father of synthetics. Whether or not he was, in his time at the Tuskegee Institute, he discovered over three hundred uses for just the peanut alone.

There is, indeed, much science in the Bible. *Isostasy* is a geology term that explains how mountains can "float" above the earth's crust. They have low-density roots, a fact not known until recently unless one reads the Bible. "He puts his hand on the flint; He overturns mountains at their base (roots)" (Job 28:9). The laws of thermodynamics find themselves referenced in the Bible, too. "That the creation itself also will be set free from its slavery to corruption into the freedom of the glory of the children of God" (Romans 8:21).

The social sciences can also find their origins in the Bible. Psychiatry is a Biblical concept. "A plan in the heart of man is like deep water, but a man of understanding draws it out" (Proverbs 20:5). Education, sociology, childrearing, and a host of other social fields are addressed in the Bible. The Bible is the foundation of all truth. But there is truth outside the Bible, too, as even the Bible bares witness to.

"And there are also many other things which Jesus did, which if they were written in detail, I suppose that even the world itself would not contain all the books which were written" (John 21:25). We don't have all of Peter's, Paul's, or John's sermons, or any other apostle's. Elijah, Elisha, Samuel, and others who were inspired of God left behind few recorded messages. Even the Apocrypha, or Pseudepigrapha, contains inspired truth. If this were not so, Jude 14 wouldn't have been quoted from one of those books: the Book of Enoch.

None of this inspired truth made it into our Bibles, though, but God did provide us with all we need. "But these things have been written that you may believe that Jesus is the Christ, the Son of God, and that believing you may have life in His name" (John 20:31). Jesus, and later, His apostles, accepted the Old Testament as inspired. II Timothy 3:15 says, "The sacred writings which are able to give you the wisdom that leads to salvation through faith which is in Christ Jesus." There's much evidence supporting early acceptance of inspiration for the twenty-seven New Testament books we possess today. This likely was by AD 130, as findings from Damascus, Antioch of Syria, and other archeological cites reveal.

## All Truth

The issue has been raised, mostly by those outside of the Church, that some inspired books were lost. The purported Gospel of Thomas is one of them. All the standards of evidence shows it was not inspired, nor was it even authentic, but there's a list of other alleged lost books as well. In the New Testament, these include a third letter to the Corinthians (I Corinthians 5:9), and the book to the Laodiceans (Colossians 4:16). Not only are both of these easily explained, as the letter from Laodicea was probably the book of Ephesians, there is also no other evidence of their existence. All the evidence from Rome or by our early Church fathers argues against any books having been lost. Regardless of this possibility, God gave us what we need to provide for our salvation and a foundation for all truth.

The Bible is foundational, but God has revealed truth outside of His Word. God told Adam and Eve to find it out and to use it. "And God blessed them, and God said to them, 'Be fruitful and multiply, and fill the earth and subdue it; and rule over the fish of the sea and over the birds of the sky'" (Genesis 1:28). God didn't put every equation or theorem in the Bible, He left it to us to do the math. He provided for us a vast amount of knowledge and truth for us to discover. "The writing of many books is endless, and excessive devotion to books wearying to the body" (Ecclesiastes 12:12). The sheer weight of available knowledge in any given field is so great that no one person can know it all.

The world is quick to focus on this indisputable reality: that no one can possibly know everything. Even the Hindu creation account recognizes this. The "Great One", or pure Braham, the invisible essence from which all things come into existence, is beyond comprehension. The earth is the universal mother of all creatures, having spiritual and creative powers as well as those of the natural order, again beyond our ability to fully understand. Truth is, by any measure, beyond our ability to fathom it all.

The world argues, based on this reality, that since no one can know all of what even can be known, every person's perspective is just as real, valid, or true as anyone else's. The Christian has no corner on truth. Other religions are just as good. If God is so great that neither the Jew, or Christian, or Hindu, or anyone else can adequately represent or fathom Him, why would He limit Himself to one people in one corner of the planet? Since God is so great, and as Christians say, loves us, why wouldn't He reveal truth to everyone? Why would He only speak His truth through the Bible alone?

While other beliefs on salvation will be taken up later, this is a point well taken. And in many ways, the Church has failed terribly in even presenting the truth that God has revealed to us; our divisions attest to this. While the numbers vary from week to week, the broad umbrella of Christendom encompasses well over one thousand different denominations, sects, and cults. Friedrich Engels (1820-1895) scoffed at the divided Church and its Bible. Christians couldn't agree on capital punishment, baptism, slavery, church authority, or a host of other issues. Truth seemed to evade the Church, he observed. As a result, he had no difficulty in rejecting the Bible or the Bible's God. Our division is our shame, to say the least. If we can't agree on truth, how are we pleasing God or rightly presenting Him to the world? We have justified the scoffer's view in two ways: that no one can know all the truth, and that we don't appear to have it. Our egos, pride, ignorance, and self will have given God a black eye.

The world, though, fails to offer this argument with clean hands, in part due to intellectual dishonesty and part due to personal sin. "As it is written, "There is none righteous, not even one... All have turned aside, together they have become useless; there is none who does good, there is not even one'" (Romans 3:10,12). If we want to understand truth, we must first accept that God's ways are not ours. We all sin and have limited perspectives, and yet, there are absolutes, and there is perfection out there if we are willing to seek it.

Over the millennia, there have been billions of rainbows. Not all of them have even been observed. Of those that have been, each of us has seen them from a different perspective. Philosophically, Plato argued that somewhere in the universe, there exists a perfect rainbow, just like there is a perfect horse or a perfect diamond. Someone might argue it was the one God gave Noah (Genesis 9:12), but while we may not all see exactly the same thing, to an honest mind certain patterns or realities can be determined. The same is true with any sincere quest for what is truth.

By all rights, since we each have a different observation point and perspective, we are all entitled to a right to be heard. Our founding fathers affirmed this in preserving for us the right to free speech. In this way, honest minds can weigh all the evidence in determining truth and a proper course of action. But the modern rationalist, or what atheists and humanists claim to be, takes this one step further. Their approach is called "values neutral". They assert, that while some observations or arguments sound better than others, all are of equal value, and there are no absolutes. By this standard, no one can stake an exclusive claim of rightness. All societies, religions, and cultures are equal; the Nazis were just as good as the Democrats or Republicans. Logically, Pol Pot, who, in the 1970's, murdered a fourth of his own people, was equal to the visionary Mahatma Gandhi or John F. Kennedy.

It must be noted that those who advocate values neutrality are openly unapologetic about the ramifications of their position, even though such logic negates any basic standard of right and wrong. It also defies logic. How can societies, as North Korea's present system, which tortures, starves, and suppresses its people be equal, values wise, to South Korea, with economic, religious, and personal liberties? It makes no provision for ranking of laws, policies, or needs. If all laws are equal, then it doesn't matter if one lawbreaker murders or another jay walks, all should be treated equally. But such logic is, in itself, illogical. If someone were stranded on a desert isle with a container of seed wheat, they probably would be a little more concerned about the laws governing evaporation and condensation, or of rain, than those of geometry or quantum mechanics. Their need is to grow a crop and survive.

Not all truth is relevant, not all we claim to be truth is so, nor are all truths equal in every way, and as has already been shown, not every observation yields truth. Louis Pasteur (1822-1895) once said, "Chance favors only the prepared mind." So truth only favors the sincere mind. If one is not open to accept truth, no amount of exposure will ever reveal it to them. Nor are all skills or expertise of value to every circumstance. A professional short order cook is definitely skilled in his field but would be no good as part of a brain surgery team. His skills and truth serve a purpose, but his counsel would prove lethal in the operating room. His opinion might be of value if the patient were seeking it, or if he was writing a letter to the editor regarding the subject of brain surgery, but simply because he has an opinion does not make his views equal to those of the surgery team.

Neither does the right to participate in discussion give anyone the right to suppress truth. If the world were to come together and vote to repeal the law of inertia, which states that a body in motion stays in motion, would that law cease to be? Denying God doesn't make Him any less God either. Truth is truth. As Biblical truth is foundational to our existence and salvation, just as scientific, mathematic, or economic truths are for our worldly sustenance and comfort. God is the author of Biblical truth, and He chose the Jews to be His mouthpiece. "For salvation is from the Jews" (John 4:22). From them, this message was to go to all the earth. It is not man's right to determine God's ways, but it is only ours to accept or reject it.

What we Christians need to understand is the importance of our position and the nature of our enemy. Our message is truth, and it is the words of life. Our enemy is Satan. He would be delighted if we came to reject the Bible as saving truth, but this isn't necessary to disarm us. All our enemy needs for us to do is to accept an argument as: Since none of us know all the truth, other beliefs are just as able to save as ours is. This values neutral "truth" forces us to surrender the very claims central to our faith. Even if our witnesses were not compromised, we run the risk of shipwrecking our salvation. Paul said, "See to it that no one takes you captive through philosophy and empty deception, according to the tradition of men, according to the elementary principles of the world, rather than according to Christ" (Colossians 2:8). The belief system of the rationalist cannot save. "You foolish Galatians (Christians)! Who has bewitched you, before whose eyes Jesus Christ was publicly portrayed as crucified...Are you so foolish? Having begun by the Spirit are you now being perfected by the flesh?" (Galatians 3:1, 3). Our only hope is in holding on with all of our heart to God's word as truth.

# III

## "IS JESUS THE ONLY WAY TO GOD?"

*"Jesus said to him, 'I am the way, and the truth and the life; no one comes to the Father, but through Me."*

—John 14:6

On Paul's second missionary journey, he and his entourage found themselves in Philippi, being followed by a demon-possessed girl. As she followed them around, she cried out, for days on end, her demonic theology. "These men are bond-servants of the Most High God, who proclaim to you A [author's emphasis) way of salvation" (Acts16:17). Paul, righteously annoyed, finally turned around and rebuked the demon and cast it out. This earned Paul and Silas a beating with broom handles or rods and a night in the pokey, chained uncomfortably to the wall. But the Jesus Paul proclaimed was not a way, He was the way to salvation and heaven. And there is salvation in no one else, for there is no other name under Heaven given that has been given among men by which we must be saved" (Acts 4:12).

The world both then and today sees all religions as being basically the same and, in value, equal. None are totally right or wrong. All seek what is ultimately the same god (God), and why would God limit Himself to just one way?

In 1977, George Burns starred in the movie "Oh God." A central theme was that Jesus was only one of many sons of God and one of many pathways to heaven. God, according to the movie, is more interested in world harmony than in doctrines. Also, God loves and saves everyone, based on their sincerity in their beliefs. Creeds aren't necessary; the sincere will find God. Christianity might be okay for some, but God is too big for one religion alone. No one has a corner on God, so therefore, all beliefs are acceptable.

In America today, seventy percent of adults who were surveyed believe there are many, or a plurality of ways to heaven. Diversity is promoted by the influential as a good, positive force in our culture. Openness and acceptance, or "tolerance," are seen as moral goodness. Religions that teach tolerance in this way are viewed more favorably than those that don't. Since Christian fundamentalists teach narrowness, it is no wonder why, even here in America, hostility towards Christians is on the rise. We just don't get it, by the world's standards.

"All rivers run into the same sea," or so the saying goes. Man is justified, as Buddhism teaches, in following the holy "Eight-Fold Path", or tenets of faith and action that earn his way to Nirvana. As all their sects teach, man must reach out either as his own god, or spirits to merit favor. The rank and file Buddhist holds to a high moral code that, to a degree, mirrors Christianity. This code condemns pride, uncharitableness, hypocrisy, and the like, and demands of its disciples forgiveness, patience, humility, love, and duty to one's fellow man. To a good Hindu, life is a pursuit of self-denial and cleansing. Every year in mid January, they honor a day of personal cleansing, if possible in the Ganges but at least in the nearest river. The highest calling is to be a truth seeker. A trek to and a journey around Nanda Devi, the mountain source of the Ganges, can merit forgiveness for a lifetime of sin. Daoists seek a universal harmony and intermingle in many ways with once rival Confucianism. Going with the flow, letting nature take its course, don't rock the boat; all reflect their seeking for this harmony. They also appease the spirit world with offerings and honors. Once again, one is called to lead a good life and merit the favor of the deities by right living.

In many parts of the world, mostly in Asia, these three ways have given up animosity and militancy towards each other. There are hundreds of millions of people, primarily in these Asian lands of China, India, and the nations to the south and east, who hold a mixture of all three, at least to some degree. In America, they are represented in the Unity and Unitarian Church movements. The criticism many of these believers have towards Christians is, if these three can join into a melting pot theology, why can't the Church? This is even more an irritant in the light of the Christian claim that their God loves everyone.

It is important to note that there is definitely some good and some truth in other religions. There is a basic knowledge of God, as was addressed earlier, to be seen in nature and our inner light. We, ourselves, are able to seek out some spiritual truths. As Paul told the Athenians, "That they should seek God, if perhaps they might grope for Him and find Him," (Acts 17:27). The Syrophoenician woman hit on another truth in her plea for Jesus to heal her daughter. "But she answered and said to Him, 'Yes, Lord; but even the dogs under the table feed on the children's crumbs' (Mark 7:28). These crumbs of God's truths have spread throughout the world, and this is reflected in many of their religious beliefs.

Other religions have offered some benefits to their disciples. The witch doctors, for example, have found some natural truths and have provided a number of herbal supplements and medical treatments. Some eastern regimens do enhance physical health and fitness, as do Yoga and other disciplines, including the martial arts. There are many now practicing these disciplines in America today. If the right God were being honored in so doing, their benefit would be significant. And also, as a caveat, some religious beliefs provide absolutely no benefits; Satanism, most modern derivatives of Humanism, and Western Wicca, or witchcraft are among these. While certain elements of other religions can offer us some positives, if in any way these benefits lead us away from the true God, they are not good.

There is one life and death difference that separates the beliefs, or doctrines of Christianity from virtually every other religion on earth. All other religions focus on man's efforts to seek out God, or a deity, and merit favor in His sight. The emphasis is on what man can do to redeem himself or earn the mercy, forgiveness, and acceptance, of the spirit world. On the other hand, in Christianity; there is a reality that we cannot save ourselves, but must believe in Christ to save us. "For we maintain that a man is justified by faith apart from works of the law" (Romans 3:28).

In verse 20, Paul says, "Because by the works of the law no flesh will be justified in His sight." Just in case any Christian is tempted to believe they can save themselves, Ephesians 2:8 adds, "For by grace you have been saved, and that is not of yourselves, it is the gift of God, through faith." It is God who empowers us and validates our salvation. We are not able to attain it ourselves.

The power of God to save us is shown by His power to raise Jesus from the grave. Lao-tse, Gautama (the great Buddha), Confucius, Muhammad, and all the other founders and shapers of religious belief are in their graves. The great leader Moses died and was buried, though no one, to this day, knows where. Only two people, Enoch and Elijah escaped death. They were taken bodily to Heaven. Even Jesus, Himself, died and was buried. The graves of many of these religious leaders are now revered as holy shrines for holding their remains. But the tomb of Jesus of Nazareth, King of the Jews and all Israel, is empty. He rose from the grave and later ascended bodily into Heaven. "And it came about that while He was blessing them He parted from them" (Luke 24:51). This claim is the cornerstone of the Christian faith. It has also been the focus of furious attack.

In fact, the questioning of the new age rationalist and humanist isn't on whether Jesus was a way for many to any spiritual peace, but if He was even a way at all. Of all the world's religions, Christianity is the least regarded. During the drift to intellectual liberalism of the 1950's and the turbulent 1960's, a great force was launched for the total rejection of Jesus, at least as the Christ. It would cut a swath across the very fabric of American society and systematically take over institution after institution. These are a few of their voices:

## *The Comfortable Pew,* 1965

In 1965 *The Comfortable Pew* by Pierre Berton was published. He openly rejected Christianity as having any claim to moral leadership in our culture. The issues of our new day, the advancement of science, education, and economic prosperity, showed that a new religious perspective was needed. The strict moral constraints of Christianity no longer fit, and a new beacon of enlightenment was needed to fit the demands of the new age. Jesus, whether dead or alive, and as he saw it in all likelihood still dead, was no longer relevant.

## Situation Ethics, 1966

Joseph Fletcher, another child of the age, wrote *Situation Ethics* 1966. He, too, condemned an organized Christian religion for its moral straightjacket of legalism. The outdated truths of Biblical Christianity had, like Jesus, met their expiration date. He conjured up for us a series of sticky situations thrust into our religiosity.

The deliberate attempt is to force the reader to think beyond a set standard of right and wrong. In these, murder, adultery, theft, and lying, were all justified depending on our circumstances. At least several of his dilemmas were hypothetical, not being real to begin with. His conclusion was all we need is "love," which he never defined and, coincidently enough, was similar to the title of a Beatles song of the day.

## Passover Plot, 1965

Hugh J. Schonfield portrays a Jesus who had every intention of beating the system. He lived the life of what a Messiah would do. To prove His *Messiahship*, He planned to go to Jerusalem and be crucified. But He was planning to be taken off the cross while He was still alive and, after a swoon, recover to claim His Lordship. Unfortunately, the Romans ruined His plan by casting a spear in His side. His body, then, was buried, and subsequently stolen by His disciples from the tomb. They then proclaimed him as having been resurrected.

## *The Quest For The Historic Jesus,* 1906

Such attacks, though, long predate the turbulent 1960's. One of the most famous of the skeptics was Albert Schweitzer (1875-1965). He was a renowned humanitarian doctor who selflessly lived his life in service in the, then, Belgian Congo. He was also a writer. In 1906 he published *The Quest For The Historic Jesus.* To him, Jesus was a historical figure, and a social visionary, who sought to transform His society. He died a cataclysmic death and was revered by His followers. He performed no miracles and there was no resurrection, but even dead, He was a hero, and inspired others to follow His vision. These disciples would work as well for the betterment of mankind. While His sacrifice for others was inspiring, it was no longer relevant today, nor did it apply to the challenges of the new age. Schweitzer's views were not foreign for his time, either. Through him and others, this belief had widespread acceptance in an increasingly humanist and secularized Europe.

## Sigmund Freud

Another famous voice in the assault on both Jesus of Nazareth, and the Bible was Dr. Sigmund Freud (1856-1939). He is the father of psychiatry and psychotherapy. A brainchild of Charles Darwin, he associated mental illness with the process of our evolution, and along humanist lines. He saw no need for, or evidence of, the positive influence of a god (God). He, as a humanist and as a Jew, totally rejected Jesus. He also rejected miracles and most, if not the entire, supernatural realm. He set forth very formidable challenges through his psychology to the assertions of Jesus and Scriptures, one of them, many Christians accept today. This was the rejection by him and his followers of any concept of demonic possession, though they were well aware that this put them on a collision course with both Jesus and the Gospels. In an age that readily embraced Darwin and evolution, and a rationalistic bias that applied to everything, he took the intellectual world by storm.

Over the next several decades, Freud's views on evil and Satan became the accepted intellectual norm. No longer did the enlightened mind have a place for the devil or the host of darkness. This belief soon found itself rooted in many mainline Protestant denominations. Even before the turbulent 1960's, evil far more frequently was psychoanalyzed than exorcised. This also affected crime and punishment; criminals were seen as more the victims of a hostile social order than tempted by a devil to do evil. Today, demonic possession is masked as just one or another mental illness or disorder. If the psychiatric community finds it can't explain away a behavior by theory, they'll just invent a new one to attempt to do so.

This rationalistic shift has rippled through the Church, and has led to a softening attitude on sin in general and the conflict between good and evil. For the majority of the mainline denominational world that long ago rejected a literal Adam and Eve, and much of Genesis, this was not a hard step to take. Along with this was a belief in a social Jesus, or one whose sole purpose was in meeting our worldly needs, feeding the hungry, healing the sick, and in forcing social change. Since so many had already cast off a Jesus who died and rose again, it should be no surprise that a number of mainline churches have rejected other standards of sin as well. For example, in an age of relativism and relevance, many denominations openly embrace sexual liberation, a redefined family, and the rejection of guilt. Even their social Jesus, as a great benevolent leader, is now outdated, His gospel message has been transformed to one of tolerance, social justice, and inner harmony. The only "demons" to be cast out are our own, those of self-doubt, of moral hang-ups, or of bad attitudes.

This shows again the devious nature of Satan. "But I was afraid lest as the serpent deceived Eve by his craftiness, your minds should be led astray from the simplicity and purity of devotion to Christ" (II Corinthians 11:3). His greatest victory is not possession, though some mental disorder is, but in deception, which He does to us all, to some degree.

## Altizerm, La Vey

The depth to which the Church has fallen here is shown in the results. While modem theologians, like Thomas Altizerm were proclaiming, "God is dead," Anton La Vey was taking the theological debate in another direction. On April 30, 1966, he launched into modern existence the Church of Satan, USA. Since so much of the Christian world had already denied that a real devil existed, and had outgrown God as well, its advent was met with only sighs. Caught flat-footed by the advent of evil for the sake of evil, these liberal theologians were put in a dilemma. Seduced by their own theology, they could not now go back to the original argument about demons and the devil, while still claiming an enlightened and relevant theological perspective. They hid their collective heads in the sand of denial.

But there is a real devil, there is demonic activity in the world, and some of that is in actual possession. By no means is this to say that even a majority of mental disorder is possession. Quite plainly, it isn't. Most autism, severe depression, even schizophrenia usually results from biological, personal, or environmental issues, but some mental disorder is from possession. One of the best ways in our society to expose oneself to possession is through misuse of mind-altering drugs. The word "sorcery" is used Biblically, as in Revelation 9:21 and 18:23, as a reference to the use of mind-altering drugs in idol worship. The actual word in the Greek is "pharmakia," from which we get the word pharmacy. Since the devil is real, our sole hope is in the existence of a saving God through Jesus, and the reality of the resurrection becomes critical.

The question, once again, has come back to the resurrection of Jesus. If He did not rise from the dead, then people like Schonfield are right, and the modern rationalist can at least claim that He is irrelevant. It would be impossible to see Jesus as a moral leader, as He made claims He could or would not keep. He would either be a liar or a deluded mental case. So, did He rise from the dead?

## *Systematic Theology,* 1989

> Rex A. Turner was but one of a myriad of responders to claims like those in *The Passover Plot.* In his *Systematic Theology,* 1989, he firmly establishes that Jesus' body couldn't have been stolen. First of all, his enemies wouldn't have done so; it would only have fueled a lie that He had risen. Logically, if they had been so foolish as to have taken the body, why not show it to Peter and John in Acts 4:10, when these men so boldly asserted His resurrection? Also, Jesus's broken and scattered disciples, even if they could have somehow pulled together, would have had to defeat sixteen determined Roman soldiers, plus probable reinforcements from the Fortress of Antonia, only a quarter of a mile away. As for the Romans, why stir up another riot, or a revolution? Any other group, once again, would have faced the might of Rome. The only logical conclusions are that space aliens from Alpha Centauri stole it when no one was watching, or He rose from the dead. Since He appeared to over five hundred after his resurrection, this becomes the only credible option.

While there have been many voices in opposition, a myriad of factual evidences support the resurrection. Among these include even the Roman historical chroniclers, Tacitus (AD 56-117), Pliny the younger (AD 61-140), and Gaius Suetonius (AD 69-140). All commented on the early days of Christianity, of Nero's fire in Rome, AD 64, and the blame and persecution visited upon them for it. So was the expulsion of the Jews from Rome by Claudius, about AD 50, because of the controversy over Christ, but none of these made any assertion to deny the belief in the resurrection of Jesus from the dead. It was common knowledge in Palestine in AD 60 as Paul reminded Herod Agrippa. "For the king knows about these matters, and I speak to him also with confidence, since I am persuaded that none of these things escape his notice, for this [resurrection, verse 23], has not been done in a corner" (Acts 26:26). Josephus Flavius (AD 37-100) offers another voice, he is better known as agnostic Jewish historian, but in response to his study of Christianity after the AD 70 fall of Jerusalem, he became one of its greatest advocates. If this were a book on evidences, as many good ones exist, as *Who Moved The Stone?*, 1930, Frank Morrison, or Josh McDowell's *Evidence That Demands A Verdict*, 1999, the rest of these pages could easily be filled.

As the risen Lord, Christ's authority is shown in His message. He preached salvation from sin and eternal life. His was not a "love only" gospel of worldly tolerance while glorifying the flesh and where all rivers flow into the same sea. He called sin for what it was: sin. God's love is shown in reaching down to us despite of our sin. "For God so loved the world that he gave His only begotten Son, that whoever believes in Him should not perish, but have eternal life" (John 3:16). His gospel was not love alone; those rejecting Him were lost. "I tell you No: but unless you repent you will all likewise perish" (Luke 13:3).

He taught exclusiveness. Interestingly enough, all rivers don't flow into the same oceans. Some run into land-locked saltine seas. In Europe, the Mother Volga runs into the Caspian, while in Asia, the Jordan runs into the Dead Sea, the Amu and Syr Daryas run into the Aral, etc. Those who advocate this belief aren't correct even from a worldly perspective. Jesus never advocated going with the flow into the seas of life. These seas weren't even where He wanted His followers to end up. To the contrary, He called for Peter, Andrew, James, and John to "Follow Me, and I will make you fishers of men" (Matthew 4:19). We are to be saved and snatched out of the seas of life, not to seek them out for our eternal destiny.

Jesus also didn't teach a gospel of either tolerance, or of sincerity alone as being able to bring salvation. These aren't able to redeem us. But, He claimed that He, and He alone was the true light and source of saving truth, access to God, and eternal life. "I am the light of the world; he who follows Me shall not walk in darkness but shall have the light of life" (John 8:12). And again He said in John 11:25, "I am the resurrection and the life, he who believes in Me, shall live even if he dies." God is a jealous and exclusive God, He alone is God, and He will not be likened to idols or other deities. "I am the Lord, that is My name; I will not give My glory to another" (Isaiah 42:8).

While God is an exclusive God, and Jesus is the exclusive way to Heaven, His offer of salvation isn't. Everyone is invited to His table. The

Jewish leadership of His day found fault with Him because He accepted everyone, regardless of their pasts. "Now the tax gatherers and the sinners were coming near to listen to Him. And both the Pharisees and the scribes began to grumble, saying, 'This man receives sinners and eats with them'" (Luke 15:1, 2). Jesus will accept anyone who calls upon Him in faithful surrender. But this doesn't mean He accepts sin, "He condemned sin in the flesh" (Romans 8:3).

Jesus calls us where we are, as He did with the woman caught in adultery, but He doesn't expect us to remain there. Beyond question, Jesus offered her acceptance and forgiveness. It didn't matter so much where she had been; His concern was in where she was going. He forgave her, but it didn't end there. He called her to a higher plane of living, and of true joy. "Neither do I condemn you; go your way. From now on, sin no more" (John 8:11).

This condemnation of, or calling sin as sin, is the very thing that leads many today to criticize the Church, the Scriptures, and ultimately the Lord. Relativism asserts that there is no sin. Alcohol and substance abuse are a "sickness." Our genetics has become a fig leaf to justify behavior, with the presence of [the alleged] gay, the selfish, warrior, or other genes. In addition, society has outgrown sexual taboos. People suffer from behavioral issues, not sinful ones. Surely, claims the New Agers, by this time a better and enlightened way to deal with these issues and cover our failings has come along. Adam and Eve had felt the same way, trying to cover themselves with fig leaves and hide from God (Genesis 3:7, 8). God showed them that the only "covering" that could deal with sin required the shedding of blood (Genesis 3:21), and then they lost paradise.

Our problem is one of the heart, "The heart is more deceitful than all else, and desperately sick [corrupt]; who can understand it?" (Jeremiah 17:9). Alcohol and other abuses may well be a sickness, but they are also a sin, and there appears to be no gay gene. With all the time and money spent trying to find it, had it been found, it would have been front-page news with headlines the size of the 1969 Apollo moon landing. Even if someone did find one, as they have the warrior (MAO-A), selfish gene (AVPRIA), among others, these only identify potential traits, they do not excuse behavior. Yet for any sin, the modernist has claimed just such arguments from genetics, especially in reference to sexual morality. They tell us to just believe those genes are there, and that one day they will be found. Therefore, they claim, to fit modern reality, it is the Bible that needs to be rewritten, to accommodate them.

The rewriting of the Bible has become quite vogue in America today. This does bring up the issue of who has the authority to do so. Since the first author died and rose again to authenticate it, who among men has the right to change it? This course of action does dovetail with existentialism, and the idea that if one doesn't like history or reality, just deny and rewrite it. There have been produced, for example, a number of "gender neutral" Bible versions today. Purging the Bible of sex gender language satisfies those who reject God's appointed order. The words "God our father" become "God our parent," "man" becomes "mortal," among other examples. Other versions deliberately leave out references to homosexuality, or sin, or whatever someone wants to alter. Thus, the Lordship of Jesus is rejected, both in the act of revising and in the revisions themselves. But He is the "Author of Life" on His terms, not ours. Christ didn't die to bless our urges and desires, but to transform our lives. By His resurrection, He proves His authority to demand it. We are in mortal danger if we feel we have the right to rewrite either His Scriptures or His Gospel to suit ourselves.

Sadly, we in the Church have been guilty of just that. One of the most famous was when the 1611 authorized King James version was published. In order to avoid the veto of the Church of England, and a potential social upheaval, the word baptize was transliterated rather than translated as "immerse." While three-fourths of a loaf is better than no loaf at all, as in this case, getting the Bible into the common people's hands, precedent was set. In 1973, the New York Bible Society International copyrighted the New International Version. In many ways, it was a very good version, even improving on some of the deliberate errors in prior versions. There is, however, one glaring imposition of theology over God's intent. This is in the term "sinful nature" from Romans 7:18 through the end of the Bible. The Greek word used here is "sarkos" which means "flesh". The authors desired to interpolate their theology into the text, and altered this word to do so. Just a reminder, no one has the right to rewrite Scripture to suit their beliefs. If there is a contradiction between the two, our beliefs are what need to be rewritten. Jesus is the way, and He is God, not us.

We who wear the name of Jesus have also been guilty of attempting to provide people alternate ways to Heaven other than by faith in Jesus. Origen (AD 185-254) had a concern for the lost. In a heartfelt interest to save those who had no saving faith in Jesus, he came up with the concept of Divine Overflow. He taught that creation itself was a result of this overflow. In time, all things would undergo universal restoration and return to God. Gregory of Nyssa (AD 335-390) expounds further. "A time will come when there will be no sin or evil existing anywhere. Every person will then be made into one body, and all humanity will be the body of Christ."

From this concept, the Roman Catholic Church established the doctrine of Purgatory. At the Council of Trent (1545-1563), this became the official dogma of the church. For those souls not subject to immediate saint-hood, they were allowed to work off their sins and advance to heaven. This whole concept opens up the door to salvation outside of only through saving faith in Jesus.

Theodosius, Emperor of Rome (AD 378-398), opened another alternative way. This was the prospect of a government-mandated salvation through a state Church. Under his reign, in 380, Christianity became the only sanctioned state religion. He didn't stop there; conversion to Christianity was compulsory for all his subjects. No longer a voluntary act of faith, "salvation," it was a state mandate, and church membership became a bureaucrat's, or officer of the state's, concern. Salvation, it could be argued, was jointly determined by the police and the priest. It had little or nothing to do with the heart or will of the parishioner, and everything to do with the bean counters. This was a policy that was to become the norm of the Church for the next millennium. Once again, salvation could be imputed by the will of man, not by faith in Jesus.

Even without of the pull of the modern world, we Christians have proved all too willing to muddy the waters of salvation, but while the world does not have a right to dictate their conditions to God, neither does the Church. This has, sadly, become an accepted view, though. Most of the Church's willingness to accept salvation outside of Christ has not been doctrinal; it has been through a surrender to the world. A full fifty-seven percent of those who claim Christianity, believe salvation can be attained outside of Jesus, not much better than the seventy percent of all Americans. We find ourselves intimidated by a world that calls us arrogant for feeling that our religion is superior and demanding that others convert to Christ. So why mess with the gods of Asia? Rather than confront this world, Christians are often content to concede that while Christianity is okay for them, it may not be needed by the lost person who puts faith in another belief system. It is okay for the world to have our endorsement of their belief in Hinduism, Islam, or Humanism. In so doing, these Christians are showing contempt for Jesus. All too often, this goes beyond just in compromising and neglecting world evangelism. Christians come to believe this open-ended salvation applies to themselves as well.

God has already answered these arguments of turf rights. First of all He claims to be God over all of the world, and more than once He has proved it "Because the Arameans [Syrians] have said, The Lord is a god of the mountains but He is not a god of the valleys [plains],' therefore I will give all this great multitude into your hand, and you shall know that I am the Lord," (I Kings 20:28).

With our contrary nature, it almost defies logic that He even gave us a way at all. Sometimes, in our hearts, we just want "Plan B" for ourselves. We will pray to God for something, and when He doesn't answer how or when we think He should, we try our own way. We can become like those in Jeremiah 11:12. "Then the cities of Judah and the inhabitants of Jerusalem will go and cry to the gods to whom they burn incense, but they surely will not save them in the time of their disaster." Not only do we fail, we show faithlessness to our own beliefs. When we show such a poor witness and lack of faith in the true God to those who trust their alternative beliefs, how can we expect them to believe?

Many in the world already view God as dead. They see Christianity as no longer relevant. While they may be intellectually dishonest in rejecting Jesus, we should not be giving them ammunition. They can already point to all of the Jimmy Swaggarts's and Jim Jones's of the Church. Will they add us, in our unbelief, to their list? Too often, are we ourselves guilty of "Holding to the form of a godliness although they have denied its power" (II Timothy 3:5). The Jesus who rose from the dead will be the world's judge on the last day. He will also be ours. Are we ready? Are we living our faith worthy of Him? On that question hangs not just the world's salvation, but ours as well.

# IV

## CHRIST OR CAESAR?

*"Then He said to them, 'Then render to Caesar the things*
*that are Caesar's and to God the things that are God's.'"*

—Matthew 22:21

In 1960, a man named John F. Kennedy was running for President of the United States. The road was not easy. He found himself locked in a very tight race with then Vice President Richard M. Nixon, and he was also a Catholic. While he was not the first, it was locked in his memory banks what had happened in 1928 to Alfred E. Smith, another Catholic who ran for President. Even at this point in US history, many voters were still biased against Catholics, and Kennedy was not about to make the same mistakes Smith had. Along the way, he was asked a question. If he were elected President, would his highest allegiance be to his church or to the nation? He responded by saying he was an American first and a Catholic second.

Like most of the rest of the nation, I, a then seven-year-old Protestant boy believed he had answered rightly. By a razor-thin margin he won the presidency over Nixon. He still had his detractors, like Norman Vincent Peale (1898-1993), who saw him as a grave threat to America. But many others voiced their belief that Kennedy had obtained God's approval and blessing for his choice of masters.

This election fell in a time frame when America was considered a Christian nation. In 1892, the Supreme Court had ruled that since our people were a religious (Christian) people, and our institutions presuppose a Supreme Being, America was a Christian nation. Throughout the 1950s Peale repeatedly hit that theme, and despite the liberal shift seen in 1958 and again in 1960, this was still an era of rising church attendance with a perceived rise in spiritual concerns. The average American on the street had a basic belief that America was on God's side (or God on our side) in her worldwide struggle with the atheistic Communists. While some still feared a Catholic Kennedy, America saw his compromise as good.

In retrospect, this compromise was anything but good. It was not good for the Roman Catholic Church. Precedent was set for other Catholic politicians to reject church values in order to win and hold political office. One good example was that of the President's brother, the late Edward "Teddy" Kennedy. He engaged in a running war with the church over such issues as abortion and gay rights as US Senator from Massachusetts. The same became true as well for otherwise Evangelical Protestant politicians, like President "Jimmy" James Earl Carter, from 1977-1981. His religious claims did not prevent him from advocating radical feminism, humanist judges, abortion, and acceptance of an anti-Christian international policy. This divorce of faith and politics, now practiced by many in both parties, has done all Christians a disservice.

It has served as well as a poor example to other Christians and to the world. If Christian values are second to the edicts of the state, then Christianity fails to serve her master. Any attempt to force the Church from her distinctive mission will only end in defeat for society and a failure for the Church. As the bride of Christ compromises, both her mission and moral "salt" (Matthew 5:13) are lost. Our light fails to shine. "You are the light of the world" (Matthew 5:14). This is exactly what happened in 1960, and in the years that followed.

This appeasement theology, as reflected in the Church, also hit at a very critical point in American judicial history. In the years prior, the US Supreme Court had been proceeding down an anti-Christian road. Many trace this to about 1940, with the appointment in 1939 of William O. Douglass (1898-1980) to the court where he served until 1975. This outspoken humanist was a key player in an unfolding judicial activism. In 1948 he helped strike down a long honored policy whereby public schools had held religious classes. In 1954 Earl Warren (1891-1974) officially became Chief Justice, a position he held until retiring in 1969. The pieces were in place for an aggressive court that accelerated a program of moving America from a Christian foundation, to the present humanist one. Not every decision of the high court of that era was bad, but the focus here is on those of a religious perspective. Judicial restraint, already under challenge in the prior decades from both left and right, died. From a Christian perspective, this assault climaxed in the early 1960s. Norman Vincent Peale's aggressive and misguided extremist position on Kennedy, Kennedy's compromise, along with the rising voices of left wing theologians had already shackled the Church with controversy, crippling her ability to respond. Two of the leading theologians of the era show yet another facet of the weight of this albatross hanging around the neck of a compromised Church.

One was Reinhold Niebhur (1892-1971). He was a Protestant leader in the years preceding this decade. Viewed as a devoutly anti-Communist advocate of reason and theological accommodation, his was a middle road between the Liberal naiveté to sin and a then sterile, conservative, narrow definition of true religion. While he authored the now famous "Serenity Prayer," his theology centered on what he called Christian realism. This included pragmatism, or practical, and often worldly solutions over theology, a little relativism, and a dash of rationalism. The resurrection of Christ was not so much "actual," but only relevant in a spiritual sense or in feeling inspired over what Jesus said and did. In essence, his theology was open to interpretation on key theological points, as with the virgin birth, resurrection of Christ, or the inspiration of Scripture. He used language in such a way that both liberals and conservatives could identify with him. He saw a mystical God, truth, and the Bible as one whose claims weren't so much literal as spiritual. His views led his followers down a road of social acceptance over moral conviction, of silence over expression of faith. Theology didn't matter as much as just getting along, hiding our faith in our hearts, and not making waves.

Paul Tillich (1886-1965) was a friend and an associate of Niebuhr, and another leading Protestant theological voice of the era. He didn't believe in a personal God, according to the Christian perspective. Nor did he accept immortality in accordance with a literal resurrection of the dead. He was a Christian existentialist, by his own admission. He was famous for among other things, his idea of a God above God. He saw God, by His nature, as limited, and another God above Him created Him. There was almost a tinge of Gnosticism in his view of a series of Gods from the highest down to man.

To a large extent, God, as we know Him, was also unknowable. Religion was not so much to be advocated or lived as it was to be felt, or believed, and also hidden in one's heart. When Chief Justice Earl Warren questioned the Christian perspective, he picked up on this concept of anyone's ability to know or speak for God, or of God even being close enough to be prayed to. He also pointed out that a God of only a spiritual nature was too mystical for human ritual. School prayer was only a form and was, therefore, irrelevant.

Strangled by theological irrationalism, the Church lacked strength or organization to deal with the now looming crisis. Under the maneuvering of Jack Pemberton, momentum was already in the ACLU's sails by 1962, by having previously won several significant anti-Church rulings. Then in "Engel vs. Vitale," or the case that determined whether or not school prayer would be allowed, the high court rejected all the precedence of its 173 years as guardian of our liberties. All official, or school-sponsored prayer, was ruled unconstitutional. The very next year, in Abington Township School District vs. Schempp, scripture reading was banned as well. An anemic and half-hearted Church did nothing to stem the tide. She was defeated from within long before this battle began by surrendering her sword to the state and her soul to mediocrity. The one victory the Church received was that humanism was also ruled to be a religion, but this was of little value. Most Christians were too comfortable in their lifestyles to offer much challenge through the Court.

One can only speculate on what might have happened if in 1962 or 1963 the Church had stood up to the Supreme Court. If compromise and subservience had not been her answer to the challenge of the world, could she have found the courage to act? If even ten million had stood together and engaged in peaceful civil disobedience, as shown by the Civil Rights Movement, refused to pay their taxes, or refused to work at their jobs until this Court imposed evil was reversed, our system couldn't have coped. This also would have gone a long way in making Christianity relevant to an age which increasingly questioned just that.

Instead, compromise to the state cost Christianity dearly, and the damage wasn't just in America. The Church throughout the western world was looking for a purpose to exist, and Christians behind the Iron and Bamboo Curtains could've used some inspiration. A stand of Christian conviction, in all likelihood, would have triggered at least a nation-wide revival, and, possibly, a national rededication to God. How many more missionary endeavors might have resulted from such a newfound fervency? How many more souls worldwide would now be bound for heaven? We will never know this side of eternity.

The 1960's Church, though, didn't do anything other religions haven't done throughout history. The Greeks provide a good example. The philosopher Socrates (469-399 BC) was once asked about a citizen's responsibility to honor and serve the gods. He answered that they had a duty to do so, but only in accordance with the laws of their country or city-state. Since each one had its own particular patron and matron deities, worship of a community's gods was also a requisite for citizenship. This was how one got along in ancient Greece, and it was also the cultural norm throughout most of the pre-Christian Mediterranean world. There was an old saying, "When in Rome, do as the Romans do." This was a reason Rome accepted any deity or religion in existence at the time she took over, and also why there was no allowance for any new religions to arise under her rule.

Patron and matron deities also ruled throughout much of Mesopotamia. After a war, sometimes the victor's deities were imposed upon the conquered, but often the vanquished were just subject to taunting, and the victor's god was viewed as superior to the loser's. This is seen in the events of I Samuel 5:1, 2: "Now the Philistines took the ark of God, and brought it from Ebenezer to Ashdod. Then the Philistines took the ark of God and brought it to the house of Dagon and set it by (beneath) Dagon." The Philistines believed they now possessed both the present and the afterlives of the Israelites. Their god was superior to the Lord, and the Lord as well would now serve Dagon. While over the next seven months God proved otherwise, it provided Israel a chance to think about the costs of their own idolatry.

We see a more aggressive policy in Babylon under Nebuchadnezzar. In 605 BC, four youths, Daniel, Hananiah, Mishael, and Azariah found themselves deported from Jerusalem to Babylon. They were very fortunate, ending up in the court of the king. But their first lessons in cross-cultural living could have undone them. They were tested in their faith regarding the un-kosher diet of the land, and there was a name change. Daniel became Belteshazzer, after Bel, Nebuchadnezzar's god. The others were named Shadrach, Meshach, and Abednego. They did win their battle over their diets. Then came another test, as some time later, the king made a great idolatrous image as much as ninety feet tall. The edict was for everyone who lived near, regardless of religion or nationality; at set times to worship it.

Shadrach, Meshach, and Abednigo refused. They had a lot to lose, jeopardizing their upper class status, and the perks that went with it. If the king kept his word on punishment, they also put their lives on the line. Yet they disobeyed anyway. Brought before the king they were given one last opportunity to reconsider. The three answered Nebuchadnezzar as one, "O Nebuchadnezzar, we do not need to give you an answer concerning this matter... Let it be known to you, O King, that we are not going to serve your gods or worship the golden image that you have set up" (Daniel 3:16,18). The three won a free trip to a fiery furnace. The king believed that as king, he had the right to do whatever he wanted to do.

In this case, it was a proud king who had to change. God delivered Shadrach and company from death in a super-heated furnace, and a mighty king was forced to acknowledge God. Policies were changed in Babylon. No longer were the Jews coerced into homage to the gods of Babylon. To the contrary, the king issued a decree: "Any people, nation, or language that speaks anything offensive against the God of Shadrach, Meshach, and Abednigo shall be torn limb from limb, and their houses reduced to a rubbish heap; inasmuch as there is no other god who is able to deliver in this way" (Daniel 3:29). Later, through Beltshazzar (Daniel), the king got another lesson in theology and ethics. He was humbled with madness until he learned "That the Most High is ruler over the realm of mankind and bestows it on whomever He wills" (Daniel 4:32). Governments derive their just authority to govern from God, not the other way around. God doesn't need authority to be God from the government or us. The Church, Christ's bride, owes first allegiance to her husband, Jesus, not to the state.

During the Christian era, many of the Pan-Germanic tribes in Europe sought their own way around this issue, and the divided loyalty of their armies. In AD 496, Clovis (466-511), king of the Franks, converted to Christ. At that time, up to twenty thousand members of his Frankish tribes also were baptized. According to at least one tradition, many of the local chieftains ordered their soldiers to hold their right hands out of the water when they were baptized. That way, their sword bearing hands still belonged to the chieftain when the time came for war.

Roughly two centuries later, Winfred Boniface (672- 754AD) was credited with converting a great many of the Germanic Tribes. His success dated, beginning in 723 with his felling of Thor's Oak, near Fritzlar. This led to mass conversions among the Bavarians, Thuringians, Hessians, Saxons, and others. He was martyred in 754 at the hand of the still pagan Frisians and later was canonized as a saint. But one issue, again according to tradition, that clouded his success was found in many of these mass baptisms. Following their Frankish counterparts, several chieftains didn't allow their soldiers to have their hands baptized. In retrospect, many, as well, involved in mass baptisms also failed to convert. Soldiers merely followed their leader's orders, and for a significant number of them, there was no saving faith in Christ.

Governmental intrusion in salvation did not begin here, or with Theodosius either. Nor does it end here. The Bolsheviks offer a recent example. When they took over Russia in October 1918, one of their first orders of business was to license the churches. Any Greek Orthodox priest who refused to comply with this, and embrace the Communist version of the Gospel, ended up in the Gulag Archipelago or the Soviet prison work camps, with most of these being in Siberia. The ones who survived were black-marked for life, though many of them became leaders in the underground church.

In the People's Republic of China, all churches are required to obtain a license through the Three Self Patriotic Movement. The state must approve of both the ministers and their messages. Among other things, they must acknowledge the government's authority as being the head of the church. A loyalty oath is also required. All those who don't are considered to be operating illegally, and the government reserves the right to close them down at any time. Their leaders face arrest and are often kept in prison indefinitely.

Chancellor Adolph Hitler, head of Germany from 1933 until 1945, also controlled the church in Germany. In 1938 he issued an edict for all the ministers of Germany to take a loyalty oath to him. A group of dissenting ministers begged an audience with him. They argued, among other things, that an independent church was necessary for the good of Germany. To this Hitler responded, "I am Germany." Once again, dissenters ended up in concentration camps where most of them died.

Romans 13:1-7 outlines a Christian's duty to the state. Peter adds, "Submit yourselves for the Lord's sake to every human institution, whether to a king, or the one in authority, or as governors sent by him for the punishment of evildoers" (I Peter 2:13, 14). A Christian is called to obey the legitimate, and even at times, unjust demands of government. This is not at question here. Granted, our unique American form of government gives us options that others don't have, but most of the basic rule still applies. Paul even exhorted us to pray for our leaders, whether we like them or not. "First of all, then, I urge that entreaties and prayers...be made on behalf of all men, for kings and all who are in authority, in order that we may lead a tranquil and quiet life, in all godliness and dignity" (I Timothy 2:1,2).

What is in question is the government's authority to intrude in religious affairs. Religious worship predates government. "So it came about in the course of time that Cain brought an offering to the Lord of the fruit of the ground, and Abel, on his part also brought of the firstlings of his flock and of their fat portions" (Genesis 4:3, 4). In as much as worshippers in any society aren't violating the basic Laws of God, their rights to do so will always take precedence over man's laws. And this applies to those religions beyond the Christian faith.

Much has been said about the rise of Islamic Fundamentalism and rightly so. It has sent shockwaves throughout most of the world, and with the exception of Antarctica, (at least when this was written), every continent has witnessed acts of terror against civilian targets, acts of war against government or military establishments, or both. In America, there have been many. Largely because of this, anyone who advocates their religious loyalties above those to the government, especially if they are Muslim, become a candidate for monitoring by Homeland Security. But any American Muslim, or Christian, or Jew who does not hold to this conviction is not being true to their faith. And unless they are violating God's moral law in their actions, it is their duty to live their faith. This is not an endorsement of salvation outside of Christ, or of suppressive and brutal actions by Islamic Fundamentalists, but of basic fairness and justice. No Muslim, Hindu, Buddhist, etc. should ever be forced to put allegiance to government above their conscience or rightful religious beliefs. Watching tanks run over unarmed civilian worshippers in Syria should be enough to drive this truth home to everyone, including the governments of Russia and China.

While it's easy for the American Church to see the evils of the compromise of conscience worldwide, it is often obscured or she turns a blind eye to this in our country. Even today, many Americans still claim we are a Christian nation. This largely is due to our Declaration of Independence, Constitution, and Bill of Rights. Now, to argue against Divine guidance and direction in their writing would be in error, but these documents aren't inspired, despite claims by super-patriots, or on the same level as Scripture. Men were led, not inspired of God, to write them, and since the 1960's, the intent of these documents has been rejected. What is today called Constitutional is not what the framers envisioned. For example, the Fourteenth Amendment was never intended to cover abortion, or the First, pornography.

Still, many view the oath of office, to uphold the Constitution and our government as being both a religious and a political statement. Military service is also viewed by the majority as a service to God as well as to America. A half-century ago, when virtually every civic and volunteer organization began their meetings with prayer, this may have been partially true, but over the years, the goalposts have moved. Today, it is almost rare for civic and volunteer groups to open with prayers. No longer does much of our culture even resemble anything of a Christian nature. To the contrary, anti-Christian values rule, from abortion, gambling, gay rights, immoral lifestyles, pornography, and sanctioned blasphemy, to mention a few. President Barak Obama actually did us a favor by saying America is no longer a Christian nation. We are no longer a nation of, "My Country Tis of Thee" or "The Battle Hymn of The Republic." Instead, John Lennon's "Imagine" or the 1960's hit "Angel Is A Centerfold" better describe us today.

While the Christian evangelicals or fundamentalists see ever less moral encouragement in our government, many mainline denominations have taken an opposing viewpoint. They have seen a fulfillment in their pursuit of social justice, environmental concerns, alternate lifestyles, and even abortion, which many view as a compassionate answer to an unwanted pregnancy. Yet, at the same time, they take comfort in laws restricting tobacco, eliminating trans fats, and other imposed safety and health mandates. Without addressing the issue of moving goalposts, or a values shift, the question needs to be asked as to what even constitutes social good, and if Christians should conscientiously be paying for it.

Moral and legal purism is probably never going to happen in this life. Even in the best of systems, there are times when even justice itself is unjust. Guilty people will be acquitted and the innocent convicted; the needy will not be helped and the greedy, subsidized. But is there a point where a Christian should say "no" to the mandates of the state? In the late 1930's and into the early 1940's under Hitler, the "good Germans" or the "confessing Church" believed that if they went along with him, they might somehow influence him for good. To a small degree they felt they did, as in alleviating some German war suffering, but their compromise did nothing to save some twenty five million plus Jews, Gypsies, Russians, or others that the Nazis beat, starved, shot, or gassed to death. Of this figure, according to *The Rise And Fall Of The Third Reich*, 1960, by William L. Shirer, Jewish deaths alone were eleven million, of which six million were gassed or worked to death. If the church in Germany had said "no" to compromise, who knows how many of these might have been saved?

The Church, both of the left and the right, does correctly understand and agree on one thing about Christ's love: He healed and fed more than souls, and His followers are obliged to do so as well. "If a brother or sister is without clothing and in need of daily food, and one of you says to them, 'Go in peace, be warmed and filled,' and yet you do not give them what is necessary for their body, what use is that?" (James 2:15, 16). The question is not in the command, it is in how it is met, and this is seen in national policy. This points to one more area of Church compromise of mission to the state, the area of social and economic justice.

Welfare was originally set up as compassionate aid for the helpless poor. Programs like Social Security and Medicare do provide a security for the aged and infirm so also Food Stamps, Medicaid, and others provide a safety net. But, over the years, even without the issue of the "Second Bill of Rights," the Church has accepted these as substitutes for Church sponsored social justice.

Unfortunately, this help not only leaves God out of the picture, it has bred a mindset of dependency. People have often made no effort to save money for themselves, believing that Social Security will provide all they need. Others, having spent years on government support, find it very hard to get off, with much of the blame falling on the government as well for making this attempt difficult. Also, for a majority, doing nothing to get their monthly support is destructive to their self-esteem. One exception is those in their golden years, who are active in community or church volunteer work. Welfare support, as well, tends to become multigenerational, locking otherwise highly capable people in a cycle of poverty.

Such social justice at taxpayer expense also leads to class warfare, as the very term "entitlement" fuels it. Those on public support tend to lose any sense of gratitude and begin to look at such aid as a right. Social Security, for all the good it's done, is especially guilty of this. Most recipients can be expected to draw out far more in benefits than they ever paid in, including any interest rightly due on this money, yet almost no one dares call it a Ponzi scheme. Most recipients feel this monthly check is something they're entitled to, and resent any effort to reform a now unsustainable system. Any politician who advocates reform does so at his own political peril. Welfare works the same way, and in time, many recipients often come to resent those "rich folks" who pay their bill every month. Very often, the rich, who are paying out of compulsion, come to resent the poor. In cold and impersonal government hands these programs only tend to alienate us towards each other, and no one really wins.

However well intended welfare might be, it reveals the failure of a Church that surrendered her mission and authority to a, godless, state, and the consequences of our surrender to the mandates of the state show this as such aid has failed to be a lifting force to bring people out of poverty. All too often, it has only served to fostering bad life choices, like immorality. This was true even in the 1930s; government works projects under federal administration, restricted employment to only one member of a family. While this may have been a prudent use of government funds, it did much to breed immorality. If a man and a woman, both employed in public works, fell in love, married, having only half the money they once had was out of the question. Instead, they shacked up. Welfare, Social Security, and other such programs also carry with them a marriage penalty. The very nature of our "social justice" is doing us all great harm with lost morality, dependency, loss of self-esteem, and class warfare. Should Christians even support, much less advocate, the very things that destroy us?

As God saw it, the assistance of those in need was a mission of the Church. It wasn't God's plan to pass it on to a cold, humanistic state, but by meeting those in need where they are. Granted, no church or even group of churches today could ever hope to step up and take over these programs as they are now administered. By abrogating social welfare to the government, we've created an unsustainable monster, that, barring major revision, not even the full force of the US economy can afford either. God knew this better than we do.

When Church charities provide for the helpless poor, aged, and infirm, they provide them as well with statement of value or worth. God values them, and His love is confirmed. God has never been as concerned about programs or wealth distribution as He is about the value of each person, including the working poor. "You shall not oppress a hired servant who is poor and needy... You shall give him his wages on his day (he earns it), before the sun sets... So that he may not cry out against you to the Lord, and it become sin in you" (Deuteronomy 24:14, 15). A bureaucracy can't meet fluid daily needs, it can only act in a legally structured way, but a church can. Neither can a government program always discern between the needy and the lazy. "If any one will not work, neither let him eat" (II Thessalonians 3:10). There's a difference between can't and won't, and most of those on disability can still do something to benefit someone. While "He supports the fatherless and the widow" (Psalm 146:9), He also condemns sloth. "Now we command you brethren, in the name of our Lord Jesus Christ, that you keep aloof from every brother who leads an unruly (in idleness) life," (II Thessalonians 3:6). God has a calling and a purpose for all of us in serving each other.

God is in the human dignity business. Most everyone is familiar with the song, "You're Nobody Till Somebody Loves You." God loves us, imputes value to us, and gives purpose. Therefore, we are somebody and called to His purpose. Paul said of a church supported widow, in I Timothy 5:10, "Having a reputation for good works; and if she has brought up children, if she has shown hospitality to strangers, if she has washed the saint's feet, assisted those in distress, and if she has devoted herself to every good work." Dorcas, in Acts 9:36-39, was a servant in her sewing. Those who provide service can feel good in meeting needs and being a witness for Christ. They are pleasing to God.

When we surrender our commission to social justice to the government, the value of the recipient is the first casualty. Governments cannot give value, not of a spiritual quality anyway. In a Christian government system, it might prove somewhat closer to workable, but at best, it's a poor second to what the Church was called to do. Even at its best, government can only administer what God has provided, and rarely do governments rightly do even that.

America will probably never again be a Christian nation, barring a massive revival, and we see all around us, an ever growing, ever demanding, ever intrusive government rising to take God's place. It also brings destruction on us, even without God's direct judgment. By doing everything for us, it's empowered to take over our liberties. If the Church were to take back social justice for the Church, this would go a long way in disarming the state. In so doing, this would offer a defining moment for both America and us. For Christians, at least, dependency would be on God rather than on the state. How great of a statement of faith would that be?

Government has nudged the church from her mission, and brought failure to society and humiliation to the Church. How can we go about reclaiming our mission? It would have to be something done in stages, but if genuine commitment were made to God to do this, would He not bless us? We can be confident of His provision. "And my God shall supply all your needs according to His riches in glory in Christ Jesus" (Philippians 4:19).

At what point a Christian should disobey the government is open to question, especially depending on the form of government we have, but there are some absolutes. In reference to the Gospel message, Peter and John said, "Whether it is right in the sight of God to give heed to you rather than to God, you be the judge; for we cannot stop speaking what we have seen and heard" (Acts 4:19, 20). Clearly, government doesn't own morality, dispense or decide our, God given, rights, rule our hearts, or have the right to limit our freedom of thought. It has no rightful authority in America to restrict our liberty, or of the worship of God anywhere on earth and will not, unless we let it. It is time for us to go on the offensive for our God, our faith, and then our nation.

Our founders understood that God was the author of government, and the ultimate authority. Here, government is by the authority of the governed, not the other way around. This served as the basis for the system they established. "For the Lord is our judge, the Lord is our law giver, the Lord is our king; He will save us" (Isaiah 33:22). God calls us to transform, not surrender; the question is, do we have the courage to make it happen?

# V

## NOTHING IS WORTH
## DYING FOR

*"And they overcame Him [Satan] because of the blood
of the Lamb and because of the word of their testimony,
and they did not love their life even to death."*

—Revelation 12:11

Back in 1968, the nation seemed destined to fall apart. The Vietnam War, according to even Walter Cronkite of the CBS News, was now unwinnable. The January Tet Offensive by the North Vietnamese and the Viet Cong finally disillusioned even him. Public sentiment reflected the deepening chasm in our society fed by the war and social differences. Our nation seemed headed for a civil war. Each traumatic event, like the April fourth assassination of Martin Luther King Jr. followed a month later by that of "Bobby" Kennedy, threatened to be the spark to set it off. On August 21, Soviet tanks crushed "Prague Spring" and Alexander Dubcek's Czechoslovakian reforms. There were the "Chicago Seven," and radical protests in that city while the Democrats were selecting Hubert Humphrey as their presidential candidate. Each confrontation edged us closer to igniting civil war or an anarchic revolution. Ironically, one of the peace slogans then threatening to destroy us was, "Nothing is worth dying for." Now it could kill millions of us.

This slogan originated as a retort to one from the 1950's: "Better Dead than Red." This first slogan was a response to the communistic encroachment of the USSR and Red China in the world. By both hegemony and naked aggression, with infiltration even into our own country; they had exploited colonial break ups and were poised as ready to take over the whole world. Under the spreading mushroom tree (the H-bomb), the threat seemed real. This slogan was a rallying cry to remind us there were things worth dying for. It was better to die in a thermonuclear war than of torture and starvation in a Soviet gulag. This also echoed back to 1775 and the words of Patrick Henry (1736-1799) in the Virginia Provincial Convention. "I know not what course others may take, but as for me, give me liberty or give me death."

The intellectual turbulence of the decades before was now bearing fruit in the convictions of the newly arrived "Now" Generation, or "Baby Boomers." The now seen as unwinnable Vietnam War "quagmire," was well into its fourth year of active combat. This generation didn't see any war, much less one in a far away place, as worth their blood. The government, and the "progressive" President Lyndon B. Johnson (1963-1969) did have its arguments for it. But his "credibility gap," as the media referred to his statements, undermined his position. One, of these was the policy of "Containment," dated from the Korean War. This set the stage for limited wars designed to do no more than halt violence. It could not take the war home to the aggressors or their Soviet and Maoist sponsors; its only hope was to outlast them. Financially, we had the most skin in the game. Added to this was the "Domino Theory," which asserted that were we not to confront aggression in Vietnam; it would lead to the fall of all of Southeast Asia to Communism, including Australia, New Zealand, and The Philippines. To the New Left, as many of these protestors were, neither of these mattered. Many even sported the slogans, "Better Red than Dead" and "Live For Today."

The intellectual dichotomy and dishonesty of their position was intriguing. The takeover of China in 1949 by the Communists under Chairman Mao Zedung (1893-1976) was accepted as reality as was the June 25, 1950 invasion of South Korea by the North, with China's aid, and other events including the French defeat in Indochina. To the intellectual left, however, all the atrocities perpetrated by Communism were categorically denied. Mao's "Little Red Book" was popular reading. What those readers blindly refused to see was that the Mao of that book and the Mao who ruled China were two very opposite people. The mindset of the "Counterculture," or much of the "Now Generation," wouldn't let them even listen to any intellectual challenge to their position or any opinion but their own. Nothing was worth dying for, "Peace at any price." Even slavery, to the Communists, seemed preferable to a far away war.

While the surface currents of this movement were primarily of opposition to this war, the growing "Counterculture" was fueled by a host of other issues as well. One was a fear of doomsday. They had grown up under the spreading "mushroom tree." Graphic images of Hiroshima and Nagasaki had implanted into everyone's minds the horrors of nuclear war. While some in the State Department tried to convince us that, as a nation, we could survive, and even win such a war, their arguments ignored reality. Americans of all generations realistically saw in any significant nuclear exchange not only death to untold millions but an end to civilization and a poisoning of the planet. Most hoped that the doctrine of "Massive Retaliation" of the 1950s would intimidate the Soviet "Bear" (the Bear is a symbol of Russia, like Uncle Sam is of us) into a less confrontational world policy.

In the summer of 1962, however, that Bear, under Nikita Khrushchev, Premier from 1955-1964, pushed us to a new level of nuclear brinkmanship. The USSR began to install nuclear missiles in Cuba, less than two hundred fifty miles from Miami, Florida. By October, a confrontation between them and us over those missiles led to a crisis. Then, an American blockade of Cuba brought us to the brink of the unthinkable: all out nuclear war. All those imprinted images of horrible death flashed in our minds. From this crisis, our whole nation began to reflect on the question of if our position was worth dying for. When a new generation began to openly question if it was, many of their parents found themselves, in their hearts, in agreement. Our growing apprehension now fueled two entirely opposite positions on nuclear arms, both motivated by fear of death.

One was a policy of strength. The idea was to create an image in the minds of the Soviets that such a war was unwinnable by either side, even if they struck first. Mutually Assured Destruction, or MAD, would hold hostage their people and assure the doomsday machine would never be used. Our arsenals needed to be increased.

The other position was disarmament, or to get rid of all nukes. It was noted that even Andrei Sakharov (1921- 1989), head of the Soviet nuclear program, was in agreement. There is some honest speculation that this might have worked, had the leadership of the USSR been open to a free exchange of ideas, but from July 21, 1967 on, they ignored, rejected, and resorted to the censorship of any appeal by Sakharov or others in their own peace movement. A one-sided disarmament would have spelled disaster to the world, though pressure in the West to do so continued to build.

As the 1960's progressed into the 1970's, other nations joined the nuclear club as well. In 1974, India joined the US, USSR, France, Great Britain, and China. At some point, maybe as early as 1976, so did Israel. The USSR and, despite our defense cutbacks, the US, were locked in an endless proliferation race. The Soviets envisioned a psychological war of nuclear intimidation. Their intent was to posture the Western World into a position of fear that would result in its collapse in any future confrontation, without the fighting of a major war. By the late 1970s the US anti-nuclear movement led US President Jimmy Carter to kill plans for the B-1 Bomber, an advanced weapon to counter the Soviet Backfire Bomber, the neutron bomb, and other programs. The dread of nuclear weapons, combined with the belief nothing was worth dying for, came close to costing us all our liberty and our civilization.

In 1989, the Iron Curtain fell, and on August 21, 1991, so did the Soviet Union. The "mushroom tree" went into decline as both the Russian leader, Borris Yeltzin, from 1991-1999, and US Presidents George Bush Sr. and Bill Clinton seemed to be racing with each other to cut these arsenals. The Peace Movement seemed to be winning, but in May 1998, Pakistan joined the club. North Korea followed in October 2006, and Iran is on the verge of joining. If not for preemptive Israeli air strikes, both Syria and Iraq would have joined as well. Fear of confrontation has kept the US and the West from preventing North Korea's entry to it, and will Iran's as well. A philosophy of "nothing worth dying for" casts a long shadow over our foreign policy and our potential survival as a society.

There is an even greater concern considering the prospects of more players at the table: the terrorist network. Much of the weapons-grade plutonium from the collapse of the USSR has never been accounted for and could end up in terrorist hands. If Pakistan was to fall to the terrorists, or if Iran supplied them one, the world would go into panic. It is feared, as shown in several strategic studies, that a nuclear detonation by an unknown group anywhere in the world would create political revolt and a surrender mindset throughout the West. Among the casualties would be our own Bill of Rights and potentially the whole Constitution in a tidal wave of panicked paranoia. Any attack on us today would most likely lead to surrender to any terrorist demands. Most of us are no longer willing to die for our beliefs or standard of living.

Our new self-focused American religions also render us impotent to meet any real crisis. In the *Declaration of Independence* are the words: "With a firm reliance on the protection of divine providence, we mutually pledge to each other our lives, our fortunes, and our sacred honor." However, this cohesive power of love for God and love for each other is now foreign to our society. Living for this life alone brings a dread of death upon us. The idea of some things being worse than death now seems strange to us. Life has become for the moment and "live for today" is a modern tenet of humanism. Sadly, this has found its way into the Church.

Back in 1997, a dear Christian lady was planning an overseas mission trip by plane. Only days before her planned trip, there was a plane crash. On August 6, Korean flight KAL 801 crash-landed at Guam, killing 208 of the 254 on board. Terrorism was suspected. Like so many other Americans, she was terrified and was strongly reconsidering her trip. She even used the words, "Nothing is worth dying for." Thankfully, she put her trust in the Lord and took the flight anyway, but she was not the first Christian to say this. This is a belief that keeps many back from committed service.

Is there anything worth dying for? And how did America get to where we are today? Is life our most important possession? What does our history teach us about our nation's past, and legacy? A common theme in our past wars was the slogan: "For God, for family, and for country." The patriot Nathan Hale (1755-1776) is famous for this shortened quip, "I only regret that I have but one life to give for my country." In his mind, country included family, and God. It's also noteworthy that, in the order of this slogan, God was first for a reason. "Do not be afraid of them; remember the Lord who is great and awesome, and fight for your brothers, your sons, your daughters, your wives, and your houses" (Nehemiah 4:14).

It must be noted that the first casualty in our new age was God. With this foundation gone, the rest soon followed. Our society now has manhood in the crosshairs. Masculinity is mocked and has almost become illegal. This reflects a historical omen, as dying civilizations tend to mock and abolish those values that once made them great. Today in America, it's hard to fight for family when mothers, wives, and daughters are out fighting with the men. This only leaves country to fight for. With the rewriting of history since, at least, the 1970s, many Americans are no longer proud of our country. This showed in the numbers of those who approved of President Obama's international tour in 2009. Each apology for America's wealth, mission, and legacy brought almost unanimous agreement from our academia and media leaders. Too many Americans have become like sheep following a shepherd. It should make us all a little apprehensive about where we are being led and by whom. In addition to nation bashing, other forces are at work.

For many in our nation, life is the most prized of all possessions. With a half-century plus of indoctrination by the religion of humanism, large numbers now view this life as all there is. An old beer commercial reflected this: "You only go around once in life, so get all the gusto you can get." With our emphasis on health, safety, security, peace at any price, self-centered distrust, and a desire to keep any threats away from us, it is no wonder this has become so important. Humanism teaches that there is nothing else, that there is no real meaning outside of us. The Humanist Manifesto I (1933) and the Humanist Manifesto II (1973) deny any purpose or value for man outride of this physical realm alone, and since 1962, the Supreme Court has systematically decreed this to be our national religion.

It's been said that if, in 1960, a foreign power had invaded us and imposed the spiritual, cultural, and moral changes of the last half-century, the whole nation would've risen in revolt. In increments, or going one step at a time, a subversive power has done just that with few doing anything about it. Why? In 1888, William Thompson Sedgwick repeated an 1872 experiment by another scientist, A. Heinzmann. A frog was put into a pan of water it could easily escape from. The water was heated at a rate of about .3 of a degree Fahrenheit per minute from a seventy-degree starting point until the frog died from the heat. While many modem scientists challenge the results, there's good reason to believe this happened. Its point has been made: slow change can usually be achieved through a steady influence by a determined source. In our case, our original values have been boiled or frozen to death by the humanist takeover of our society.

From a Christian perspective, there are many things worth dying for. For me, I'd gladly give my very existence to have my nation restored to being a Christian one again. In 1861, many Christians saw at least two things to die for. For many Christians in the eleven southern states, secession from the Union was not over slavery, it was over the moral belief in self-determination and providing a future for their children, wrapped up in the term "States Rights." They felt a potentially crushing imposition on themselves of tariffs, regulations, and national interference that was gradually impoverishing them and destroying their way of life. With a precedent set eighty-five years before by our Declaration of Independence, and a belief that God was on their side, they acted on their convictions. Others, however, did have less altruistic motives, these being slavery and an exploited wealth, as well as a Southern pride that bordered on elitism.

In the North, many Christians believed, first and foremost, in a duty to defend their county. The preservation of the Union was what their government was defending, and as Christians, they were called upon to obey (Romans 13:1-7). Many also saw slavery as a moral evil, and they were willing to invest their blood to free others from it. They, too, believed God was on their side. Before it was over, a million Americans lay dead, two-thirds of them combatants, but God's favor was on those who sought Him, and He was on the side of righteousness and justice. Four plus million people were endowed with liberty. The North underwent a spiritual revival and devotion to a dignity that eventually would include all peoples.

Our families are worth dying for. Ask almost any mother or father. In 1967, a New York woman made the news. Her toddler was trapped under the rear end of the family car. This one hundred and ten pound woman proceeded to lift the back of that vehicle to pull her child to safety. This is a love that husbands are to have for their wives as well. "Husbands love your wives just as Christ loved the Church and gave Himself up for her" (Ephesians 5:25). To die for family is a death well approved.

Many of our Christian values are worth dying for as well. Famous evangelist Billy Sunday (1862-1935) once said, "The streets of America will [would] run red with blood before we [Christians] allow the Bible to be removed from our schools." Evidently, the modern Church didn't agree. They didn't see the eternal life of their children as worth dying for. As a logical result of this choice, about one in four have died to abortion since the 1973 Supreme Court ruling on Roe v. Wade. Even in Christian homes, another third are lost spiritually to the humanist world. Since we wouldn't die for them, now they are dying for us.

With the Bible no longer worth our dying for, neither is our Constitution. Also forsaken is the American spirit it once stood for. Once again, even among many Christians, what is feared most is death. Our health and safety policies have come to reflect this. Safety and security have become gods, as is shown in many ways. One is seen in the death of the Constitution itself. The Fourth Amendment says, "The right of the people to be secure in their persons, houses, papers, and effects, against unreasonable searches and seizures, shall not be violated, and no warrants shall issue, but upon probable cause." Some criminals even use this protection to argue against being harassed by overzealous law enforcement surveillance, but today, America has fallen in love with having a watchful eye monitoring every one. Now, all of us, unless we never leave our homes, will have our picture taken by multiple security cameras every day. It's next to impossible to buy gas, groceries, go to a bank, government office, school, shopping mall, or parking garage without encountering them. Several cities now monitor their downtown areas as well, and this doesn't count things like airport security. With a combination of cardio sensors, thermal cameras, eye trackers, and high-resolution video cameras, the threshold of reading our minds is about to be crossed.

This monitoring is not limited to just cameras. Thanks to the Patriot Act and Homeland Security, cell phones can be used to track about ninety-five percent of us. Computers, bank accounts, library patronage, automobiles, and any other travel can be monitored as well. Most Americans now have On-star or GPS (Global Positioning System) in at least one vehicle. In addition, local law enforcement agencies are required to keep lists of potential security and terrorist threats. People can find themselves on it simply for being a member of a religious group outside of governmental accepted norms. Any civic, volunteer, or activist group member, especially to include almost any "right wing" organization, is now seen as a potential security threat. Being tagged as extremist, as large numbers of conservative Christians are labeled, will get them on this list. To a large degree, this negates the Fifth and Sixth Amendments as well.

This encroachment is not limited to the public sector, the private does this too. Background security checks, drug tests, and a credit rating report are often conditions for employment. At the time that this is being written, a statewide background check can be had for $12.95 and a nationwide one for $16.95. With each passing year, the information gathered, or at least sought, is ever more intrusive. Questions may even cover one's diet, TV and entertainment choices, friends, and spending habits. It is argued that if someone objects to this, they must have something to hide. Corporations like Hewlett Packard are developing commercial scanners, as well, to some degree, read our minds as we enter a business or exit into the public. Our liberty and privacy no longer is sacred or even an option.

Ironically, though, while government and employers have the power to know all about us, we are increasingly isolated from each other. Government is to blame for much of this social shift. The FERPA, or Family Education Rights Privacy Act, of 1974, in protecting student rights, imposed extreme privacy access rules beyond any reasonable shield for our children. HIPAA, or the 1996 Health Insurance Portability and Accountability Act, in protecting patient rights, does the same thing. The privacy of medical information even prevents family members from knowing about a person's health issues, yet health insurance companies can access this same information for marketing purposes. The super-rights of the perverse are protected, however. While, at this point, the exact status of a 2011 Missouri law that made it illegal for teachers to interact with their students on Twitter is in question, the ACLU is forcing these same schools to allow homosexual pornography access to students via the Internet.

In other ways we've done this to ourselves, in our new age of fear. It used to be that if someone wanted to get in touch with another person, a phone book provided their number and address. For a small fee, calling information would do the same for one in another city. Granted, some people did have unlisted numbers for protection or privacy, but now, with the proliferation of cell phones, finding someone is getting less and less possible. This only serves to weaken community ties. Privacy has come to divide us and make us even more dependent on the government.

Public safety is another area showing our safety-security paranoia. Years ago, for example, the standard for food and product safety was one of reasonable expectation. While we were protected from the unscrupulous that would adulterate, dilute, and deceive, there was still a degree of "caveat emptor," or buyer beware. If something didn't look, smell, taste, or feel right, the consumer had a responsibility to take it back or throw it away. Fear of injury or death has moved this standard to one of zero tolerance, even to the point of legal liability for consumer carelessness or misuse; hence, a $2,700,000.00 cup of McDonalds coffee.

This fear of death and injury safety standard has now come to apply to personal choices. In the 1980's, seatbelt usage went from voluntary to mandatory. The government decided, via a bureaucracy, to take away an American right of self- determination. It knows better than we do what is best for us. This self-ascribed mandate is seen in the multiplication of antismoking (of tobacco, anyway) campaigns, growing legislative efforts to regulate obesity, limit consumption of trans-fats, salt, sugar, red meats, etc. A rising tide of behavioral concerns are being scrutinized as well, from exercise programs to our social circles, and marked for future regulation. Government has become our security.

Our founders, who believed their cause was worth dying for, said, "God is our security." Government today intrudes on our rights in claiming to protect us from everything. Benjamin Franklin (1706-1790) said, "He who trades a little liberty for a little security (or safety) will soon find he has neither." Sadly, the Christian community has acquiesced to the government; these rights seem no longer worth fighting or dying for. Rather than see the dangers, Christians all too easily give in and let someone else be responsible for them. It has long been believed by many theologians over the centuries that when the "Mark of the Beast" (Revelation 13:16-18) comes along, it will not be a significant shift from what the Church has already compromised into accepting. Loss of liberty is not just temporal, it has spiritual connotations. Voluntary slavery has consequences. Remember the frog in the water?

If we're willing to surrender what we value and live as slaves just to live, then we have already submitted to slavery in our hearts. In I Corinthians

7:21, Paul exhorts us to go the other way. "But if you are able also to become free, rather do that." To get a balance, Esther 7:4 "…Now if we had only been sold as slaves, men and women, I would have remained silent, for the trouble would not be commensurate with the annoyance to the king." should also be read, but with consideration for the government they were under at that time. Our Constitutional Republic, on the other hand, was founded and amended by blood to uphold liberty, and our liberty itself was the gift of God.

Our surrender results from our not having died to self. Our lives are unfruitfully wrapped up in pleasing the flesh, and society provides us this very well. "Truly, truly I say to you, unless a grain of wheat falls into the earth and dies, it remains by itself alone, but if it dies, it bears much fruit. He who loves his life will lose it, and he who hates his life in this world shall keep it to life eternal" (John 12:24, 25). Christians, too often, fear the wrong death.

In all our worry, compliance, or surrender to the world we really cannot benefit ourselves, anyway. "And which of you by being anxious, can add a single cubit to his life span?" (Matthew 6:27). And again Jesus said, "No one can serve two masters; for either he will hate the one and love the other… You cannot serve [both] God and mammon" (Matthew 6:24). By fearing the things of the world, we pay homage to the wrong master. "I tell you My friends, do not be afraid of those who kill the body, and after that they have no more that they can do. But I will warn you whom to fear; fear the One who after He has killed, has the power to cast into Hell; yes, I tell you, fear Him!" (Luke 12:4, 5).

It has been said, "Unless one is ready to die they are not really ready to live." Earth is only our temporary abode. The Psalmist, in 90:12, said, "So teach us to number our days that we may present to Thee a heart of wisdom." God is the author of life. He, not the government, determines mortality rates. A selfish clinging to this life, as if it was all we have, destroys true happiness and purpose, and also, our witness. It is rather hard to share our faith in a better place while selfishly clinging to all this life has to offer.

A selfish fear of death cripples, or at least impedes, our family relationships as well. Self-love convinces us to look out for number-one. This unhealthy view of life and self makes us takers, not givers. Marriage becomes contractual, a fifty-fifty agreement, not a covenant of love, honor, and consideration. Since husbands are to be the head of the home, the first example must be theirs as they are charged with the protection of their families, physically, emotionally, and spiritually. "You husbands likewise, live with your wives in an understanding way, as with a weaker vessel [fine china] since she is a woman, and grant her honor as a fellow heir of the grace of life, so that your prayers may not be hindered," (I Peter 3:7). Love is, by its very nature, sacrificial; it is a death to self and to the world. Strange as it may sound, a feeling that nothing is worth dying for and the rampant break up of marriage both trace back to the same root, a wrongful, self-centered love. The person consumed with it is out to get all they can get in life. Sacrificial love is the answer to these problems.

This affects our children too. Earlier, it was stated that most fathers and mothers would die for their children. A fear of death and its inherent selfishness is what prevents others from doing so. In fact, with self-centered love, the exact opposite is true. The leading reason for abortion is a fear of losing the things of life that the parents are not willing to give up. When this life becomes all one values, this "burden," or unwanted baby, must be gotten rid of so one can live as they wish. Mother Teresa of Calcutta (1910-1997) said as much: "It is a tragedy that a child must die so that you might live as you please." There's a double tragedy here as well. This choice doesn't bring happiness. Instead, it brings anger, depression, and guilt in many cases with Post Traumatic Stress Syndrome, as well as a lonely longing about what might have been. Fulfilling happiness comes only in giving that child life and in either raising it in a loving home or giving it to another home where this can be found.

Fear of death has also led to some of the greatest atrocities of history. King Jehoram of Judah was a man out of touch with God, and fearful for his life. "When Jehoram had taken over the kingdom of his father and made himself secure, he killed all his brothers with the sword, and some of the rulers of Israel also" (II Chronicles 21:4). He had paranoia that one or more of his brothers might conspire against him at some point in the future. Also, his wicked wife, Athaliah, had abetted him in idolatry, and his trust was not in the Lord.

People who believe there is absolutely nothing they are willing to die for, and have a dread of death, all too often have a totally different opinion when it comes to the lives of others. Soviet Premier Joseph Stalin (1979-1953), who ruled from 1924-1953, had a terrible fear of death. His resulting paranoia led to the murder of twenty-four to thirty million of his own people including repeated purges of any deputies or party officials who got too close to power. During World War II, he wasn't afraid to mass sacrifice whole armies to halt the Nazi invasion. Of the estimated total twenty-two million plus Russians who died to the invaders, a third to a half were sacrificed unnecessarily. Even as he lay dying in 1953, the best medical team in the USSR was assembled and was told that if they allowed him to die, they would die with him.

This is not to say that everyone who believes that "nothing is worth dying for" is divorced, a lousy pro-abortion parent, or a mass murderer, but these things do go with the territory, and under the right circumstance, often come out. Such cowardice also brings slavery, not just to the powers above us, whether physical or spiritual, but to the dreads within our own minds. Fear usually hurts us more than reality ever could, but a Christian has no reason to fear death. God is our future and our life.

If we have truly committed all to Him, then we understand this is something worth giving our lives for. He approves of our death if it is for the right reasons. Family, country, and our sacred values, all have been addressed, but there is the issue of property. Should a Christian be willing to kill or die for worldly possessions? The key here is attitude, and the purpose being served by it. Soldiers, for example, are frequently called upon to defend both life and property, as are fire fighters, police, and others. But wealth can be our worst enemy. "For what will a man be profited, if he gains the whole world and forfeits his soul?" (Matthew 16:26). Wealth can keep us from true service to God, as the Rich Young Ruler showed, in Matthew 19:16-22. Sometimes it takes a cataclysmic event to remove things from us and free us to open our spiritual eyes. Noted poet and songwriter, Francis "Fanny" Crosby (1820-1915), testified to this spiritual truth. Her blind eyes brought her a greater vision to her soul.

There are times property is definitely worth dying for. The defense of property from thieves is sanctioned by God (Exodus 22:2, Matthew 24:43). He also approved of it in times of war (Joshua 1:9), and in defending the property rights of others. This may be in a Church mission role. Paul took an entourage with him when he took the Gentile offering to Jerusalem in Acts 19:21-21:18. Jesus also showed this, by His example. His Father's "property" was the Temple. When He cleansed this Temple, driving out by force all who wrongfully profited at God's expense, in essence, He signed His own death warrant (Luke 22:1-5).

All that God values, we too must value. We were worth His sending His son to die for us. His glory and His purposes are worth our dying for. "Greater love has no man than to lay down his life for his friends" (John 15:13). Jesus didn't just die for His friends; He also died for His enemies. Thus, our willingness to die must also include our enemies as well. "Love your enemies and pray for those who persecute you" (Matthew 5:14). Jesus did this from the cross as He died for them (Luke 23:34). They were worth Jesus's life; they are also worth ours. There probably is no greater thing worth dying for than to save our enemies, or anyone else, from hell. We can see Jesus's excitement and approval in the death of Stephen. "But being full of the Holy Spirit, he gazed intently into Heaven and saw the glory of God, and Jesus standing at the right hand of God" (Acts 7:55). Stephen's death for his enemies brought Jesus to His feet. This approval of Jesus is definitely worth dying for.

# VI

## HE WHO LOVES FAMILY MORE THAN ME

*"He who loved father or mother more than Me is not worthy of Me; and he who loved son or daughter more than me is not worthy of Me."*

—Matthew 10:37

When Jesus spoke these words, most of His followers had very little understanding as to what they really meant. John the Baptist was in prison, but this was said before his death, and many still felt the Messiah would save him. All of the organized opposition and plots by the Jewish hierarchy to destroy Jesus were also, mostly, in the future. Jesus had already ruffled their feathers on multiple occasions, however, and His disciples were beginning to feel the heat. "But beware of men; for they will deliver you up to the courts, and scourge you in their synagogues" (Matthew 10:17). Most, though, held in their hearts the belief in a conquering Christ and didn't really feel Jesus would allow things to get too far out of hand. These words didn't really sink in. While they had come to experience some sacrifices of discipleship, none really believed, at this point anyway, that they would be called upon to die. They weren't to the point of "booking plane tickets" for their coming worldwide mission. It would still be some time before Peter would say, "Behold, we have left everything and followed you" (Matthew 19:27).

It didn't take long, though, for these words to hit home. The time of excommunication from the synagogue worship began even as Jesus still walked in Palestine. the Jewish leadership made a determined effort to silence Jesus's supporters: "And there was much grumbling among the multitudes concerning Him... Yet no one was speaking openly of Him for fear of the Jews [leaders]" (John 7:12, 13). When Jesus healed the man born blind in Jerusalem, the Jewish leaders asked his parents about the incident. They told them to ask their son for themselves. "His parents said this because they were afraid of the Jews, for the Jews had already agreed that if anyone should confess Him to be the Christ, he should be put out of the synagogue" (John 9:22). Because of his statement of faith, the healed man was cast out.

Synagogue excommunication very soon led to family expulsion as well. Judaism was as much about culture, economics, and family as it was religion. It was a way of life. Persecution would come to the Church on all levels, all too soon.

Many of those who became Christians on the Day of Pentecost soon found themselves both excommunicated and homeless. Their loved ones, either by their own zeal and personal convictions or under pressure from the Jewish leadership, would have a mock funeral for the new Christian. From that point on, they were considered dead to their families. All of their possessions would be removed and placed outside of their homes. They would either be left in the yard, nearest street, or maybe in the burning trash heaps in the Hinnom Valley. The message here would have carried yet another connotation, the Hinnom dumps had given rise to the term Gehenna, or "fiery hell" (Matthew 18:9). There is probably little that would hurt a person more than for their family members telling them to, "Go to hell!"

This loss of home was not the only suffering these new converts faced. If this family member had a job, very often they lost it. Many of their jobs were family or clan oriented. For those that were not, they were still usually with Jewish employers. These bosses also would have feared, and followed the Jewish leadership and did not want their displeasure. This often led to dismissal. To all society, they often became dead. Ironically though, many could still go to the Temple to worship, as did Peter and John, with frequency.

The early Church was forced into immediate action. A safety net was quickly set up to keep the dispossessed from falling through the cracks. "And they began selling their property and possessions, and were sharing them with all, as anyone might have need" (Acts 2:45). In having all things in common, this meant more than just food. They practiced hospitality by opening their homes. The Church learned early on how to be a community, or a family. It was only later, in Acts 6:1-6, that it developed into an organization.

If it hadn't have become a family, the Church might very well have died out. To begin with, at that time, Jerusalem and all of Palestine was overpopulated. As many as six million people were crammed into an area that was not much bigger than Massachusetts. Much of the land was unfit for agriculture or even the grazing of livestock. Poor parents often didn't even name their small children until they were five or six, as so many died early. Twenty children might result in three or four reaching age twenty. The Jewish leaders definitely didn't care if a few heretics died. As for Rome, they weren't in the charity business, and the Jews were not their favorite people anyway. If a few rebellious Jews died, it was no great loss to them.

This was one reason for Jesus's answer to Peter's statement (Matthew 19:27) of having left everything to follow Him. "Jesus said to him, 'Truly, I say to you, that you who have followed Me in the regeneration when the Son of Man sits on His glorious throne...everyone who has left houses or brothers or sisters or father or mother or children or farms for My names sake, will receive many times as much, and shall inherit eternal life'" (Matthew 19:28, 29). Even the Apostle Paul, upon his return to Jerusalem after his conversion, was in all likelihood cut off from much of his family. "More than that, I count all things to be loss in view of the surpassing value of knowing Christ Jesus my Lord" (Philippians 3:8).

While it did exist, this ostracism, as the Gentiles would call the cutting of a person off by family and society, was far less common in the Roman world and, later, all of Europe, but it did happen. One noteworthy example was in Scandinavia around AD 990. In the preceding years, Christianity was brought to the Vikings (Scandinavia) largely through the capture of Christians from their homes via Viking raids. In general, the Norse were tolerant to the religions of others, and Christianity took hold among many of them as well. As time went by, this led to Bluetooth, a Christian king, coming to the throne of the Danes, or one of the three major segments of the Vikings. But his son, Sweyn, known as the "King of the Norse," sought the reinstatement of worship of the pagan Norse deities upon his realm. In the process, he divorced his Christian wife, Gunhind, according to the records, because of her faith in Jesus. Both she and her young son, Chanute, were banished to her native Poland.

About thirty years later, in 1019, this Chanute became king over Denmark and a domain including much of England, which he had taken in 1016. His realm and the influence of his faith, in time stretched to most of the Scandinavian world. This is the king who, in about 1030, while at Thorney Island, or Westminster, was one day challenged in his soul by those who ascribed greatness beyond what he felt he was due. In response to them, he commanded the seas by ordering the tide to not come in. When it did anyway, he said, "Let all men know how empty and worthless is the power of kings, for there is none worthy of the name but He whom Heaven, earth, and sea obey by eternal laws." How much different would history have been if no one had taken him and his mother in years earlier. When he died in 1035, he left behind a Christian legacy that has endured the test of time.

In our era, it is quite common, especially in Asia and North Africa for Christians to be excommunicated from their society. Hindus, and in some cases, Buddhists show ever growing anti-Christian militancy. The majority of the Muslim world has long been notorious for disowning, and even killing, family members who convert to Christianity. Meanwhile, those who are Christians continue to face ever-increasing pressure to deny their faith. In several Muslim lands, most noteworthy in Pakistan, long distant family members have reduced the Christian community to slavery, in essence, to punish them for their faith. What is strange about this is that, even in the Qur'an, Christians are listed among the accepted people of faith or "of the Book." Regardless, though, family can be one's own worst enemies.

Even in the, supposedly, religiously open Western World, including America, this happens. While there usually is enough support to help these Christians, this is an area the Church needs to meet. While these outcasts very often make the most convicted, and often fruitful, of all Christians, they won't be if no one steps in to sustain them. We are under obligation to act to preserve them. What if one of these rejected Christians was potentially another Chanute? Or Apostle Paul? Or an angel? "Do not neglect to show hospitality to strangers, for thereby some have entertained angels unawares" (Hebrews 13:2).

Disowning is but one tool Satan uses against the Church. He knows what works best in any given culture to ensnare or defeat us. "And brother will deliver up brother to death, and father his child, and children will rise up against parents and have them put to death" (Mark 13:12).

But there are different types of family persecution that have different affects on the Church. All too often, an unbelieving husband has withheld financial consideration from a believing wife. There have been numerous cases of physical violence perpetrated against believing wives and children. In several cases, believing children have been denied college, prep school, or have been excluded from a family business or inheritance. I am aware, personally, of more than one case of both violence and financial exclusion, but they wish for anonymity.

Usually, family persecution is more subtle: "If your brother... or your son, or daughter, or the wife you cherish, or your friend who is as your own soul, entices you secretly, saying, 'Let us go and serve other gods,' (whom neither you nor your fathers have known)" (Deuteronomy 13:6). The pull is usually to compromise "just a little" in some area of life. This might be in a family's choice of entertainment, magazines that are purchased, movies that are rented or viewed, or TV shows that are watched. There are many ways Satan seeks to demolish family faith from within, with a subtle lure or pressure we often don't even see until the damage is done.

Subtlety works very effectively, at least most of the time, and this is especially true in family relationships. Confrontation, while it can be effective, as in kicking a believer out of the family, also tends to polarize. The attacked person becomes more deeply convicted and becomes a greater witness as well. Threats, hatred, and abuse often galvanize faith. Congeniality, on the other hand, tends to bring compromise or reconciliation. "A gentle answer turns away wrath, but a harsh word stirs up anger" (Proverbs 15:1). While this verse was meant to enhance Christian relationships, it can be used against us. Kindness, empathy, and friendship are tools to be used for good or for evil. Many a person has been talked into something against their better judgment because someone befriended them, whereas confrontation usually goes the other way.

Family relationships were intended by God to be powerful tools in affecting someone's behavior, and we learn that very young. Babies usually learn to get attention and what they need via their vocal chords. In time, most of these infants learn how to throw in a little anger or yell a little louder. As they get older, these tykes may hold their breath, kick their feet, throw things, lock doors, etc. By this point, a prudent parent has an arsenal of adverse actions to meet the child's antics with unpleasant results. Giving in to bad behavior usually will only lead to more of the same.

However, children also learn how to ask nicely and play the charm or the cute card. Cute, especially with girls, will often achieve desired goals. Boys can sometimes accomplish the same by charm, in imitating daddy, or trying to act all grown up. Children acquire skills to get what they want by negotiation and compromise. Depending on how or what is being negotiated, this can either be good or bad. In a positive way, it can aid in a child's maturity, in learning how to succeed in the real world, and building self-confidence.

Compromise can also be bad. Parents sometimes will allow a child to negotiate around moral safeguards. A child can end up in a situation that they cannot handle. Parents might think, for example, their daughter looks cute in a bikini without any thought of the message this is sending. In this field of sexuality, well meaning parents have put, or allowed temptation into their children's hands that results in moral compromise. This however, is not just the fault of parents. Our society at large has pushed us into moral compromise for all its worth.

The automobile is one such opportunity for moral compromise. For all the good it provides to society, it has the distinction of being one of the three biggest contributors to our moral decline. They have also served as one of the greatest battlegrounds between Christian parents and their worldly torn teen. Young people need to learn how to responsibly use autos, and to some extent, enjoy the freedom they bring. Some of this will involve interaction with the opposite sex. But parents fail their children, and the Lord when they allow their children too much freedom and opportunity before they are ready for it. If, and when, this opportunity leads to immorality, a change occurs in the heart of their child, one that will never be undone. "Surely she [the immoral woman] lurks as a robber, and increases the faithless among men" (Proverbs 23:28). This "faithless" can and does apply to both sexes, and even if the young person repents, this indiscretion puts a spiritual scar on their hearts which will never fully go away.

Too often, well meaning parents will sin by giving in to their children simply out of a desire to get along. They are more afraid of losing their child's affections than in offending God. Peace at any price applies to family as well as international affairs. Often we rationalize that with all of the hassles of modern life, any battle avoided is a battle won.

This may be what "father" David was thinking with his children. His oldest, and in all probability crown prince, son Amnon, had, with the help of peer pressure, sexually molested his half sister Tamar. Then, to add insult to injury, he totally rejected her, and had her physically cast out from his presence. Whether this was out of the guilt that sets in after the deed or contempt for her as a person, he brought upon himself the pernicious hatred of Tamar's full brother, and next in line after him for the throne, Absalom. "Now when King David heard of all these matters, he was very angry" (II Samuel 13:21), but he failed to act in a meaningful way. His own guilt over his past indiscretion with Bathsheba probably inhibited his own judgment.

Unfortunately, unresolved guilt can cloud a parent's judgement as well. Years ago, Planned Parenthood Corporation of America played on that guilt in encouraging teenagers to ask their "prude" parents what they were doing when they were growing up. The intent was to shame parents into silence so that PPC could sell more condoms, birth control pills, and abortions. For David, this guilt, plus a little more guilt over his parental neglect, combined with his desire to get along with his family, led him to do nothing. He just hoped that, in time, it would work itself out. In so doing, he put misdirected love of family ahead of God and disregarded God's commands. At the very least, he should have gotten with the priests and honored Leviticus 18:11 with its curse on incest. Honoring Deuteronomy 22:28, 29, he would have forced Amnon to marry Tamar to take away her disgrace. He also would have sent him away, at least for a time, and he would have forfeited his crown prince status.

By doing nothing, he didn't bring Amnon to repentance or family harmony. Absalom's hatred festered over the next two years, as did his growing contempt for his father, David. David soon lost his crown prince to Absalom's murderous rage and lost the loyalty of many of his own countrymen. If there had been a recall election, David would have lost the throne. Five years later, he almost did lose it to a revolt fostered by Absalom, who now utterly hated his dad. When he defeated this crisis, another revolt soon followed as Sheba, the Benjamite, challenged him. Though he reestablished his reign, things were never the same again.

Today, there are a host of challenges to our families and our love for God, as well. As children grow up, other people and things come to replace much of the moral and emotional support once provided by the parents. Peer pressure plays a big role and so does TV. Many parents come to see television as a cheap and effective baby sitter. It can also be a very dangerous guest, or intruder, into our homes. It has the status of being the second major pillar in moral decline. The third one, by the way, is coed public swimming. If parents are judicious about what and how much their children watch, TV can be of some benefit, but all too often, through parental compromise or neglect, this window to the world leads to a worldly contamination of their children's minds and hearts.

Working parents often rely on day care as well. Here, their children become a member of a group with peer pressures. Depending on day care, they may well be indoctrinated with, at best, values neutral training. Many of these are guilty of confusing and compromising their child's gender identity, moral beliefs, and even their faith in God. Even before they get to kindergarten, these children have been deeply indoctrinated in the worldly concepts of tolerance and acceptance of sin. It is no wonder that before they are teenagers, so many are already in trouble, including those raised in Christian homes. This is a tragedy that might at least be mitigated if Christian parents sought out Christian day care and private education if their public school proved unable to reinforce godly values.

At the same time, parents allow themselves to be disarmed by intellectual, cultural, and legal influences. Parents can also find themselves overwhelmed by the multiple demands of job, family, and society. This leaves them wide open to the claimed intellectual challenges of humanist experts and their attacks on Biblical concepts. A classic example of this battleground has been over child discipline. Dr. Benjamin Spock (1903-1998) authored multiple editions of his book, commonly called *Baby And Child Care*, from 1946 until his death. One point he is most famous for was his rejection of spanking and corporal punishment. Due to his work, and the movement he helped foster, at least twenty-seven states now impede, in some cases severely, parental authority to spank their own children.

Among the arguments against it is a fear of damaging a child's self esteem. Yet, at the same time, our children are being pressured to give up their faith in a loving Jesus, and they are indoctrinated to embrace a cold concept of having a rock as their first parent ancestor. A dinosaur is a long lost relative and life just is, it has no ultimate purpose. Yet, we seem clueless as to why our children suffer from esteem issues. Spanking will not deflate a broken spirit, nor will its absence inflate an esteem that no longer exists. In reality, in a godly setting, the exact opposite is true; corporal punishment affirms our value, purpose, and our belonging. "My son, do not regard lightly the discipline of the Lord, nor faint when you are reproved by Him. For those whom the Lord loves He disciplines" (Hebrews 12:5, 6).

The modern rationalist argues that violence only begets violence. If, indeed, we lived in a values-neutral Camelot world, where good and evil had no spiritual root, this might have a hope of being true. However, to break this hypothetical chain of violence, first and foremost all the world's militaries would have to disband. Then, all police departments must close, and everyone must turn in all their guns, knives, peppered mace, rocks, or anything else that can be used as a weapon. At that point, as the theory goes, violence eventually will disappear from the world, and we will all live in peace.

Reality paints a different picture. In 2009, the death rate for the American military in Iraq was eighty-eight per hundred thousand. In Washington DC, under the strictest gun control in America, it was twenty-four per hundred thousand. A peaceful and disarmed city still has a violent death rate well over one fourth of that in a war zone. Michigan laws are among the strictest in the nation on spanking. Yet the Detroit homicide rate was forty per hundred thousand, or nearly half that of a war zone. If there were any truth to the arguments against child spanking or by removing all threats of parental violence to children, this would not be.

Reality, though, shows just the opposite to be true. As spanking has declined, the incidence rate of children striking adults has exploded. A half-century ago, about the only time a child struck an adult, or their parents, was in a sports or play setting. Why the change? Violence is not a values-neutral action. For one thing, there is good violence and bad violence. As the good violence has declined, bad violence has skyrocketed to take its place. What is good violence? Romans 13:4 speaks to one: "For it [the governing authority] does not bear the sword for nothing, for it is a minister of God."

So, also, spanking is good violence. What is frightening is how many Christians now disobey God by buying into a wrongful love of their children and humanistic fallacy. Solomon said, "He who spares the rod [spanking] hates his son, but he who loves him disciplines him diligently" (Proverbs 13:24). One of the High Priest Eli's sins was against his sons in failing to restrain them (I Samuel 3:13). To not correct bad behavior, by force if necessary, shows, at best, misplaced and wrongful love for our children and putting their feelings ahead of God. Do we fear the world and our children's temporary anger, or do we fear the Lord? If we fear our children, then we've already lost them to the road of moral compromise.

It can't be emphasized strongly enough the dangers of moral compromise in any attempt to appease or retain relationships with our children or any other family members. This doesn't mean attempting to control every aspect of our maturing kids' lives. There are many things outside our control to begin with, and wise parents pick their battles well. Also, spanking is not the answer to everything, especially as children mature. Emphasis should be put on moral and spiritual concerns. There is a big difference between godly concern and mother-henning our children. To better understand this, we should realize that they aren't really ours to begin with. God has loaned us our children. We are stewards and accountable to God for their lives.

Hannah understood this. Some believe that it was easy for her to commit to God something she didn't have, like someone in poverty who promises that if God gave them a million dollars, they'll give it back. But it was not easy for her to promise. "O Lord of hosts, if Thou wilt indeed look upon the affliction of Thy maidservant, and remember me, and not forget Thy maidservant, but wilt give Thy maidservant a son, then I will give him to the Lord all the days of his life" (I Samuel 1:11). It was harder to keep that promise, and allow her son to be adopted into the High Priest family, than most could imagine. Do we look at our children as ours and ours alone? Now, I wouldn't have minded keeping mine little for at least twenty more years because I enjoyed them so much, but to view them selfishly is to set ourselves up to lose them. First and foremost, giving them to God offers a greater promise of keeping them.

If our daughters are God's, and under our stewardship, do we permit them to constantly twitter, or shop at Victoria's Secret? Especially with our money? Do we look the other way when our sons bypass v-chips and view pornography over TV or the Internet? or let them "hang" with the drug, alcohol, and violent crowd? Also, if God has entrusted His property to us, what kind of example are we? Are we "legally" addicted to painkillers or antidepressants? Is our heart addicted to the things of the world? Do we secretly have our own idol shelf of morally compromising material? "You, therefore; who teach another, do you not teach yourself? You who preach that one should not steal, do you steal? You who say that one should not commit adultery, do you commit adultery? You who abhor idols, do you rob temples?" (Romans 2:21, 22). We can't be good stewards for God if our "house" is full of idols.

Another way we can fail Jesus is by trying to buy our children's love with things rather than investing in them with our hearts. The generation that raised mine, the Baby Boomers, endured the Great Depression, World War II, and the onset of the Cold War. They proved as well to be quite industrious in building a nation of wealth, power, and innovation unlike any the world may have ever known. They wanted our generation to have all the things they couldn't afford, but they were often too busy for relationships. Things, or wealth, became a convenient substitute, not unlike what happened in Joshua's day. "And there arose another generation after them, who did not know the Lord, nor yet the work which He has done for Israel" (Judges 2:10).

This problem has only multiplied. Many times today, we are guilty of the same thing. Even Christian parents have succumbed to "child worship," and they dote in every material way on their children. Interestingly enough, this same thing is happening in the People's Republic of China. Frequently, these values are only measured in dollars, social status, or worldly accomplishments. Once again, we love our children in the wrong ways, and allow them to become our idols. What parents do in moderation, children tend to do in excess. The Baby Boomers showed this, taking the sins of our parents, they multiplied them so the world couldn't help but see. And for us, if we neglect spiritual values a little, our children will neglect them a lot. The spiritual and moral crises in our families are often self-inflicted.

In all fairness, we do live in an age where, no matter how good a job of parenting we do, many of our children go astray anyway. As mentioned before, we are losing about a third (34-36%) from Christian homes, but we can do better. We can face up to the challenges, through standing by our convictions, seeking Godly advice from others who have had to deal with these problems and, if necessary, with a little "tough love." Two issues that many parents are forced to deal with are gay children and live together relationships. In our age of tolerance and relativism, parents are being pressured to accept these things. After all, we are told, the world is changing, and many fear they will lose their children entirely if they don't accept their kids as they are.

For a parent to cave in to this is devastating. Often, the child is still engaged in a personal war of conscience or just lost to rebellion. Either way, they find themselves assured of a family blessing. It is hard to see how many of them will ever find their way back to the Lord when parental love gets in the way of spiritual discipline. The father of the Prodigal Son grieved and longed daily for his son (Luke 15:20) but did not go to the "far country" with him to smooth his way. Had he, his son's repentance and return would have been problematic at best. It could have led his other son astray, by his example of "tolerance." A bad example would have been set as well for the society around him.

To accept our children's sin destroys them. Affirming a love for them, while making it clear that certain behavior is unacceptable, is a must. And if they still live at home, they can be reminded that such behavior will not be tolerated in that home. This does not mean we should ever stop loving them, nor be unwilling to meet them with love when they see their sin as sin, but an acceptance of sin only reinforces it. We also divide our loyalty between the Lord and our children. While we may think this compromise brings peace, it doesn't, and it violates our relationship with God. Even if it does not lead us personally into committing the same sins, it makes us a friend to the world and an adversary to God. "You adulteresses, do you not know that friendship with the world is hostility toward God? Therefore, whoever wishes to be a friend of the world makes himself an enemy of God" (James 4:4). It becomes easier for sin to take hold of the entire family.

The Church is also wounded. Sin and a tolerance to it will creep in secretly, but it doesn't stay that way. "Your boasting [acceptance] is not good. Do you not know that a little leaven leavens the whole lump of dough?" (I Corinthians 5:6). The damage is done in multiple ways. Parents who accept their children's sin begin to wince when those sins are mentioned from the pulpit. They either will drop out, or change churches, or form an animosity towards the preacher and church leadership. The leaders become pressured to accept this sin and the unrepentant person as well. Parents begin reinterpreting the Bible to suit their situation, including a misuse of Matthew 7:1, "Do not judge, lest you be judged," whenever their children's lifestyles come up. They forget, "By faith Noah... prepared an ark for the salvation of his household, by this he condemned the world" (Hebrews 11:7). The church also comes to accept, and is tempted to follow by example, rather than stand by conviction. If another young person sees a condoning of sin for others, why shouldn't they follow as well?

One huge reason why sexual immorality and gay rights have swept the nation is because the Church has refused to stand against it. A critical part in this has been the cave in of Christian parents to the life choices of their children. Gays didn't obtain social acceptance, come to serve openly in the military, or get married because of the courts or the Democrats. They do so because the Church, starting with compromising parents, surrendered on the issue. What would have happened in AD 35 if new Christians had caved in to the demands of their families and compromised their beliefs? There would be no Church. We stand today in the same gap for the Lord. Jesus knew what His command would cost, but He also knew the cost of disobedience. If we wrongfully allow a love of family priority over our love for Jesus, it costs us so much more, both our Church and our civilization. We can do better than losing a third of our children to the world. It all begins with our convictions.

# VII

## THE LUST OF THE FLESH

*"Do not love the world, not the things of the world. If any one loves the world, love for the Father is not in him. For all that is in the world, the lust of the flesh...is not from the Father but is from the world."*

—I John 2:15, 16

### Lust

When the word lust is mentioned, usually the first thing that comes to mind is sexual lust, or the misuse of our God ordained sexuality Sex is our second strongest human drive, right after survival. We are bombarded with it constantly; it's on TV, in our magazines and newspapers, and embedded in most of our entertainment. It is also available online. It takes a disproportionate share of our conversations and, on a negative note, all too often works its way into the Church. If anyone doubts this last statement, have a conversation with a church gossip and see what topic comes up most often. Sex sells; Madison Avenue figured this out in the 1920's and made it a major theme in the recession years just after World War II.

The appeal of sexual lust is not new. It was the same two millennia ago. "And the scribes and the Pharisees brought a woman caught in [the very act of] adultery" (John 8:3). The most obvious draw is to the woman. After all, she was the one caught in sin. What is often missed is the sin of the Jewish leadership. To begin with, they would had to have been familiar with her reputation. There would have been gossip or some other communication of a dark nature. In addition, there had to be an awareness of, and some form of complicity with, the man involved. "If there is a man who commits adultery with another man's wife, one who commits adultery with his friend's wife, the adulterer and the adulteress shall surely be put to death," (Leviticus 20:10). Here, only one, the woman, was present. Adultery, in the form of "one night stands" very rarely occurred in Jesus's day. To catch them in the act, a deal or plea bargain had to be made to let the man go free. Their goal was to catch the woman, and force a dilemma upon Jesus. There also was a certain amount of voyeurism on the part of the Jewish leadership, otherwise, it would have been almost magically serendipitous to catch them in the very act. If, by chance, her husband had walked in on them, either both of them would have been presented to Jesus, or they would be dead. It was all too convenient to just be occurring for the first time, when Jesus just happened to be in town.

The Jewish leaders had their own lusts of the flesh that they were trying to mask while springing this one on Jesus. On more than one occasion, Jesus called them on their hypocrisy. "Beware of the scribes, who like to go about in long robes, and love respectful greetings in the marketplaces, and chief seats in the synagogues and places of honor at banquets, who devour widow's houses [for money] and for appearance's sake offer long prayers" (Luke 20:46, 47). They loved wealth, comfort, honor, and the easy life. Jesus posed a threat to their schemes to live off others in the name of God. Lust of the flesh takes many forms, and the Jewish leaders knew most of them very well. All revolved around their love for the world.

## False Hopes

In the beginning, God created us in His image. "Then God said, 'Let us make man in Our image, according to Our likeness" (Genesis 1:26). He put man in a land of opportunity, blessed them, and provided all that was needed to make it a paradise. The only choice Adam and Eve had was whether they would discover, subdue, and advance in this creation God's way or Satan's way. God had put one test in the garden: "The tree of the knowledge of good and evil" (Genesis 2:17). Eve looked with longing on this tree, and Satan picked up on this. He assured her that no bad consequence would happen if she ate it, but only good things. "When the woman saw that the tree was good for food, and that it was a delight to the eyes, and that the tree was to be desired to make one wise" (Genesis 3:6), she accepted Satan's counter offer. He was offering one tree he really didn't own, in exchange for her fellowship with God, paradise, perpetual youth, vigor, and true happiness. He also offered her a mental image of an escape to a secret place of "fantasy and desire". He substituted wantonness and an unhappiness for her present state, instead of "Godliness [which] actually is a means of great gain, when accompanied by contentment" (I Timothy 6:6).

With a lust for all the good things that she was sure God was holding out on her and that sin had to offer, she made a selfish choice, a deal with the devil, and she ate. So did Adam, as he shared, at least for a moment, in her grasp for a nonexistent ecstasy. In return, they lost paradise, both eternal physical, and spiritual life and received a broken, or at least marred, relationship with each other. They now lived in a cursed and fallen world and suffered the loss of ownership of their home. Not only was Eden lost, so was the world as well. "For it [the world] has been handed over to me [Satan], and I give it to whomever I wish" (Luke 4:6). Whether Satan actually owns it or if God does is another issue, but Adam and Eve gave it up for one act of spiritual infidelity. We all know the rest of the story.

The workings of Satan are worth noting here. He was able to get them to trade all they had for nothing but trinkets. If it is still taught in our schools, back in 1626 the Dutch purchased Manhattan from the Indians for about $300.00 worth of trinkets, beads, and cloth. Today, some of the land on Wall Street alone is worth multi-millions per square foot. A fortune was sold for glitter, but this is nothing when compared to the bargain Satan made with Adam and Eve, and it is the same one we are being proposed today. He lures us by offering a mirage of a temporary world with fleeting pleasures in exchange for our own eternal spirits. In many cases, Satan is offering us something we already either now, or in the future, will possess, if we only chose to remain faithful to God.

Entrapment in the lust of the flesh is usually the result of a process. Psalms 1:1 points to this progression: "How blessed is the man who does not walk in the counsel of the wicked, nor stand in the path of sinners, nor sit in the seat of scoffers." Whether lust is sexual, greedy, for wrongful power, or the pursuit of pleasure, we first desire to go see what it looks like, kind of like spiritual voyeurism. Later, we come back to look again and get a better idea, playing with it in our minds. We linger, and try to rationalize on how good it would be, how it really isn't so bad, and why we should have it. Then, we figure out how to get it. Then, we sit down with it and, in the process, lay aside our spiritual armor so we can be comfortable. We make it our abode. At that point, we can no longer run, we are in its midst, and it has us.

As Christians, we would like to think that this entrapment is a problem the world has and not us. We think that somehow we are above it all. The lost have this problem, or the rich, or maybe the denomination down the street, but not us. Satan already has the world, however, the bars, nightclubs, wild parties, or other fields of sin, and these are low priority. In a military perspective, far fewer soldiers are required to guard disarmed prisoners than to attack enemy strongholds. His targets are those not yet ensnared by sin. We need to remind ourselves of this.

## Mindset of the Flesh

The builders of the Notre Dame saw that as well. There is a lot of history behind its being built in Paris. Initially constructed from 1163-1245, it was completed (about) 1345. During the 1789 French Revolution, it suffered deliberate damage, only later to be restored. Among its most famous features is of the gargoyles, or demonic images, on its outside. One legend for this refers back to St. Romanus, Chancellor of Merovingian (631-641AD). He was credited for capturing all the fire-breathing dragons in the realm and posting their heads as trophies on his cathedral walls. Accordingly, Notre Dame had to have the same, but a better explanation offered was that the designers were reminding us that the devil is always watching and waiting. That these gargoyles were also used as water drains and gutters brings to mind the phrase: "To have one's mind in the gutter." Our minds can become our own worst enemy and often serve as a channel for Satan's assault. He is indeed watching and waiting, as with Eve, to entice and destroy us.

As a Church, we are not immune. Sinful lusts seem right at home in our midst. Covetous, selfish lust, sexual, or otherwise, is the greatest enemy of marriage. According to the "USA Today" from March 14, 2011, the US divorce rate hovers right at 50 percent of all marriages. Among professing Christians, it is 42 percent, or only eight points lower than the national average. Alan Guttemacher is the official statistician for Planned Parenthood, PPC, America's leading abortion provider, and next to the Center for Disease Control (CDC), probably the best source for all abortion information. By their count, more than one in five abortions are performed on professing evangelical, or "Born Again" Christians. Approximately 26 percent of Americans are in this group, and they are 77 percent as likely to have an abortion as any other women. They also report the Catholic rate as virtually equal to the national average. To deny this is to hide our heads in the sand.

In our lust for more than what God offers, according to a December 9, 2009, internet poll, 23 percent of Christians believe the planets and stars affect their lives, as opposed to 25 percent of all Americans.[9] Not only are Christians into astrology, they are into gambling as well. According to the Barna Group, 23 percent of all Christians, and 15 percent of born again ones will play the lottery in any given week. This compares to only 12 percent of atheists and agnostics, and 10 percent of those of other faiths.[10] Those who wear the name of Jesus are just as likely as non-Christians to read their daily horoscopes. It is 36 percent for both groups. Those buying at least one lottery ticket per week number 27 percent for everybody, while for Christians it is 23 percent. Even worse, nationally, 33 percent of all Americans will cohabitate with a member of the opposite sex, either premarital or without the intent of marriage. For Protestants the rate is 30 percent and, for Roman Catholics, 36 percent. It has been said, to our shame that the primary difference between a Christian and a non-Christian is that Christians presume that God will forgive them. All too many view grace as a credit card rather than a get out of jail free one.

---

[9]  Pew Research Center's Forum on Religion & Public Life. http://pewforum.org/ Government/Global-Restrictions-on-Religion.aspx.

[10]  www.barna.org/barna

The Christian community must also take its share of blame for the quality of TV programming and of movies as well. This was blatantly displayed during the Michael Eisner era (1984-2005) as Chief Executive Officer of Walt Disney Corp. Under his auspices, Disney became an advocate of among other evils, the Gay Rights Movement. Primarily due to this, and secondly, their anti-Christians bias, several Christian groups, including The American Family Association, called for a boycott in the early to mid 1990s. Many rank and file Christians paid lip service to the idea that "other" Christians should stop buying Disney products, but this didn't include themselves. Most continued to go to Disney World, buy their movies and other products, and Disney barely felt a ripple in sales.

The same is true in Christian response to the rest of our entertainment industry. In February of 1999, ABC Corp. was called to the carpet over an episode of "The Practice" where a gay mother wanted her son to change the laws so she could marry her female partner. Among those complaining about the show's content was Coach Jim Neugent, then of Mena, Arkansas. ABC's response to him was: "How about getting your nose out of the Bible... Or better yet, try thinking for yourself and stop using an archaic book of stories as your lame crutch for your existence. You are in the minority in this country and your boycott will not affect us at ABC or our freedom statement." According to the ABC Webmaster, Tuesday, April 27, 1999, the employee who sent this reply was terminated, and ABC apologized to Neugent. By all appearances, it didn't affect programming, at least not in a positive way. There has been a marked increase by all three networks in promoting gay agenda issues favorably, with ABC among the worst. When Christians watch the same filth on TV, read the same publications, and participate in the same entertainment as the world enjoys, it looks like the lust of the flesh is winning.

There are many in the Church who convince themselves that, as long as they stay just a few steps behind the world, they are okay. They feel they can enjoy the same fads, fashions, and popular trends as the world does. Granted, not all culture or entertainment are bad in themselves, Christians can go to games, most civic events, and even see some movies among other things, but there is definitely a difference between basketball cagers and cage fighting, and our consciences will tell us this. Some sports offer a somewhat positive form of entertainment, others offer nothing but an appeal to our darker nature, as blood lust in cage fighting. There is a pull to fulfill the flesh in all of us. This carnal desire may be for racy entertainment or buzz drunkenness, addictions to prescription painkillers, stress, or anti-depressants. In all of these, our flesh demands to be pleased.

The carnal Christian tries to hide behind their supposedly discrete indulgences of the flesh. They might argue that their entertainment isn't X-rated, they aren't smashed drunk, or doing illegal drugs—of course, everyone knows addiction to prescription drugs is different than that to street drugs. However, isn't there a commercial that asks, "Who is more dead?" of two "drugees" in a morgue setting. "The one who took the street drugs or the one on prescription ones?" Both the prescription drug and the illegal drug can kill, and according to the CDC, the prescription varieties took over fifteen thousand lives in 2009. This death is spiritual as well as physical, however. Being run over by only one steamroller will not render us any less dead than two. Being a socially accepted sinner will render us just as lost as a debauched atheist.

## Idolatry

Living for the world, regardless of degrees is still living for the world. "For those who are according to the flesh set their minds on the things of the flesh, but those who are according to the Spirit, the things of the Spirit. For the mind set on the flesh is death" (Romans 8:5, 6). The "those" here, isn't directed as an attack on worldly people walking according to their "lostness". In the lust of their flesh, Paul is talking to Christians. He adds, in verse 7, "Because the mind that is set on the flesh is hostile toward God; for it does not subject itself to the law of God, for it is not even able to do so." Seeking the in-crowd and enjoying for the moment the fleeting pleasures of sin in moderation is still sin, and unrepentant sin still kills.

Fleeting pleasure is well in line with existentialism, or a "live for today" mentality, but it also appeals to us all. Sin is fun, its pleasant, and it brings pleasure and fulfillment to the flesh. If it weren't, then people wouldn't do it. "Stolen water is sweet, and bread eaten in secret is pleasant" (Proverbs 9:17), but, Solomon adds in 20:17, "Bread obtained by falsehood is sweet to a man, but afterward his mouth will be filled with gravel." Not only does sin become an addiction, it's a purchase we never quit paying for. It's like buying a new iPod on payments, and forty years later, long after it is in the junkyard, we're still paying. And this is just the physical and mental consequence. The existentialist and atheist and all too often Christians are mistaken in assuming their actions only affect us here and now. We are eternal beings, and there are spiritual consequences as well.

Sin, or lust of the flesh, also leads to idolatry. This results in a love for the world and lust of the flesh that is greater than our love for God. When we think of idolatry, we have mental images of idols and charms, and the ancients did have their household gods and idol shelves. For collective worship, they had their sacred pillars, altars, and temples, but we modern Americans think we are too smart for that. We even tend to look down on people who sacrifice a chicken to appease the spirits and bring for themselves success or put food in a cemetery for an ancestor, but idolatry is when a person allows anything else to become more important to them than God. We, so called sophisticated Americans, have our own church of the two goal posts (football). Then there's our shrine of the Wall Street gurus, devotion to the one-eyed talking box (TV), and any other unhealthy attachment to our bodies or for comfort. Jokingly, rock stars and Hollywood celebrities are called idols, but with our infatuation with every detail of their lives, they have become just that. A huge number of Americans would gladly compromise their morals to spend a day with one of them. This is really no different than what an ancient Middle Easterner would have done in their worship of Baal or Asherah.

Since so many Americans are now so involved in gambling, this lust of the flesh and of the spirit has become almost a trillion dollar industry. It is also addicting, both to our spirits as well as our minds, and it does involve idolatrous deities. Gamblers often appeal to "Lady Luck," or other forms of "destiny," to give them a winning roll or hand. Very often, a person will have a favorite lucky trinket, shirt, cap, or something else to bring success. They may clutch, rub, kiss, or in some way touch these religiously as they gamble. In other cases, a special fetish, or compulsive action (ball players do this too) is done. Admitted to or not, this is an appeal, or offering, to bring their lucky stars into alignment or call on lucky spirits. This too is idolatrous. "But you who forsake the Lord, who forget My holy mountain, who set a table for Fortune and who fill cups with mixed wine for Destiny" (Isaiah 65:11). When the ancients gambled, they paid homage to Lady Luck and their lucky stars, too.

## Worldly Attachments

In addition to appealing to, or fulfilling, the lust of the flesh, idols served at least one more purpose as well: they symbolized a possession of at least a part of the world. When Rachel stole her father Lahan's, household gods in Genesis 31:19, she was taking more than the value of any stone, gem, or metal they may have contained. Contrary to what many may think, she didn't steal them for the purpose of worship, but to claim her father's possessions and disarm him in any future confrontation. Those household gods, or *teraphim*, functioned as a title deed as much as an object of worship. She may have been aware of God's promise to Abraham, "On that day the Lord made a covenant with Abram [Abraham], saying, 'To your descendants I have given this land, from the river of Egypt to the great river, the River Euphrates'" (Genesis 15:18). She wanted a dowry for herself and her descendants.

These household idols could be today translated as "turf rights." While these images were the god or lord of that place, they symbolized an acknowledgement by the holders of these idols that the land really didn't belong to the people possessing it. God also told Israel this, "The land moreover shall not be sold permanently, for the land is Mine; for you are but aliens and sojourners with Me" (Leviticus 25:23). A spirit would claim ownership, but by possessing the household gods, a person claimed power from the god of that place. A spirit could bless or curse the possessor, but there was an implied binding of the spirit as well. A land "owner" could call on it, not quite, but something along the line of calling on a genie in a bottle. By taking Laban's idols, she got his attention and an unpleasant response.

God claimed a higher authority to that of these turf right deities. When His people were to enter the land of Canaan, they were solemnly commanded to destroy all the idols of the inhabitants (Deuteronomy 6:14, 15) and not to make any of their own. "You shall not make for yourselves idols, nor shall you set up for yourselves an image or a sacred pillar, nor shall you place a figured stone in your land to bow down to it" (Leviticus 26:1). God was the owner and their portion, their title deed of possession, was a faithful obedience. Their real home was not of this world, nor was worldly possession to be their first love. The same concept applies to Christians in our looking for an eternal dwelling place. "Now faith is the assurance [or standing, title deed] of things hoped for, the conviction of things not seen" (Hebrews 11:1). Any household idol was a door to the lust of the flesh, the spirit world, and showed unfaithfulness to God.

## Unfaithfulness

Unfaithfulness plays right into the lust of the flesh. Adam and Eve showed unfaithfulness to God in being seduced away by the devil. Idolatry has a very close parallel with adultery. Both involve unfaithfulness and a breaking of a sacred commitment. They are a violation of the ability to trust, as well, and pose a question of integrity. As a side note, a person who will commit adultery ultimately can't be trusted to keep any commitment of faith, including business or professional ones. God provided us a good picture of unfaithfulness in the book of Hosea, "Go take to yourself a wife of harlotry and have children of harlotry, for the land commits flagrant harlotry, forsaking the Lord" (Hosea 1:2). God uses Hosea as an object lesson to show how their wantonness, or lust of the flesh, was a craving for happiness, love, fulfillment, and affections outside of their sacred vow of fidelity. Israel, Samaria, craved this fulfillment outside of God. They had put other deities ahead of the Lord like a wayward wife puts other men ahead of her husband. It is also no coincidence that immorality was destroying Samaria as well. "I will not punish your daughters when they play the harlot, or your brides when they commit adultery; for the men themselves go apart with harlots, and offer sacrifices with temple prostitutes" (Hosea 4:14). As America has fallen farther into a love for the world, it is no wonder both idolatry and immorality are so prevalent.

It is true that we are in the world, and this is the only home and physical reality we have ever known. It is hard to set our sights on something none of us have ever seen. We also crave comfort, so we want our homes to be as pleasant and comfortable as possible. Everything that we see, hear, feel, smell, and taste is through the flesh, and as a result, we think of the flesh quite frequently. God did design it this way. When we are hungry, we eat, when thirsty, we drink. So also heat or cold, pain or exhaustion affect us. If you think you can get around the pull of the literal flesh, hold your breath for ten minutes (unless you have a health condition). See if very soon, in the effort, your body doesn't force you to breathe. It is easy to see why the flesh has such a strong influence on our behavior.

For most people, the mind is the second main conduit of what most affects us. Not only are we always in touch with our bodies, we are always thinking something. This is even true for at least much of the time we are asleep. Try another experiment here. Sometime, when you have a few minutes free of activity, try not to think at all. You will find this impossible. Whether we read, watch TV, or are in a conversation, our minds are engaged, even if it is nothing more than processing data.

Our spirits quite often are relegated to third place on this list. It gets crowded out by what affects us most, just like the urgent tends to crowd out the essential, if we are not careful. This, in part, explains why the Lord God walked in the Garden of Eden in the cool of the day, to keep an abiding fellowship with Adam and Eve. Unless we make a conscientious effort to pray, read Scripture, and meditate, this most critical part of our being can be ignored. This is truer for men, since women tend to be more spiritually and relationship driven. For all, a commitment to daily prayer and Bible reading, and frequent Christian fellowship are vital.

## Spiritual Drift

We also need some knowledge on the workings of Satan. All that is needed sometimes to lead us astray is a subtle nudge off our course, a fleshly teaser, or appeal to an area of weakness that even momentarily steals our hearts and plants a seed and the process is begun. We then begin to drift. "For this reason we must pay the closer attention to what we have heard, lest we drift away from it" (Hebrews 2:1). The moral decline of America did not happen overnight, it was a process and a steady stream of factors. The rise of leisure time, or an excess of it, was one of them. So, as already mentioned, are the car, public swimming, and TV. Coed dormitories, living arrangements, and unisex workplaces have added to it. The spoiling of our children to the point of prolonged adolescent behavior has promoted both hetero and homosexual behavior issues. Birth control, while of benefit to married couples, has made immoral behavior much easier. Other factors have been dress codes, or the lack of them, pornography, strip clubs, etc. Add to this a myriad of so called intellectual voices over the years who have openly advocated immorality and perversion. Some of these names are easily recognizable. Over the last century, a very limited roll call of the perverse includes, among others, Ellen Keye, Havelock Ellis, Sigmund Freud, Margaret Sanger, Alfred Kinsey, Phil Donahue, Shere Hite, Hugh Hefner, and Oprah Winfrey. All these have helped to advance sexual immorality. A similar list could be compiled for other lusts as well.

Add this to the continuing temptations of our enemy, and it is clear to see the deck is stacked against us. Throw in the present social trend toward the marginalizing of Christianity and the Bible, both in the world and in our lives, and those who hold to Christian moral standards are seen as strange by the world. Today, we are encouraged to look out for self, or number-one, and if self wants physical titillation and satiation, then the world says go for it. Throw in Hollywood and its mentality as well. All one needs to do to fall is to allow worldly thought patterns to invade their minds and the flesh takes over. Less than this concoction of fleshly allure has resulted in moral compromises in the past. "Now when evening came David arose from his bed and walked around on the roof of the king's house, and from the roof he saw a woman bathing; and the woman was very beautiful in appearance. So David sent and inquired about the woman," (II Samuel 11:2, 3). If we are not on guard, the same surrender will happen to us.

"Then when lust has conceived, it gives birth to sin; and when sin is accomplished, it brings forth death" (James 1:15). For us Christians, this makes our reliance on the power of God through His Holy Spirit critical to our strength. Feeding our spirits can't be emphasized strongly enough. It also hones in on the value and importance of a pure thought life. "Finally brethren, whatever is true, whatever is honorable, whatever is right, whatever is pure, whatever is lovely, whatever is of good repute, if there is any excellence, if there is anything worthy of praise, let your mind dwell on these things" (Philippians 4:8).

## Wrongful Cravings

The lust of the flesh is seen in our love for possessions and pleasure. This is summarized well by the Chase Bank commercial song lyrics, "I want it, I want it all, and I want it all now!" Ours is an age of not just of gratification, but also of total instant gratification. Consider just the field of entertainment. If someone were to be born today and lived to be one hundred, with only our present amusement forms to select from, they could live their whole life being entertained, twenty-four-seven, and never see or do the same thing twice. If they just limited themselves to watching either live or taped shows of every professional football, baseball, and basketball game, there are not enough hours in a year, only 8,766 of them, to watch them all. This doesn't even touch other sports, theme parks, gambling facilities, amusement facilities, nightclubs, or any other form of entertainment.

The craze for possessions is just as great. So many young people want to start life with the best of everything. Many will literally max out on every access to credit they can obtain. They have bought into the belief that they must have the best, look their best, and enjoy the most right now. Why work for years to have something if all one has to do is whip out plastic and have it all now?

Satan also wants us to go for it all right now. This is one of the traps that can keep us spiritually shallow and worldly-minded. He also wants us to live for today, or for the moment. This fits with the lyrics from Expose's "People Change": "I'd sacrifice tomorrow just to have you here today." By keeping us on "today" we never see a need to deepen or mature our character. We never have longings for spiritual things. We never find that hunger for God, His righteousness, or His kingdom. Satan pawns on us a few trinkets in exchange for our potential possession of the riches of heaven.

He wants us to believe that this world is all there is or, as a humanist would say, all that is important. Spiritually, the devil is succeeding admirably through their movement, but if, by some chance, one still feels a spiritual yearning, a counterfeit is offered to them here as well. St. Augustine (AD 354-AD 430) spoke of a God sized emptiness, or vacuum inside each of us. This inner need for God, our enemy will gladly fill it in us with drugs, pleasures, or possessions and the like, but if all else fails, we can get just enough of a glimpse of a spiritual realm of the devil's design. This was shown in the beliefs of Sir Alfred R. Wallace (1823-1913), a competitor of Charles Darwin in offering a theory of evolution. He believed in a spirit consciousness, or the Force, as *Star Wars* later made famous. This was a vast entity, like a nirvana, that we all one day would join. It is along the lines of spending all we have in a video arcade here and then, when this is over, go home to a spirit world to recharge so we can do it all over again.

## True Happiness

God, on the other hand, wants what is best for us. He wants our ultimate happiness, which can come only through Him, our designer. Our fulfillment isn't here. "For our citizenship is in Heaven" (Philippians 3:20). Our purpose is not wrapped up in the things of this world, and we should be grateful it is not. Our entire created order of existence is destined for a fiery destruction. By giving us a different destiny, we are offered an escape as well as an eternal home. We are in, but not of the world.

Deferred gratification makes one appreciate what they have. Too often, parents feel that giving a child a new car, especially a racier model, will somehow be good for them. Quite frequently, it ends up dented, broken, and in a junkyard. All too often, and tragically, the young driver is damaged or killed in the process. On the other hand, a young person who has to work for his wheels, even if they are used, will appreciate them and take care of the vehicle. This is an analogy of how our spiritual character is built: by sacrifice, suffering, and labor. It develops in learning to overcome the urges the devil plays on and by growing up to look outside ourselves to the needs and hurts of others. It is somewhat similar to the process of physical conditioning and mental development of a football player or soldier "And perseverance proven (produces) character, and proven character, hope" (Romans 5:4). Life is a journey, not a destination," said Ralph Waldo Emerson [1803-1882], and this world is a testing ground.[11] It is also a war zone between the flesh and the spirit, and between the spirits of good and evil.

We can't live for the world and also for God, these are opposites. Choosing God will make us an enemy of the world. We may even earn the title of "fanatic" and see the world unite against us; it also united against Jesus. God promises joys beyond comprehension, however, way beyond the fleeting pleasures of this world. "Delight yourself in the Lord, and He will give you the desires of your heart" (Psalms 37:4).

There is one last point. Adam and Eve not only lost a world, they became slaves to sin. Those who obey the flesh become a slave to the flesh. "Do you not know that when you present yourselves to someone as

[11] "Goodreads." Accessed August 20, 2012. http://www.goodreads.com/quotes/24142-life-is-a-journey-not-a-destination.

slaves for obedience, you are slaves of the one whom you obey, either of sin resulting in death, or of obedience resulting in righteousness?" (Romans 6:16). Ego was never on the throne in their lives, unless for the brief moment. They had to choose masters. It will either be God or Satan. The same is true for us; we are never really lord of our lives, except to choose which master we serve. Lust of the flesh, like drug addiction, will destroy us, both here and eternally. Only slavery to God can bring us fulfillment and life, and true joy. Maybe one way to see this is to try a little experiment. Next time you feel the urge to buy something for yourself, give the same amount of money to someone you know who has a genuine need. See which one provides the greatest happiness. Both Satan and the world can only offer something for the moment, but God offers us eternity.

# VIII

## CHOKED BY RICHES

*"And the one on whom seed was sown among thorns, this is the man who hears the word, and the worry of the world and the deceitfulness of riches choke the word, and it becomes unfruitful."*

—Matthew 13:22

Americans live in an increasingly polarized country. Both sides of this divide are quick to put labels on the other side, liberal and conservative are two of them. Both sides feel they have little in common with the other. In dealing with our federal deficit, the opposing camps show the depths of their differences. One phrase used by the liberals to justify tax increases to balance the budget is, "The rich should pay their fair share." The conservatives retort to this call for tax hikes as, "A job killing destruction of incentives to produce more wealth." Like it or not, both sides have this in common, their positions are half-truths. They also share in common something called "greed," and they both are choked by riches.

Most people will point at the rich and say that, in their case, greed is obvious. Many rich do have a relentless and insatiable desire to have more. "He who loves money will not be satisfied with money, nor he who loves abundance, with its income, this too is vanity [futility]" (Ecclesiastes 5:10). There is always a desire for more. In the back of a CEO's mind is

98

always a nagging feeling about labor costs being too high or profit margins being too low. There is always a drive to stay one step ahead, or catch up to, their competitors. Others might ponder about where they might have been if only they had ventured into the right initial public offering of a stock and made a killing. They always are worried about the potential for a disaster, shortage, market crash, or just something going wrong. "But the full stomach of the rich will not allow him sleep" (Ecclesiastes 4:12). Their excess is not just their security, it is also both their enemy and their master.

But this is not always true. Some do come to a point of satiation. "A sated man loathes honey" (Proverbs 27:6). Without mentioning names, two billionaires in America today have given away a fortune, and have successfully challenged a number of others to join them in "The Giving Pledge." For one, his legacy was fulfilled more through his proving to the world that he could obtain it, than in his possessing it. There often is a prestige and a power that comes with wealth, or the ability to succeed, and this can be very satisfying. But there have also been many cases of Christians who have viewed their wealth as a stewardship, and an opportunity of service, and have not fallen into its snares.

In general, though, money or riches tend to make the owner very conservative and defensive to any change or challenges outside his control. Wealth does not like market uncertainties or volatility unless it feels it can play these to make more of itself. Money seeks stability and this is right in the center of the hearts of most who possess it. Any restrictions on its growth, whether by excessive taxes, regulations, or other challenges, make it uneasy. Right now in America, we are seeing a perfect example of how this works. US corporations, including the banking industry, are sitting on over two trillion in cash reserves. The demands and uncertainty of regulatory policies on how it will affect future business and profits has made many companies unwilling to invest. Some of these rules, as with the Dodd-Frank financial institution reforms, have effectively frozen assets that could otherwise be loaned out. Others are paralyzed by the impositions of national health care, the Environmental Protection Agency, and others. This not only affects profitability, but the whole economy as well. Then there is the fear of tax policy.

Tragically, we all pay for this. If business were to invest this money in capital expansion, even if each new added job cost one hundred thousand dollars, this money could create twenty million jobs. Unfortunately, the powers that be in Washington DC are unwilling to agree to a more favorable regulatory policy, create an economic climate, or only propose tax increases that will not retard economic growth. But on the other hand, in our post-Christian America, many of these corporations cannot see beyond their own immediate bottom line.

Money tends to flee unprofitable or dangerous markets for safer and profitable ones. In Great Britain, in 1974, the Labor Party under Harold Wilson took over the reins of power. Among an assortment of ideas to raise tax revenues, a possessions-property tax was passed to get more from the rich. As a result, Great Britain suffered from wealth flight. It was not until 1979, when Margaret Thatcher took over, that Britain reversed or ended several excessive tax policies. Italy, at about this same time, endured the same problems. She responded by placing limits on the amount of money anyone could remove from the country.

Revolutions tend to create financial instability. The French Revolution of 1789 called for a socialistic system and sweeping wealth redistribution. This, in turn, led to a massive wealth flight. Nobles and others fled with, by today's standards, tens of billions of dollars in gold, silver, gems, and other capital. The same thing happened in Russia after October 1917 when the Bolsheviks took over. This drain also greatly exacerbated the poverty and misery in both countries, as did the breakdowns in the production and economic activity that money fosters. This, in turn, fueled anger and only contributed to the reigns of terror in both nations. By all appearances, Egypt, since February 11, 2011 when Hosni Mubarak was deposed from power, is going down the same road. The money drain has not helped the economy, and a now poorer people are angry and looking for targets on whom to take out their frustrations on. This exposes another form, or manifestation, of the chokehold money can have on people.

There are those who argue that only the rich can be greedy or choked by riches. This is like saying that only people who are suffering from floodwaters need to be concerned about how much rain falls. For those in a drought, their desire might be for a different weather pattern, but their concerns about rain are just as real as those who are being flooded. The greed of the poor may manifest itself differently, but whatever greed they have is just as real. For them, one manifestation of it is their incessant demands for wealth redistribution. Such people, and their political representatives, are commonly called economic liberals, or sometimes progressives.

Since America is a Democratic Republic, and poor outnumber the rich, the power of the vote can often provide this for them. Over the years, the percentage of those who benefit from wealth distribution or government assistance has steadily grown. Statistics vary, depending on how or what questions are asked, but from corporate welfare to Social Security, food stamps, housing, transportation, health care, school lunch, and other subsidies, the vast majority of us now benefit in some way from one type of assistance or another. Not all of this should be classified as greed, nor should the unemployed who can't find work be allowed to starve, nor is the Church ready to step in any time soon to take care of these needs, but each outlay creates a dependency, and it makes the next one that much easier to happen as well. Greed plays its role. Greed is not prejudiced toward Blacks, Whites, Indians, Asians, or any other ethnic group, nor is it prejudiced toward the rich, poor, or the middle class, it is an equal opportunity sin. Jesus warns us all: "Beware and be on your guard against every form of greed, for not even when one has an abundance does his life consist of his possessions" (Luke 12:15).

The middle class is always seeking a comfort zone. Since prosperity is always just around the corner in an expanding economy, they feel it is within their grasp. At these times, they tend to vote for stability, or with the rich, for more conservative politicians. When the economy is bad, they fear falling into poverty, and then they tend to vote more with the poor, or liberals. The economy will usually determine how they vote by who will do them the most good at the time. They serve as a buffer, and a decline of the middle class poses grave danger to our system. Usually the only exception to the middle class voting patterns is if they feel one or the other side is not responsive to what they feel are their values.

The majority of all three groups tend to live for, and vote, their pocketbooks over their convictions. There are exceptions, but by and large, in any election cycle, economic issues determine the outcome. It is interesting, though, in those times when the economy is bad and a liberal leader is up for reelection. All of a sudden, unless our leftist media provides another scapegoat, those who are hurting transfer their economic faith to the conservative position, kind of like a brokenhearted lover, hit by a rebound affect, dotes on the next available person. All amusement aside, Christians tend to vote their pocketbooks over their beliefs as well, and our morally wishy-washy politicians are only giving us what we deserve. Greed divides us from ourselves, or what we should be, and our convictions for the Lord. "For the love of money is a root of all sorts of evil, and some by their longings for it have wandered away from the faith and pierced themselves with many pangs" (I Timothy 6:10).

Divided servitude both dilutes and diminishes our ability to advance the cause of Christ. First and foremost, it strains our relationship with Jesus. He loses His importance to us as other things take His place; also, we fail to render our worship due Him. "In the course of time that Cain brought an offering to the Lord of (some of) the fruit of the ground, and Abel, on his part also brought of the *firstlings* [author's emphasis] of the flock and their fat portions. And the Lord had regard for Abel and his offering, but for Cain and for his offering He had no regard" (Genesis 4:3-5). Both brought to God out of their career choices, and God did accept grain offerings (Leviticus 2:1 and following). Why did God not regard Cain?

Cain brought to God what he felt God should have been willing to accept. He gave out of his surplus, or leftovers, just enough to get by. His counterparts in Jesus's day were the Pharisees. "Woe to you scribes and Pharisees, hypocrites! For you tithe mint and dill and cumin" (Matthew 23:23). How long would it take to count a pile of dill seeds to make sure God got His fair share, and only, His fair, legal share? But Abel brought God the best he had to offer, the first fruits and the choicest portions. He wasn't choked, or blinded by self-gain. His desire was to show thankfulness and devotion to God, and God gave him His favor.

Our divided heart is shown in our giving as well. It has been said that if all American Christians today were to suddenly find themselves on welfare, and began to tithe, Church giving would rise significantly. Part of this is our love for, and focus on, worldly things. We always seem to crave more. This strangles our ability to love or care, as we should, about the things of God. In our desire for a personal comfort zone, the average American is $43,874.00 in debt, or $175,496.00 for a family of four. This is 122 percent of the average person's share of disposable income by 2010 statistics. A rate of 100 percent is considered to be the highest sustainable level. Personal debt is $8,270.00 per capita, and of that, $4,700.00 is credit card debt, by 2011 figures. This doesn't include monthly installment payments for Cable TV, cell phones, Internet service, or a host of other diversions. God is left with the remainder.

The choking of riches affects us personally in our spiritual walk with Christ. "If then you have been raised up with Christ, keep seeking the things that are above, where Christ is, seated at the right hand of God. Set your minds on things above, not on things that are on earth" (Colossians 3:1, 2). If a person is heavily in debt, it is very hard not to be constantly thinking about it. As if prayer didn't already have a selfish tendency, this anxiety causes it to be ever more lost in focus on the needs of the body and the payment of debts. These are not the "debts" Jesus was referring to as needing to be forgiven in the Model Prayer (Matthew 6:12), but they very often cause a spiritual debt through our failing to honor God, as we should.

Somewhere along the line, Christians who are deeply in debt need to take a reality check on the direction their lives are headed. Are they the master, controlling their finances, or does their financial situation control them? Stewardship involves acknowledging that our wealth is a trust from God. He is the owner, and we are the trustees. He is supposed to call the shots on what we have and what is important. While He allows us some liberty, our duty is to manage it in such a way as to build His kingdom and bring glory to Him. Living only for the purpose of having and paying for riches makes us a slave to wealth and reduces God to the position of a concerned third party. Jesus counseled us about the consequences, even here in this life: "Do not be anxious then, saying, 'What shall we eat?' or 'What shall we drink?' Or 'With what shall we clothe ourselves?' For all these things the Gentiles eagerly seek, for your Heavenly Father knows that you need all these things. But seek first His kingdom and His righteousness, and all these things shall be added to you" (Matthew 6:31-33). And again, "For what does it profit a man to gain the whole world, and forfeit his soul?" (Mark 8:36).

The illustration of choked grain is one that almost half of Jesus's crowd could relate to; they were farmers. Palestine was well known for two things: rocks and thorns. It was a precarious existence, depending on the mercy of the weather, and it was very labor intensive in milking every kernel of grain out of the soil. Each weed or thorn had to be pulled by hand. If they got too big, they smothered the wheat, barley, or lentils in the field. Today, billions of dollars are spent in America alone to control weeds. Not all of this is by agribusiness, as gardeners and homeowners also deal with weeds, and everyone is familiar with crabgrass. While starting out small, it quickly spreads, sending down thread-like roots each place a stem touches the ground. These only enable it to grow faster and get even larger. Those tough, fine roots make it very difficult to remove and give it a competitive edge to deprive other garden plants or grasses of water and nutrients. Any field or garden infested by it loses productivity.

In the African Sahel and Equatorial Africa, many subsistence farmers grow sorghum, corn, and milo for food. Here, another weed has taken a devastating toll: the striga plant. It is a parasite that lives off the roots of other plants, especially these grain bearers. These parasites attach themselves and gradually suck the life out of their host, literally strangling, or choking out the grain. Also, as it is killing its host, each parasite plant can produce up to ninety thousand seeds, which can live in the ground for at least twenty years.

This illustrates another way that the choking of wealth damages the Church. While it is gradually, spiritually strangling its host, it is also highly contagious. This reveals a side of our nature shown in the old saying, "Keeping up with the Joneses." We see it frequently played out suburbia. One person mows their yard, and in short order, half of the neighborhood is out doing theirs. No one wants to stick out as having the scrubbiest yard. If there is a social circle, and one of them gets a new vehicle, high tech toy, or even plan a weekend trip, all of a sudden, everyone in the group has to as well.

The Church is not immune to this. These social cliques don't just affect the adults in them; it also contaminates their children in devastating ways. Those whose have parents who can't keep up often become the least popular in the youth group. Their parents also risk being shunned by those in their own social circle, and the spirit of fellowship is weakened; Church unity is cracked, and in a crisis, fractures. Paul addressed this problem in Corinth, "For in your eating, each one takes his own supper first, and one is hungry and another drunk" (I Corinthians 11:21). People feel more comfortable associating with those of their own socioeconomic group, but often, this leads to the hurt of the body. The pursuit or the choking of wealth only intensifies this. Those who live in nice homes and drive nice cars tend to be drawn into fellowship with others who live in nice homes and drive nice cars. A whole group gets caught up together in this choking. Those outside of it are forced to at least consider spending more on things in an effort to measure up. It can cause them to lose their self-esteem and feeling of belonging since they are not accepted on personal levels. It is sin if we allow other Christians to become disenfranchised and fail to fully function as a body. "Be of the same mind towards one another; do not be haughty, in mind, but associate with the lowly. Do not be wise in your own estimation" (Romans 12:16). It is also a misuse of Christian liberty. "For if because of food [wealth] your bother is hurt, you are no longer walking in love. Do not destroy with food him for whom Christ died" (Romans 14:15).

The choking of riches also damages a Christian's witness to the world. Norman Vincent Peale did a lot of good in his ministry, but his message bordered on one of God blessing materially those who followed Him. This caused a mis-focus among the middle and upper classes, it created doubt of salvation and God's love in the lower classes, and it gave non-Christians a wrongful concept of the Gospel unto salvation.

Often, the only Bible the world will ever read is the lives of those Christians that they know. The "Bibles" these believers offer is in how they live, and this is a testimony to what they value and believe. When a Christian is choked by the love of wealth, the values they show are worldly, not spiritual. These are the same ones the world has, and sometimes feeling guilty about. A nonbeliever who sees this example will rightly conclude that they are just as good as the Christian, and share the same core, or applied religion. This Christian doesn't really put much value in Jesus, heaven, or the kingdom of God, except maybe as a way of getting out of debt. They are just playing the same game as everyone else is. Such testimony won't lead too many unbelievers to want to become Christians.

A wealth-choked, or driven Christian, will probably not stand too strongly on Christian principles on the job, either. They often will try to convince themselves that they are just honoring the Lord by being good employees. "Slaves [employees] in all things obey those who are your masters on earth" (Colossians 3:22). But they are inclined to leave out the last part, "But with sincerity of heart *fearing the Lord* [author's emphasis]" (Col. 3:22). In reality, their fear isn't of Jesus but of losing their jobs and a paycheck. This, not Jesus, keeps them close to the vest on all company policies, even those contrary to the will of God. Granted, Christians are supposed to be model employees in their honesty, work ethic, and loyalty, but their call is to serve Christ first, even if this is in contradiction with their bosses. Note the example of the Church in Corinth.

In Corinth, during Bible times, idol temples dotted the city. In addition to service as places of worship, these also functioned as social halls. Various employment guilds would periodically meet at these temples, and often, business deals were made there. Absence meant no contracts and no work, so all guild members wanting in on the action were present. Employees of bosses or guild members were also expected to attend; absence risked the forfeiture of their jobs. At the temple, a sacrifice would be made to the deity it represented, and all present would be expected to partake in an appeal for contractual blessing by that god or goddess. On this policy, Paul addressed the church, "You cannot drink the cup of the Lord and the cup of demons, you cannot partake of the table of the Lord and the table of demons" (I Corinthians 10:21). Paul was not on a campaign to be voted their favorite preacher, but rather, to save their souls from undue worldly snares and demonic service.

Even for a Christian employee, free from the snares of choking wealth, a decision to follow Christ in situations like this is quite difficult. To one ensnared, this becomes realistically impossible. They will seek some way to compromise their convictions to keep their jobs. If business policy is to promote gay rights, this Christian may find themselves called upon to abet or implement it. Their choice is obvious: obey their boss and keep their job or obey God and lose them, or at least destroy any hope of advancement with that company. Worldly snares will lead Christians today to obey their boss and then pray for forgiveness, change churches if anyone finds out, and search the Scriptures to justify their compromise.

This same pressure to compromise is usually forced on education professionals. They will be handed a textbook that advocates evolution or other humanistic doctrines. A health teacher will be told to promote immoral choices, such as birth control or access to abortion. Every year it seems the list of anti-Christian laws and edicts only increases. Christian educators are under immense pressure to compromise their faith to keep their jobs.

Every so often, an employee somewhere will vocally or visibly stand up for their faith. A recent case was that of Trevor Keezar, an employee of Home Depot in Okeechobee, Florida, that is, until October of 2009. For well over a year, he had worn a lapel button, which said, "One nation under God, indivisible." This was tolerated until he began bringing a Bible to work and reading it on his breaks. At that point, he was terminated. The message was clear, Christian faith, values, or convictions are to be parked at the door and will be not tolerated by employees of a growing list of corporations, nor are not welcome at many other companies in the American business world, either.

The world will claim there is no discrimination here, only a protection of someone else's civil rights or an official policy. Action is taken against the Christian not for simply having their beliefs, but in their advocating of them. In one small way, this is partly true, no one is forcing a Christian to offer a literal sacrifice on a literal alter when they walk through the door. What the world is demanding, though, is for them to park their beliefs at the office, factory, or school door. Back in 1993, the Equal Employment Opportunity Commission (EEOC) under then President Bill Clinton proposed regulations geared to address what was called, "Hostile work environment harassment." To protect the civil rights of nonbelievers, these rules would have covered all religious displays on the job. This would include everything from broadcasting Christian music over the intercom, to Christian employees witnessing their faith, or wearing religious personal belongings. While public outcry led to a scaling back of the proposals, this concept is now in effect in many businesses. In 1991 in Bissell vs. Kaleidoscope Inc., precedent was set to label any witness of faith by a Christian potential harassment. These, and other actions, have only made it easier for employers to pressure Christians to hide and compromise their beliefs. The real problem is with our response as Christians.

If a Christian accepts the claim that while they are at work their employer has the right to expect them to compromise their faith, then they're not being faithful to Jesus. Accepting any surrender of what we are violates our values and beliefs.

Just doing wrongful things, as in being immoral, unethical, or deceptive, is not the only way to cave in to the world. Allowing an employer, governmental policy, or anything else to become our god instead of Jesus is compromise in itself. This is especially tragic in a nation founded on that very religious liberty. If we are snared or choked by riches, the pressure to "pay the devil his dues" is unbearable. Such a believer will cave in, surrender, and compromise their faith. Addiction to wealth breeds spiritual inertia, or a spiritual conservatism, that resists any threat to itself. Greed, or covetousness replaces Jesus in our hearts just as much as if we were worshipping in an idol's temple. We fear what its loss will mean to our lives, and it, not Jesus, becomes our focus, while at the same time, we pay lip service to God. It separates us from Jesus. "For this you know with certainty, that no immoral or impure person or covetous man, who is an idolater, has any inheritance in the kingdom of Christ and God" (Ephesians 5:5).

Granted, Jesus called us to wisdom as to how and when to display our faith. "Behold I send you out as sheep in the midst of wolves; therefore be shrewd as serpents and innocent as doves" (Matthew 10:16). The question is, will we love God above all else and live for Him?

This may sound like overkill, but our failure here has given immense power to Satan to disarm our witness and corrupt our nation. Are we so ensnared that we fear our employers more than God? Or are we willing to risk possessions for a statement of what is right? What means more to us, Jesus or wealth? There was a young man who came to Jesus late in His ministry. Jesus gave him just one command. "And looking at him, Jesus felt a love for him, and said to him, 'One thing you lack; go and sell all your possessions, and give it to the poor, and you shall have treasure in Heaven, and come follow Me'" (Mark 10:21). God may be calling many Christians today to do the same thing.

The Church, or kingdom of God, was built by people committed to Jesus. One who was an inspiration to me was a young, unemployed college professor in the summer of 1971 named Richard Harsh. He had lost his job at the local college because of his faith. While he did obtain a job in Northern Michigan, he suffered much, as did his wife and young son, for his convictions, yet his faith never wavered. He remained bold in his faith and has now gone on to meet his Jesus. A conservative fearfulness or a spirit of cowardice has never built the Church. "For God has not given us a spirit of timidity but of power and love and discipline" (II Timothy 1:7). There was nothing conservative in launching missionary journeys to take the gospel to the far-flung regions of the known world. There was nothing fearful in standing up to the leaders of both Judea and Rome. The only "wealth flight" was that of its use in meeting the needs of the gospel, either in saving an important church in Jerusalem or of offering the opportunity of salvation to both slaves and lords.

It took a bold step into uncertainty for Abraham to leave the safety and security of Haran to follow God's calling into places unknown. He literally risked everything to face a world of idol worshippers, especially in the land of Canaan. They seemed to have a fear for every god but his (Genesis 20:11). It is easy to overlook his willingness to give up everything because God did bless him, Genesis 13:2, with material things, but his first wealth was always heavenly. "For he was looking for the city which had [unshakable] foundations, whose architect and builder is God" (Hebrews 11:10).

God has always called men and women to step outside of their comfort zone. By faith, they are called to trust Him to take care of them in another one, their survival zone. Riches blind us to seeing what this one has to offer. It is here that one finds purpose and meaning. Wealth dulls our spiritual senses. It is like a struggling strawberry plant in an unweeded garden. Its view is blocked of the sun and its roots deprived of nutrients by those weeds' strangle hold. The Christian's release comes in pulling these choking weeds, and like the strawberry plant, then we are free to reach out and expand our existence.

There is a short cut that does tempt us, it involves wanting the best of both. The world is full of self-help gurus who preach a gospel of deliverance from our mental state of anxiety over wealth and our possessions. The Scientology and Christian Science movements are famous for identifying mental attitudes, memories, or scars that can inhibit a healthy mind. In some cases they are right, as in dealing with long forgotten memories that inhibit us. In others, they are very wrong, as sin is sin. And not all illness is caused by poor mental attitudes; God, not us, is our healer. Some guilt hang-ups are good. God put them there to lead us to change our behavior. If we are relieved of guilt over the problems wealth causes us, we're less likely to solve the problem. True liberation comes by repentance and experiencing the forgiveness of sins.

Liberation is in Jesus, "Do not work [as priority] for the food which perishes, but for the food which endures to eternal life, which the Son of

Man shall give to you" (John 6:27). Freedom can only come by letting go of a snare not by denying it exists. There is something about laying all on the alter to follow Jesus that brings joy and true wealth. When Jesus called the Rich Young Ruler to sell all, give all, and follow, He gave a promise: "And you shall have treasure in Heaven; and come follow Me" (Mark 10:21). There's a saying, "You can't out-give God." This doesn't mean, as some hustlers in the preaching business say, "Give me a hundred dollars and God will give you a thousand dollars." These are people, as Paul warned: "Men depraved in mind and deprived of the truth, who suppose that godliness is a means of gain" (I Timothy 6:5). It means that a surrender of all to God opens our lives to His true riches.

If those choked today would seek this liberation, they would find themselves free and fruitful, some one hundred fold, some sixty, and some thirty. Weeds prevent fruit and can kill, but God promises to sustain us if we bear fruit. He will preserve us as His word promises. "Let your character be free from the love of money, being content with what you have; for He Himself has said, 'I will never desert you nor will I ever forsake you'" (Hebrews 13:5). He will not give us all we want, but He will provide all we need.

# IX

## ASHAMED BEFORE MEN

*"For whoever is ashamed of Me and My words, of him will the Son of Man be ashamed when He comes in His glory, and the glory of the Father and of the holy angels."*

—Luke 9:26

### Pride

Most people will put on display and show off what is important to them. An educator, doctor, or other professional will often display their various awards and degrees on their office walls. Of course, most of us have seen the Norman Rockwell picture of the boy reading the diploma of the doctor who is about to give him a shot, but doctors and others are usually proud of what they have accomplished. A professional ball player will post his awards, championships, most valuable player awards, and all-star awards, usually, somewhere on his "turf." A mechanic will post his awards. A soldier will proudly wear his ribbons and medals. In some parts of the world, worshippers will display their idol shelves, often with the same pride as a hunter or fisherman will with their trophy catch.

Accomplishment is definitely a topic some people can talk and talk and talk about, especially if it is their own. The higher some people get in their chosen field, the more some of them do brag. Even if they don't, the higher they go, the more it means to them. This is a value that cannot be measured in dollars and cents, but it may mean more to the possessor than all the money they have in the bank. It also shows a lot about the recipient's character. On February 5, 2005, the Pittsburgh Steelers won the Super Bowl over the Seattle Seahawks. Wide receiver Hines Ward won the MVP (Most Valuable Player) award for his forty-three yard touchdown reception to ice the win. In his post-game interview his praises went to Coach Bill Cowher and the team. He made special mention to the ball thrown to him by Antwaan Randle EL. Head Coach Cowher couldn't put enough praise on the team and was humbled in giving the Vince Lombardi trophy to team owner Dan Rooney. Others have shown the same spirit, among the greatest was Kurt Warner, and a now retired quarterback of the Arizona Cardinals. For all his accomplishments and Super Bowl appearances, his praises were always to God.

All too frequently, though, a person's focus is on self-glory. "And Samuel rose early in the morning to meet Saul; and it was told Samuel saying, 'Saul came to Carmel, and behold, he set up a monument for himself'" (I Samuel 15:12). In Saul's early days, it was important to him to bring praise and offer service to God, but as time went by, he began to put his faith in himself and his army, and God went to the back burner. His focus became more and more on himself and what others thought of him. While God might not have come to the point of being an embarrassment to Saul, He was definitely not at the top of Saul's priority list. Saul might not have been a narcissist, but he had definitely developed a big ego. Now, in a defining moment, he failed in his disobedience by blatantly sparing the best of Amalek when he was told to destroy all, and then by glorifying himself for the victory.

Pride, as Saul displayed, is a feeling that someone has outgrown God and are now denying Him. It is a self-seeking, self-focused, and self-fulfilling spirit. There is no room to credit anyone else, especially God. God even becomes an embarrassment, like parents are to a teenager, but beneath the facade of self sufficiency is a character paradox. The proud person actually has a deep insecurity that shows itself in an unwillingness to acknowledge their inabilities, self-doubt, and weaknesses. It would have shamed Saul to have to ascribe God as the source of this victory. Saul's faith and acknowledgement of God went into hiding.

One ingredient of pride is a craving not just of self-accomplishment but of self-glory. There is a pride in self-accomplishment, in being able to tie one's own shoes or bake a pie solo. We like to feel we can take care of ourselves, but this can get out of balance and take on a self-glory focus. The American concept of rugged individualism is a manifestation of this. We can come to feel that there is nothing that we cannot do by ourselves, and we need not depend on anyone for anything. Sometimes, family and those close to us can be a contributing factor in this. It's very important for a parent to not allow their children's needs to be seen as a burden. It's also essential to help them view most accomplishment in a "we," as opposed to in an "I" setting. An emphasis is best if it includes God, family, and friends, and how accomplishment is both in part from them and for them and not just by or for self. This doesn't mean a child can't have any purely personal victories, but "we" is almost always better than "I".

Pride leads us to a false view of self. We affirm value on ourselves as opposed to having our value given to us by God (or family). Uzziah had a problem with this. "But when he became strong his heart was so proud that he acted corruptly and he was unfaithful to the Lord his God, for he entered the Temple of the Lord to burn incense on the altar of incense" (II Chronicles 26:16). Pride is a false view, an elevation of self that, ultimately, results in self valuing. It is humanism on a personal level, but in its manifestation it can be masked, as it can be displayed in both arrogance and in self degradation and abasement. Both deny God His role in affirming our value and focus us inwardly. Very often, as a result, proud people are deeply lonely and insecure inside.

It probably should be noted that not all pride is bad, nor is all self accomplishment evil. Good pride leads us to do our best to not bring disgrace on others, especially on God. It focuses us on the source of our ability. "But he who boasts, let him boast of the Lord" (II Corinthians 10:17). It affirms our value and place on the team, or in the Church.

## [FEAR]

While pride is one way to deny Jesus, so, as well, is fear. This was true in Jesus's day just as much as it is true today. "Nevertheless many even of the rulers believed in Him, but because of the Pharisees they were not confessing Him, lest they should be put out of the synagogue" (John 12:42). From an early age, we are taught, or learn by trial and error, the benefits of getting along with others. Basically, this is good. Imagine a world where no one wants to get along. But it also has its drawbacks, as when the value of getting along with others becomes greater to us than the value of doing right. One manifestation of this today is the Christian fear of being labeled as a fanatic.

This reflects on an admonition most of us learn early on regarding topics of conversation. To apply the art of accommodation, there are two that we should never discuss in a social setting: politics and religion. Between the two, religion is clearly the most taboo. In fact, with the attitudes most Americans have toward Washington DC right now, politics, especially in a complaining way is kind of in vogue.

I remember a rebuke that I received years ago after giving God the glory for something I accomplished at work. "I don't give a *!@% about your beliefs, all I care about is your getting your job done!" my boss retorted. Quite honestly, there may have been a little bit of overzealousness on my part; God and Christian friends have helped to bring about a little more discretion in my witness, but this was merely a reflection on what I most valued, salvation in Jesus. It hit a nerve. A readiness to seek God, or think about eternity, isn't a subject most people want to face.

This reflects another truth. While people want to talk about things they value, the exact opposite is true about things they don't, or at least not in a positive way. They may complain about their job, spouse, neighbor, car, or life in general, or if they don't feel positive about these things, they won't mention them at all. The boss noted earlier, "didn't want to hear about God," but on the other hand, he had little problem in using God's name in another way. It is also curious to note how our feelings of the things we value can change over time and not always in a positive way. Newlyweds will usually chat to and about their spouses in an excited way, but for many, this flame fades, and all too often they start to find fault, or just begin to take one another for granted. They also can get too busy for each other and begin to drift apart and the conversation changes.

This can put us on dangerous ground. In most cases, married people will, at some point, be presented with an opportunity to be unfaithful. In a world where we are constantly being jostled and interacted with by people of the opposite sex, this is not rare, and it can be flattering, but experts will tell us the best way to cool passions on both our part and the solicitor's is to begin talking favorably about our spouse. Not only does it send a signal of our unavailability; it also provides a positive feedback in our own minds and makes cheating harder to do. If our talk is negative about our spouse, or we don't mention them at all, the odds of getting into a destructive situation are much greater. Eve's response to Satan was in adding unfavorably to God's command, "You shall not eat from it nor touch it, lest you die" (Genesis 3:3). Neither reflected on positive feelings for God, nor helped her to resist sin.

Here, we see that same principle is true in our relationship with God. Granted, we are not individually the bride of Christ, the Church is (Ephesians 5:25-32), but Jesus is supposed to be our best friend, and our friendship is part of a sacred partnership with God, a good parallel to the American Indian rite of being made a blood brother. In our case, Jesus's blood made us brothers. The temptation to sin, or violate this covenant, is common to all of us. If we are silent and ashamed of Him, or hide our faith, then this temptation is far more likely to defeat us. While it might bring snide remarks from those around us, talking about Jesus, or how sin displeases God, greatly increases our success rate.

Playing defense alone rarely works, at least not for long. If a baseball team cannot score, no matter how good its defense, that team will never win a game. History is the enemy of those who rely on defense alone. The Hadrian Wall was built across northern England in the AD 120s to keep out the tribes of Picts and Scots. It worked for a while, as long as Rome could keep an army tied down there, but when they withdrew, it failed. The Great Wall of China, built in the latter part of the third-century BC, also did work to keep out Mongol invaders. Again, in time, China failed to properly garrison it, and it was breached as well. It has been said of the terrorists, like Al Qaeda, that if America built a fifty-foot high fence, they would make a fifty-one-foot ladder and find a place we weren't looking.

This is what the devil does to us spiritually if we only play defense. We cannot defend every point of our life at all times when we play defense. The only way to win is to actively live, witness, and display our faith. "I press on toward the goal for the prize of the upward call of God in Christ Jesus" (Philippians 3:14). Paul was not ashamed of Jesus and was never content to play defense.

Lot wasn't either. According to one tradition, when he dwelt in Sodom (Genesis 13-19), he would carry around a sign that said to the effect, "God will destroy all the immoral and perverted: repent now!" People in town would mock him, asking why he would carry a sign when no one was paying attention. His reply was that, in so doing, at least he would not himself get swept away by their evil. He wasn't as much concerned with popular opinions as he was of God's. While this story may not be true, Lot's concern for God did get him in trouble. "This one came in as an alien, and already he is acting like a judge; now we will treat you worse than them" (Genesis 19:9).

In America today, there is one word that all too often holds a Christian back. It is the fear of being called the f-word. This is not the one most of us are thinking about; this word is "fanatic". No one wants to feel ostracized, either on a professional or a social level. Great modern theologians like Reinhold Niebhur preached a non-controversial Christianity, and at work, any display of our faith can put us outside of the loop in a heartbeat, often even with those who profess to be Christians. Oddly, the only time this word, fanatic, ever gets used is on Christians. Even terrorists are called kinder things, like "enemy combatants." No one on the left, not even the most extreme animal rights activists or militant environmentalists are called this, either; only Christians get this distinction. In a way, this is quite similar to the scarlet "A" on the character Hester Prynne in *The Scarlet Letter*, by Nathaniel Hawthorne.

In 1850, he wrote this book, to a large degree, to show that labels, even in Hester Prynne's case, are not always right. She had been guilty of adultery and was forced to wear the "A" as a result, but by her gentle spirit, serving character, and humble nature, she eventually won over her fellow townspeople. Similarly, the fear of the label "fanatic" should not keep a Christian from humble and faithful profession either. If they truly live their faith, opportunities for love and service will arise, just as it did with Hester Prynne. And while neither the vegans (vegetarians), socialists, nor gays share our label, our coworkers and others will feel a greater comfort in the presence of someone who loves them than they will of someone who threatens their lifestyle or comfort zone. God may open for us opportunities by hospital visitation, fixing a meal in an hour of need, or other areas of service. Even the world craves for, and recognizes, love.

No Christian is immune from assault if they live their faith. This may be a good test to see if we are a witness for Jesus or not. Paul said, "And indeed, all who desire to live godly in Christ Jesus will be persecuted" (II Timothy 3:12). It is a sign of our belonging to Him, as it also was for George Washington Carver. "The New York Times" assailed him for his religious conviction. They rebuked him for his "complete lack of scientific spirit" and warned that he would bring discredit to both his people and the Tuskegee Institute. "Real chemists rely on science, not inspiration," and with Christianity under assault, they believed his fall would be soon.[12] When this did not happen, the powers that be in the media and academia determined to rewrite his life to marginalize his religion.

Failure to stand up, as one should, was not new even in Jesus's day. One example was of Abraham. There was a famine in the land of Canaan, and the family was forced to take refuge in Egypt. His fear led him to hide behind his wife. "And it came about when he came near to Egypt, that he said to Sarai [Sarah] his wife, 'See now, I know that you are a beautiful woman'...'Please say that you are my sister, that it may go well with me because of you, and that I may live on account of you'" Genesis (12:11,13). God was able to display His glory in Egypt, but only in spite of Abraham. However, his cowardice forever closed for him a mission field as Pharaoh sent him out, to never return (Genesis 12:19, 20). His character did little to influence anyone for God. How much more might God have been honored and worshipped if Abraham had shown some courage, even if he did feel dropped "cold turkey" in Egypt?

Jesus did not send us out "cold turkey" to face a hostile world. In addition to the Holy Spirit, we have His example of leadership. "For consider Him who has endured such hostility by sinners against Himself, so that you may not grow weary and lose heart. You have not yet resisted to the point of shedding blood in your striving against sin," (Hebrews

[12]    "Men of Science Never Talk That Way." The New York Times, November 20, 1924

12:3, 4). In much of the world, the Church has testified in blood for her faith, and in all likelihood, barring a massive revival in America, we also are soon headed there again. If Christ died for us, however, can we expect any better treatment? In reality; there is no greater gift or offering we can give to Jesus. Tertullian (AD 160- AD 220) in his *Apology 50* said as much: "The blood of Christians is seed," or as others have said, "the seed of the Church."[13] A testimony given, even once, in the depth of trials means immensely more than a thousand times preached in comfort to the choir. A persecuted Paul said, "For I am not ashamed of the gospel, for it is the power of God for salvation to everyone who believes, to the Jew first and also to the Greek" (Romans 1:16).

While Jesus calls His followers to courage, He also warns them to be prudent. "He spoke another parable to them. 'The kingdom of Heaven is like leaven which a woman took and hid in three pecks of meal, until it was all leavened'" (Matthew 13:33). Leaven works in secret. Common sense would dictate to us that we should not to go to downtown Pyongyang, North Korea with a bullhorn and start preaching the gospel in Korean. The only exception would be if, like Jonah, God gave us a special commission.

There are times to go underground, as today in North Korea, where Christians are forced to meet in total secrecy. As the Roman persecution became more and more sophisticated in the third-century AD, going underground happened in the Roman world, but it did not stop the witness of Jesus. That "leaven" eventually took over the empire and, by AD 378, right or wrong, became the state religion under Theodosius.

Persecution did not begin with Christians. In an earlier note we saw it happen under Nebuchadnezzar about 600 BC with Shadrach, Meshach, and Abednego. Another famous Old Testament example occurred in about 475 BC in Persia, as recorded in the Book of Esther. As the story unfolds, by appearances, the Jews were getting mixed reviews in their society. While in most places, as in Susa, they seemed to be accepted on a street level (Esther 3:15), they were not so highly esteemed by the powers that be. These were the days of Ahasuerus, or Xerxes, who had invaded and lost in Greece in 480 BC. It is very possible after this defeat that he blamed, or took out his contempt on, Zoroastrianism, a religious belief with many

---

[13]    Jonathan Hill, The History Of Christian Thought, (Downers Grove, IL: InterVArsity Press, 2003), 33.

similarities with Judaism. At the very least, he would have been looking for scapegoats or causes for his defeat as he prepared for his next action with the Greeks. It was at this time that Xerxes promoted Haman the Agagite an astrologer who was probably from the district Agag or Agaz, which was near Persia. While this may not have the sermon appeal of the more conventional view that he had descended from Agag the Amalekite, it makes better historical sense, as Hammedatha, his father's name, was Persian. But the net result was the same. Hate knows no boundaries, it is an equal opportunity sin, and he hated the Jews. Fear and hate led Mordecai to tell Esther to conceal her identity and not advertise her beliefs (Esther 2:10, 20).

Later on, the feared persecution was legislated by the king's edict. Mordecai warned her of their grave danger. She was afraid before men, or in this case, the man who was king. She hoped to escape by her position of royalty, but Mordecai prodded her to put her faith on the line. She could not save her life by hiding what she was, nor could she keep her salvation by disobeying God, she would perish. He also assured her that if she were fearfully disobedient, God would raise up deliverance without her: "And who knows whether you have not attained royalty for such a time as this?" (Esther 4:14). She heeded the calling, and by her action, both she and her people were delivered.

In the Christian era, persecution has gone far beyond the confines of Western history. Of all places, China has been an interesting study. Introduced in the first-century AD, it gradually grew and flourished, greatly expanding under the Tang Dynasty (AD 618-AD 907). Persecution by the Buddhists and Daoists, plus the watchful eye of various emperors, led it to accept, or be coerced into submitting to, state sanctioning. State approval became a condition of her being tolerated in China, but when Emperor Wuzong withdrew this approval in 845, she almost went extinct. Later, the Mongols, under Genghis Kahn (1162-1227), crushed China and the Daoist, Confucian, and Buddhist power bases. This brought revival, as many of the Mongols were Christian, and Genghis was a firm believer in religious tolerance. The Mongols, however, treated the Chinese like second class citizens in their own country. When the Ming Dynasty came along in 1368, this old resentment, plus the hatred by China's other religions, led to renewed oppression. By the time Roman Catholic missionaries returned Christianity to China, about 1600, the rest had virtually all but died out. All other factors aside, these earlier believers seemed all too willing to attach their fortunes to the governments in power to avoid persecution. When governments changed, or opposed Christianity, the Church collapsed. Conviction fell by the wayside to state sanction, and when that, in turn, fell to disfavor, the Church fell with it.

Today in China, two Churches exist side by side. One is the official state sponsored organization. After the Tianamen Square massacre of June 4, 1989, the Chinese government intensified efforts to control the growing Church. The China Christian Council (CCC), an association of churches, has the sanctioned approval of the government. This sanctioning is on the condition of its acceptance of the Communist Party, and not Jesus, as the head of the church. It has as many as fifty thousand congregations with a total membership of about twenty million.

The other Chinese church is the Free Church. This house church movement encompasses between seventy million to one hundred thirty million Chinese. This underground, or Free Church, is not only exploding, but right now, it is very popular with the middle class. It is also officially illegal. In December 2010, the Chinese government, still officially controlled by the Communist Party, launched "Operation Deterrence." The goal was to force all these house churches into the fold and be incorporated into the CCC and the Three Self Patriotic Movement, the official government sanctioning agency. The outcome of all of this is still to be determined, but the repressive arrests, beatings, torture, and death are not new to the Church in China. If the Church flourishes, it will not be by sanction, it will be by its witness.

The success of the modern Church has its roots in events of a little over a half a century ago. In 1949, when the Communists under Chairman Mao Zedung took over, estimates were up to a maximum of four million Chinese that were Christian. At that time, all foreign missionaries were jailed or exiled, Church leaders were killed or arrested, and churches were closed. Over the next several decades, China endured the "Era of Criticism," purges against the "counter-revolutionaries," and the Cultural Revolution with its bloodshed. During this time, the leaven in the flour of China exploded in numbers because of the conviction and testimony of the persecuted Church. After Mao's death in 1976, the Communist Party, out of respect for this conviction, gradually warmed to and accepted this faith. Those Christians who were still imprisoned were released. The Church was still watched and, officially, was required to get state approval for its policies and doctrine. Hence, the tale of two churches: while the official one grew to meet a spiritual need, the underground one exploded to fully fill that hunger. In this environment, she had learned how to hide, meet in secret, and creatively proselytize. One can only wonder what might have been if the earlier Church had stood convicted for Jesus, not depending on the state, but on the Lord for its official sanction.

What, as well, might have happened if those in positions of influence in Jesus's day had feared God more than the praises of men? About one third of the Jews in the first forty years of the Church became Christian. 'This is seen as a fulfillment of Zechariah 13:8, "And it will come about in all the land, declares the Lord, 'That two parts in it will be cut off and perish; but the third will be left in it.'" But how many of these Jews perished spiritually because their leaders failed to heed the calling of Esther 4:14. "For if you remain silent at this time, relief and deliverance will arise... from another place and you and your father's house will perish. And who knows whether you have not attained royalty for such a time as this?" Those in leadership are accountable for the blood of many of them. They recognized Jesus as being from God (John 3:2) and could not hide the facts of His gospel or His death, burial, resurrection, and salvation by faith. Instead, they hid and gave cover and an example for other timid souls to hide as well. It is possible some of these leaders repented later: "And a great many of the priests were becoming obedient to the faith" (Acts 6:7). The place these Jews could have had in the early church, however, never happened. Although it was in God's plan was for their glory, "For salvation is from the Jews" (John 4:22), it instead, went to the Gentiles (Romans 11:17).

What does this say to Church leadership today? One of the greatest trials can be the ones inflicted by those who should know better. This was evident in the rejection of so many because of the actions of their leaders. Much of the cowardice displayed by rank and file Christians often mimics what they observe in the behavior of their leaders. Fearful of the possibility of losing their leadership position or being driven completely out of the professional ministry has led to a cowardly stifling of what needed to be said or done. Instead, they preach a feel good gospel to keep everyone happy. When was the last time you personally heard a "hellfire and brimstone" sermon? How often do the topics of abortion, adultery, and homosexuality get mentioned from the pulpits of the American Church? And what about those who deliberately omit or alter the plan of salvation to avoid controversy? We leaders are doubly accountable for our message. "Let not many of you become teachers, my brethren, knowing that as such we shall incur a stricter judgment" (James 3:1). James is not telling us to stay out of leadership but to teach in the fear and admonition of the Lord. We leaders are accountable for those in our charge, and we will be judged for confessing or denying Jesus in our messages. "My people are destroyed for lack of knowledge; because you have rejected knowledge, I also will reject you from being My priest" (Hosea 4:6).

There is no excuse for the damage that all of us can do to each other in the body. Not only do we seek ways to get around the command to confess Christ before men, but also, we are often an impediment to those who do. In today's world this often involves many who wear the name of Christian but have also made peace with the world. In a conversation years ago with one of these Christians, he made an interesting observation. By not in any way advocating, or advertising his faith, he had done well in the world. He was actually convinced that God had blessed him for this. He enumerated his blessings of money and a career, wife, kids doing well and accepted at school, and a generous comfort zone.

This person was not alone. Many Christians today fear any antagonism against whatever power is giving them their comfort. By sitting on the sidelines and not antagonizing either God or the unbeliever, they feel they have made peace with both. Since they hold church affiliation, they believe that they will escape eternal destruction. They tend to look with a contemptuous pity on Christians who have been bold for the Lord and have suffered for it, but they only fool themselves in believing that they have an allegiance to Jesus. "He who is not with Me is against Me, and he who does not gather with Me, scatters" (Luke 11:23). While being a spectator sports fan is okay, there is still the cost of a ticket or a TV. Being a spectator Christian can cost a person eternity.

In the Old Testament, there were those who attempted the same thing. "We have made a covenant with death, and with Sheol we have made a pact. The overwhelming scourge shall not reach us when it passes by" (Isaiah 28:15). The exact interpretation of what is meant in this covenant has varied explanations, but these people believed they could escape by doing nothing or not taking sides in the wars around them. They believed they could hide, and they were wrong. Our enemy will gladly give us a measure of peace and may even allow us a little prosperity, provided we cause him no trouble. He may even do this to discourage the zealous believer who suffers for their testimony, but the end result is enmity with God, emptiness, and spiritual judgment.

All too often, Christians like these can be the worst nightmare for a sincere believer. They feel that since they have made their peace, they don't want their boat rocked. When they are met with a zealous believer, animosity will often be the result. The guilt over their own compromise and apprehension over the fear of their own comfort zone being threatened is often taken out on the challenger. This anger is hard for a Christian to grasp; it is like being wounded by a fellow soldier. This is close to the worst hurt we can feel, but we are not alone. First of all, we still have Jesus. Secondly, others have endured this as well. "For Demas, having loved this present world has deserted me... Alexander the coppersmith did me much harm; the Lord will repay him according to his deeds" (II Timothy 4:10, 14). In Paul's darkest hour many of his fellow Christians gave him no light, and even Jesus was betrayed by Judas and abandoned by the others.

Paul, though, loved Jesus more than anything else. This is our challenge: to love and honor Him more than job, government approval, social circles, or family. All the philosophies of man or the popularity of sin will one day be out of vogue. All these are like: "The grass withers, and the flower falls off, but the word of the Lord abides forever" (I Peter 1:24, 25), but our gospel will never fade. Those who argue that the Church must either change its message to accommodate our modern, sinful age or be silent will, themselves, stand silent before the throne of God (Habakkuk 2:20). If time permits, our nation and civilization itself will fall into the dust, but our love and conviction for Jesus will sustain us.

Another "must" for every Christian is to seek out and embrace other Christians in both word and deeds. This involves sharing in ministries, and includes financial aid if necessary. Being of mutual support is what the Church is all about. No one is an island. God will provide all we need to be sustained if we are in His will. Very often, a large part of this support is through the encouragement of other believers. Satan wants to isolate us. As mentioned before, this is a very effective tool used to break people down. The support of the body is one of the best ways to build conviction and camaraderie as both they and we are mutually encouraged.

Christianity took over Rome and is now taking over China because generation after generation of believers were willing to stand firm for Jesus, no matter the cost. In modern days, a good parallel is seen in the actions of the American Civil Rights Movement. On December 1, 1955, a black lady, Rosa Parks, refused the order of bus driver James Blake in Montgomery, Alabama, to ride in the back of a bus. This act was the spark that launched the Civil Rights Movement. Through acts of nonviolence, civil disobedience swept the South. The 1960 Greensboro "sit in" was classic. When one person was arrested and went to jail for taking a seat in a "white's only" restaurant, another would take their place. The jails could not contain them all, and step by step, these discriminatory policies fell. The song "We shall overcome... someday" became reality. Rosa Parks heard the challenge of Esther 4:14.

This is also why Christianity is not overcoming, at least in America. When one Christian takes a stand, most of the rest run for cover. We are not called to hide, but to overcome. "For whoever is born of God overcomes the world; and this is the victory that has overcome the world, our faith" (I John 5:4). We are called to be victorious, to be overcomers. Who knows whether you have not come to the kingdom of God for such a time as this?

# X

## PROXY CHRISTIANITY

*"No, but there shall be a king over us, that we may be like all the nations, that our king may judge us and go out before us and fight our battles."*

—I Samuel 8:19, 20

In President John F. Kennedy's (1961-1963) inaugural address were the words, "And so, my fellow Americans, ask not what your country can do for you. Ask what you can do for your country." There's always been a calling for good people to rise up and serve to the benefit of the nation. There has always been a calling to meet an endless stream of social ills. After our revolution, one of these was the mistreatment of the loyalists, those who had sided with Great Britain during that war. Two others that modern Americans readily identify with were slavery and the mistreatment of the Native Americans. There also was the issue of the pervasive poverty of most Americans in our first century as a nation. This one even brought a quip from Abraham Lincoln, our 16th president, who was in office from 1861-1865. "God must have really loved poor people: that's why He made so many of them." Each era has had its own special needs.

## Illiteracy

One social inadequacy was illiteracy. In a crusade to overcome this, one man gave virtually his entire life in an effort to change his world. In 1837 Horace Mann (1796-1859) resigned his law practice to actively lobby the need for universal education and literacy, taking the position of Secretary of the Massachusetts State Board of Education. He recognized the pathway education provided for the young out of poverty and the growing economic abuse, fueled by the industrial age. He was known to have said, "Be ashamed to die until you have won some victory for humanity" Resigning that post in 1843, he continued the fight for free and universal primary education. He was a catalyst for Massachusetts becoming the first state in the US to have compulsory primary education in 1853.

## Abolition of Slavery

Then there was the issue of abolition of slavery. Again, one man stands out for his total devotion to this cause. William Lloyd Garrison (1805-1879) was a steady conscience and activist on the issue and was faithful to his God, whether it was popular or not. He was a pacifist and never voted. He believed that all manners of righteousness would prevail through the tireless and wholehearted efforts of those committed to its cause. "Preach the word; be ready in season and out of season; reprove, rebuke, exhort, with great patience and instruction" (II Timothy 4:2). In 1831 he began publishing "The Liberator," an antislavery newspaper. This he continued until 1865 when the Thirteenth Amendment to the Constitution officially ended slavery that December. "The success of a moral principle has not depended on guns or popularity," he wrote, "The success of any great moral enterprise does not depend upon numbers," according to brainyquote.com, "but on devotion, justice, and resolve."[14] To his chagrin, the final success of this issue took both conviction and combat.

These two felt called by God to special missions; ones outside of the doors of their own churches. God is still calling among us in the same way, today. His call may be for us to make our life's mission the meeting of a

---

[14] Life Quotes, "William Lloyd Garrison Quotes." http://lifequoteslib.com/authors/william_lloyd_garrison.html

social need or an injustice. Granted, our prime directive is to win others to the Lord, but He will use social issues as a channel to bring others to salvation and declare His glory among the lost. Whether or not this is our specific calling, we are called to support those who are, both in prayer and in active participation. "We're all called, as Christians, to ministries of prayer, support, and activism. "For just as we have many members in one body and all the members do not have the same function, so we, who are many, are one body in Christ, and individually members one of another" (Romans 12:4,5).

Our physical bodies were created by God to work as a team, under the authority of our head, or brain. The Church is the same. "But speaking the truth in love, we are to grow up in all aspects into Him, who is the head, even Christ, from whom the whole body, being fitted and held together by that which every joint supplies, according to the proper working of each individual part, causes growth of the body for the building up of itself in love" (Ephesians 4:15, 16).

All of us know of someone whose body doesn't work properly. It may be blindness. In this circumstance, the other parts of the body try to compensate for the nonfunctioning part. The blind usually develop a keener sense of hearing as the brain literally rewires itself. But while such a person may excel, there will always be something they are unable to do that they could have if they had their sight. The same is true in the Church, as one part will try to pull for a nonworking member, something is always lost. And there are limits, feet can't digest food, nor can ears run a race. An incomplete body can't do what a complete one can. Church missions suffer when some parts fail to do their duties.

There are some functions all members are called upon to do, in Matthew 5, Jesus mentions two. In verse 14: "You are the light of the world. A city set on a hill cannot be hidden."

Every part of the body is involved in metabolism, the process of giving off heat and energy that maintains survival and, in the proper stages of life, to grow. We are all this light and are called as well in verse 13: "You are the salt of the earth; but if the salt has become tasteless, how will it be made salty again?" Salt's functions include; a seasoning, a preservative, and as a cleansing agent. As a preservative, it kept food from becoming corrupt and rancid, and as a cleansing agent, it purged wounds especially of potentially lethal bacteria. This parallels moral preservation, as in the Church's role in purifying and preserving our world. Just based on these verses alone, there is no ministry of pew sitting, nor are there proxy organs. No one is called to sit back and do nothing.

It's often been said that the two most lethal threats to the sustaining existence of any institution are apathetic laziness and willful ignorance. No system of government or church is better than those involved in it. Strength and function depend on active involvement, just as muscle strength is to usage, interest is tied to investment. The more one puts into something, the more concerned they are in the outcome. This is true in both spiritual and physical things. Jesus applied this to both our labors and our investment strategy. "For where your treasure is, there will your heart be also" (Matthew 6:21).

In both society and the Church, we often either abrogate our responsibilities, pretend they don't exist or to substitute them to another. The issue of abortion comes to mind. The Christian will call this a political issue in efforts to avoid any involvement in this controversial issue. The politician will retort, only slightly more righteously than the Christian, it is a moral, or Church, issue. God help us all for turning our backs on these unborn "orphans." Sir Edmond Burke [1729-1797] warned us that, "For evil to triumph, all it takes is for good men to do nothing."[15]

When responsibility is forsaken, vested interest is either transferred or lost. It's no longer "our" problem even if it directly affects us. Instead, it becomes "their" problem. As a result, often no one steps in to fill the void our absence leaves. Try filling a glass half full of water and insert your finger. The water relies on your finger to fill space and raise its level. Remove your finger and see how quickly the space is filled and how the level drops. Without your active presence, the glass is emptier and so is the Church. We each have a God-assigned mission to fill. When we fail to keep our place, the ministry level of the whole drops off. This also is reflected in our becoming net takers of the now reduced blessings of the faith. But, in one sense, we all are takers, in our relation to Jesus. Our cost to God for our redemption was greater than anything we could ever do to even try to repay it. "So you too, when you do all the things which are commanded

15    Life Quotes, Edmund Burke Quotes." http://life-quotes-lib.com/authors/edmund_burke.html.

you, say, 'We are unworthy [unprofitable] slaves, we have only done that which we aught to have done'" (Luke 17:10). But, in the body sense, we can become lazy and do nothing but absorb the service of others. Church giving usually drops, as does our interest in God's word, so long as we are being taken care of. This ignorance is glaring in the American Church today. The agnostic humanist Cal Sagan (1934-1996) would shame even the average preacher, much less the average Christian, with his knowledge of the Scriptures. Proxy faith destroys us, and this problem is not new.

The people of Israel in 1050 BC were tired. They were tired of defeat, especially at the hands of the Philistines. They were tired of God giving them judges, which He didn't seem to be giving them enough of, but they weren't tired of the idolatry and slavery to sin that got them into trouble to begin with. They lacked the conviction to stand up in faith and take responsibility for themselves; instead, they wanted a proxy. They cried for a king. Samuel warned them of the ways of kings, but they were in no mood to listen. "No, but there shall be a king over us, that we also may be like all the nations; that our king may judge us and go out before us and fight our battles" (I Samuel 8:19, 20). They willingly gave up a measure of their liberty to rid themselves of the burdens of personal responsibility. It was a decision that they came to regret over and over again, and that failed to provide them the destiny God had intended for them.

Our own political system was designed as a Constitutional Republic. While leaders are elected and judges appointed, the bulk of responsibility for our success and prosperity lays in the hands of the people. This was the theme of the, now ignored, Tenth Amendment, which reserved powers to the states and people. This was why people like Garrison and Mann were able to act and accomplish what they did, but over the years, this has been lost. As mentioned earlier, the problems of fracturing and paralysis within the Church has led to our surrender of liberty and the acceptance of proxies to meet our duties and determine our values.

This is what happened in 1962 and 1963. A hopping mad nation of pew sitters, rather than act in a determined and organized way, chose to pawn off their responsibilities to their elected officials. After the Warren Court struck down prayer and our Christian heritage, Congress was inundated with appeals and proposals to reverse these rulings. None were ever passed, though one man, West Virginia Democrat Robert Byrd, was a hero in his repeated efforts. He proposed a prayer amendment in 1962, but other pressing issues, including the October Cuban Missile Crisis, overshadowed this proposal, and it died. It continued to be a hot issue, as opinion polls over the next few decades showed overwhelming support for it, but all efforts over those years fell short. In 1998 it was brought up for the last time. In a Republican controlled House of Representatives, the amendment failed, getting only 224 votes out of 435, far short of the 290 needed for a two-thirds majority. This was its last hurrah, the indoctrination of our nation had led to a rewrite of our beliefs.

Even though all efforts to restore a godly foundation and school prayer met with failure, Christians continued to seek proxy solutions for this issue. Many will argue that this is the proper way to go about this. This isn't without some merit, as in our system, the ballot box is the instrument of change. But our moral compass wasn't stolen via the ballot box; it was through our apathy, the overreaching Supreme Court, and a society in drift away from God, that gave a strategic victory to the forces of darkness. Also, elections are limited in their effects. Most voters are not one-issue voters, unless the issue is their pocketbooks, and moral issues tend to be of a limited draw. When a politician is elected, they are immediately and overwhelmingly beset upon by swarms of lobbyists and special interest groups. These either cancel or drown out moral concerns and, at best, put them on the back burner.

If this policy were to work at all, it would have in the 1980s. In 1980, Under Jerry Falwell (1933-2007) and the "Moral Majority," we came as close to a "Divine Election" (and proxy Christianity) as we were ever going to get. Ronald Reagan, president from 1981-1989, ran as a social conservative and won election. To Christians in America, it seemed that a host of moral wrongs would now be righted. We were poised to see America restored as a Christian nation. During the Reagan presidency, repeated efforts were made to ban pornography, halt the gay rights agenda, and reverse our slide into moral decadence. In 1983, an effort to amend the Constitution on abortion, the Hatch-Eagleton bill, was offered. It simply stated, "A right to abortion is not secured by the Constitution." In a Republican controlled Senate, it failed forty-nine to fifty, far short of the sixty-seven needed to pass that chamber. In 1982, Robert Byrd also made another attempt at a School Prayer Amendment, which failed. By 1989, proxy Christianity had accomplished virtually nothing.

In that decade, the Evangelical Church also nearly forgot her prime directive, to build the spiritual kingdom of God. Since Jesus sought to transform men's hearts, our first duty is to bring people to Him. Granted, in both society and the Church there must be rules, but a sound moral compass is not so much something that can be imposed from without as through a change in our hearts. In times past, as in the Middle Ages, there were attempts by the Church to impose its rules on both believers and nonbelievers. These edicts went far beyond any rightful laws of the state. While this kept a standard of social behavior for a time, it did little to restore souls to God.

By changing hearts, society changes. This has been seen in a negative way as a consequence of the tidal wave of victories by the secular humanists, existentialists, and atheists. Even secular society has observed our social and moral decline. "The Wall Street Journal" said, "The nation seems to be on the wrong track, and not just economically... The leveling or deterioration of public behavior has got to be worrying people who have enough years on them to judge with some perspective."[16] This is not to diminish a Christian's vote or advocacy for common morality. We are the salt of the earth. Social issues are critical to both basic justice and economic prosperity, but to allow them to become our mission does a disservice to the lost, and fails to honor the Jesus who died for them. To sit back and entrust to politicians or others our mission voids our responsibilities as servants of Christ. It also reduces the Church to bondage to a state instead of to our Savior. Our mission is hijacked by the powers of man.

Throughout history, the Church has found herself hijacked by kings, chancellors, prime ministers and presidents to exalt the purposes of men. Even Joseph Stalin released thousands of imprisoned church ministers during the Second World War in an effort to inspire his battered nation. During both World Wars, almost any American would tell you that God was on our side, and in World War II, both the Germans and Japanese were cruelly barbaric. The rape of Nanking in China, beginning on December 13, 1937, which ultimately resulted in the murder of three hundred thousand, is proof of this. Yet, God allowed the initial success of these evils as He did the atrocities of Stalin, Pol Pot, the Rwanda massacre, and all the

---

[16]  Noonan, Peggy "America's Crisis of Character." Wall Street Journal, April 20, 2012. http://online.wsj.com/arti-cle/SB10001424052702303513404577354221282508372.html

evils in the world today. God has purposed the evil and unjust governments as well as those we call good. While it may trouble us, He does, at times use the most evil to punish those who have deceived themselves into thinking that they are good. "Woe to Assyria, the rod of My anger, and the staff in whose hands is My indignation" (Isaiah 10:5). Few, if any, on earth could compare to them in cruelty, yet they served God's purpose in destroying those who rejected Him. Such evil also serves as an illustration of the evils of hell. God may stand on one side or another in wars between nations, but His purposes are not necessarily ours.

Christians need to beware of ever allowing their faith to be conditional on the success of their nations. The same is true whether or not their government upholds their beliefs. Those who would force Christianity into the position of propping up nationalism, an economic system, or a political party will only bring a distressing humiliation to God's people, the Church. A good example is found in I Samuel 4. The Israelites, in the days before the kings, had been severely humiliated by the Philistines in battle. They attempted to answer this in committing God, by coercion, to their side. "As the ark of the covenant of the Lord came into the camp, that all Israel shouted with a mighty shout" (I Samuel 4:5), but a short time later, God allowed it to be captured, Israel routed, and the wicked priests Hophni and Phinehas, Eli's sons, to be slain. The whole Israelite nation had every reason to believe God had forsaken them, and their faith was crushed. We face the same danger today if our faith is in Christian America rather than in a Christian God.

This is not to exclude Christians from the political process. One factor in our nation ending up in the mess it has was that, for most of the twentieth-century, politics was seen as dirty business. Christian men were strongly discouraged from getting involved. This left the field all too often to the corrupt and unscrupulous. If any good can come from Christian involvement, we still have a system of government designed to allow this, but our primary mission is spiritual, the salvation of the lost.

A foolish trust in others to fulfill the mission God has entrusted to us can be deadly, as history shows us. The advent of Christianity in AD 380 as the state religion under Roman Emperor Theodosius put a person's spiritual destiny into the hands of a mutually concerned bishop and emperor. Not only did this blur the distinct roles of both the Church and State, it established false doctrines as legitimate and incorporated them into the Church. One example is if governors could confer the favor of the Emperor on the common person, so also could priests confer favor, or the forgiveness of sin on the parishioner. In fact, only through official Church channels was it offered to anyone.

The Papacy soon rose to fill the vacuum caused over the next few centuries, by the collapse of a strong, unifying, government. In China, the exact reverse happened, as the State twice took authority over the Church and proved disastrous on both occasions.

For the Greek Orthodox Church, marriage of the Church to the state also proved catastrophic on two occasions. The first, in 1453, was with the fall of Constantinople to the Turks and the subsequent massacres of Christians in retribution for their long opposition to Islam. The second, in 1917, was when their second spiritual capital, Moscow, fell to the Bolshevik Red Army. Heavy persecution again followed.

A Church-State marriage in Africa brought one of the greatest disasters in all of Church history. The Coptic Church of Egypt, and the lands to the south, had a theological dispute with the Church in the rest of the Roman world. Without getting into details, in a growing spirit of intolerance to anything not accepted as orthodox beliefs, the Coptics were persecuted after the Council of Chalcedon in AD 451. There, the Coptic beliefs on the nature of Christ were declared as heresy. Under the dual authority between the Coptic Patriarch and the Byzantine Eastern Roman Empire, Coptics were imprisoned and tortured as so-called Christian persecuted Christian. In AD 639, a Muslim army, at one point only four thousand strong, under Rashidun, invaded Egypt with her millions of people. The Coptic Cyrus, Patriarch of Alexandria, and his followers gave no resistance and, many times, even came to the aid of these Muslim invaders: They were viewed as liberators from their Byzantine overlords. By AD 641/642, Rashidun captured Alexandria and, over the next few decades, captured the rest of North Africa. This gave the Coptics four centuries of relative peace until Islam took up where the Byzantines had left off.

If Christians believe that a government, even a declared Christian one, will guarantee their success, they put trust in a false hope. First of all, God created government to rule the body, and to some, degree, mind of man. The Church, on the other hand, He created to rule over the spirit, with a resulting authority over the mind and body, but not to the wrongful impingement of that of the state. Trust in the state violates this God-ordained arrangement and puts faith in the hands of fickle men. If the Church yokes itself to one political party today, it might find itself out of power in the next election cycle. By taking sides, it invites political backlash when this happens. Trust in man becomes our undoing. "Woe to those who go down to Egypt for help, and rely on horses, and trust in chariots because they are many... But they do not look to the Holy One of Israel, nor seek the Lord" (Isaiah 31:1). Where is our trust in God in such an arrangement?

There is another type of proxy Christianity, or divine election, that we engage in that cripples the Church's mission as well. It's obvious that the kingdom of God can't be voted into power, neither can it be delegated to others through elevation of Church leadership, to accomplish what others are too lazy or apathetic to do. This isn't an attack on rightful Church leadership or our duty to obey them. "Obey your leaders and submit to them; for they keep watch over your souls, as those who will give an account" (Hebrews 13:17). Too often, those in the pew convince themselves that they can hire a minister to do their service for them. As a result, the work of the kingdom goes undone. Jesus didn't call us to hire lackeys; He said, "Whoever does not carry his own cross and follow Me cannot be My disciple" (Luke 14:27). This puts in question the salvation of those who would pawn off their ministries.

Once again, we don't all share the same ministries or responsibilities. Not all are called to foreign mission fields, or to be a William Lloyd Garrison or Horace Mann, but every one is called. There are many support ministries; sometimes we have to read between the lines to see them. There were the women who ministered to Jesus and the disciples (Luke 8:2, 3), the man who owned a boat (Matthew 8:23), or a donkey, an upper room for the Passover, and others; these were the unsung heroes of the Bible. This was also true in Antioch of Syria. "And while they were ministering to the Lord and fasting, the Holy Spirit said, 'Set apart for Me Barnabas and Saul for the work to which I have called them'" (Acts 13:2).

An *out of sight, out of mind* mentality follows with those who fail to fulfill their supporting ministries. Little investment means little interest, and as mentioned before, those of this mindset also tend to be net takers or absorbers of the blessings of the faithful. This only further weakens the efforts of the Church to win the world. This also leads to a mentality of the Church as an organization of *them*, and not a body of *us*. The Church is obliged to serve them, rather than their being active in serving Jesus. This Church, in their view, provides the money, prayer, support, and moral encouragement for missions, and when these missionaries return, they can raise their own support, or the Church can furnish them a retirement home somewhere, "Just not in my backyard." With this spiritually and emotionally sterile mindset, it is truly amazing what God can do in spite of us.

To be disconnected from what doesn't involve us is only natural. The only times we may take interest is for amusement, or trivial pursuit, but we are not called to do what is natural; we are called to be spiritual, and our purposes are to seek the things of the Spirit. "But I say, walk by the Spirit, and you will not carry out the desire of the flesh" (Galatians 5:16). A worldly, self-centered encapsulation rationalizes away individual accountability. Such a Christian may vote for a politician who promises to close all of the casinos for them and get rid of all the riff-raff; they may attend a church that condemns it, and expect their minister to work to end it as well, but when this doesn't happen, this Christian blames them for the failure. It doesn't matter that they personally never took any initiative to talk to others or to advocate their views. It isn't their concern, and it's the preacher's and politician's faults.

Often, what happens next is that this believer becomes allured by it, and yields to the temptation of gambling. They then are only too willing to blame the preacher and politician for failing to close the casinos and, thereby, posing an undue temptation. This weakness to gamble isn't their fault; nobody took this temptation away from them. They then vote to fire the preacher and oust the politician. This can apply to any sin, if we assume no responsibility to overcome evil, it will overcome us.

Often, this same proxy mindset is applied in dealing with sin when it arises within the Church as well. Confrontation is not an enjoyable action to begin with. As a minister in a small church in Northern Missouri in the early 1980s, this was thrust upon me. It didn't matter that the individual involved was defiantly unrepentant, I ended up losing sleep and weight over it, even as the Holy Spirit confirmed to me that I was "speaking the truth in love" (Ephesians 4:15). But to have not confronted this situation would have been sin. Cleansing is essential to the spiritual health of the body. Jesus furnished us a process to do this. "And if your brother sins, go and reprove him in private; if he listens to you, you have won your brother" (Matthew 18:15). If someone in that church had taken this first step, it is possible this person would have repented or at least been open to correction and healing. All of us have a responsibility to love their fellow brother or sister and to bring healing and unity in love. By delegating this problem to someone else, they fail their brother. Often, do they not only fail in this, they are the very ones who compound the injury through gossip. Even if they do not gossip, they do not love. A lack of commitment leads to a lack of love, and this holds true in the Church, politics, or personal relationships. By hiding, rather than confronting, they give silent approval to the fallen brother to continue their wrongful lifestyle. This tacit approval does nothing to reverse the moral decline around us, nor does it save souls.

When we transfer our duties we also surrender ownership and accept servitude. A slave loses any right to determine outcomes or protest costs. In the case of Israel, Samuel warned them of the ways of a king. There would be taxes, eminent domain over the best of their lands and possessions, a military draft, bureaucracy, greed, and lust. All victories would be in the king's name. Not only would they be his slaves, they were liable for his poor choices. This had spiritual, as well as physical, consequences: They abrogated their destiny nationally, and individually, to the actions of their king.

God also warned them through Samuel that, once they got a king, He would not heed their complaints and remove him. After one-hundred twenty years of Saul, David, and Solomon, the kingdom would divide. With all their cries under Solomon, God did allow the Northern tribes to cast off that dynasty but only to be replaced by another. For the next two centuries, they suffered under one king and dynasty after another until 721 BC, when that nation ceased to exist. Their remnant was scattered among the nations.

Christians today play the same game, delegating their destiny to rulers and church councils. We even proxy our thinking on matters of our own salvation, and God allows us to see the fallacies of our choices. The advent of the National Council of Churches (NCC), chartered on November 29, 1950, is one. This happened because Christians first proxied their liberties to local ministers, who, in turn, did to an ecclesiastical hierarchy. These hierarchies embraced a position of rejecting Jesus. To this, the Calvinist, Dr. R. J. Rushdoony (1916-2001), father of *Christian Reconstructionalism* wrote; alluding to the National Council of Churches, "The beginning of true liberty is Jesus Christ. And therefore the first and last target of all subversion is Biblical faith. Hence, it is, that the Church has been the first target of infiltration and subversion, and is the most subverted institution in the US today."[17] The NCC is an institution devoid of the very reason for her existence: the Lordship of Jesus.

The Episcopal Anglican Church, a part of the NCC and also of the Church of England, has proven this true. In 1998, their body, at the Lumbeth Conference, voted 526 to seventy to affirm their position that the homosexual lifestyle is contrary to the teachings of the Gospel of Christ. Yet in 2003, the English hierarchy elevated an openly gay man, Jeffry John, to be Suffragon Bishop of Reading. That same year, Gene Robinson became bishop of the New Hampshire Diocese. Openly gay, he is now "married" to his partner. The American Episcopal Church also now has the pro-gay Katherine Jefferts Schori as her head. While this has splintered the denomination, both in the US and worldwide, one can only imagine what might have been if Christians had honored their calling in Christ.

Dependency on others for what we should do for ourselves is slavery. Samuel emphasized to Israel: "And you yourselves will become his servants" (I Samuel 8:17). This was contrary to God's intent for them, as it is for us. "I am the Lord your God who brought you out of the land of Egypt so that you should not be their slaves, and I broke the bars of your yoke and made you walk erect" (Leviticus 26:13). God calls us to liberty. He calls us to accountability, and He calls us to love His people and His kingdom.

There is a Michael Jackson song called "Man in the Mirror" that goes, "I'm starting with the man in the mirror, I'm asking him to change his ways." Before we can change our nation, we have to begin with the Church, and before we can change her, we have to change ourselves. We dare not proxy to another our salvation; it is between Jesus and us. We can't elect someone to do what God has called us to do for ourselves. Who knows if we might he called to be the next Rosa Parks, Thomas Mann, or William Lloyd Garrison? God alone knows what can be done if our lives were totally committed to Him.

[17]    "Apostasy", reformed-theology.org, Issue 2007

# XI

## FORSAKING THE BODY

*"Not forsaking our own assembling together, as is the habit of some, but encouraging one another; and all the more, as you see the day drawing near."*

—Hebrews 10:25

Emotional and psychological independence is one goal in modern psychotherapy. Patients are counseled to arrive at "maximum individual autonomy" (Humanist Manifesto II, 1973, The Individual, paragraph 5). The goal is the elimination of all feelings of dependency on anyone for emotional security, yet ironically, their policies encourage greater dependency on the state. Psychiatry is not alone in pushing this personhood. Individualism, with its resulting emotional isolation, was a growing goal in America before the 1973 *Manifesto* position was penned. Before cigarette ads were removed from TV, Virginia Slims aimed at both this and feminism in their jingle: "You've come a long way baby, to get where you got to today. You've got your own cigarette now baby, you've come a long, long way." In another ad a few years ago, the US Army ran a recruitment slogan: "An army of one." They also ran another one: "Be all that you can be." From different angles, the focus is on the individual autonomy of the person.

Most of us remember John Wayne (1907-1979). While his beliefs would kill his acting career today, he was a star bigger than life in his own day. He portrayed a mentality of rugged individualism, primarily for boys and men. Success depended on brains, guns, guts, and as seen personified in one movie, *True Grit*, determination. Real men never let anyone see them cry. A man has to do what a man has to do, and his life was his, and no one else's business. A real man always made his own way in the world. He stood on his own two feet and needed not to depend on anyone for his personal happiness.

To a degree, this fits with the Now Generation phrase: "Do your own thing." While the intent was to reject the demands of parents or of society, it also applied to one's view of self and in relationships with others. Sexual liberation shows this better than any other way. With easy access to birth control, the sexual revolution shook the foundations of both the traditional family unit and social cohesiveness more than anything else did.

The very advancement of our modern life has promoted the rise of self as well. Our society has provided us with multiple time and energy-saving devices, which greatly enhance prosperity and our quality of life.

But, says Martin Pawley, "There is something else about our economy of means, or possessions, by which such cheap implements as the refrigerator, the TV, and the car can undo: the social patterns of centuries that makes them seem like tools designed especially for the job. These things were designed to reduce human contact, to reduce the amount of time spent worrying about the goodwill or hostility of others."[18] One example is the car itself, which is a very effective tool in offering an isolating personal environment.

In the decades prior to our modern advances, women especially were likely to perform many of their chores in a social setting. In some parts of the world, women still get together on laundry day as they communally take their wash to the creek, watering hole, or washing spot. In some places, this provides safety, but in all places, it offers fellowship. They usually go as a group to draw water as well. This is what made the Samaritan woman so unusual. "There came a woman of Samaria to draw water. Jesus said to her, 'Give Me a drink'" (John 4:7). This was a clue to, in her case, a sinful life which had separated her from the rest of her community.

---

[18] Martin Pawky, The Private Future, (Random House, 1974), 45.

Since the 1970s, our drive for personal fulfillment, identity, and privacy has continued to progress. Only the issues of safety and security seem more important to most of the population. Government, as mentioned before, by its policies, only seemed to amplify this through legislated privacy. In many ways, this form of privacy has abetted the dividing of families. Abortion is a prime example. A minor child doesn't even have to discuss their use of birth control or abortion with their parents. Governmental privacy greatly weakens the development of relationships, both in and outside of the Church, but much of this we also do to ourselves.

The home computer umbrella, including cell phones, laptops, etc., has greatly improved the efficiency of our society. It also provides benefits, the ease of access of information for example, that past generations could only dream of. This has allowed people, from the privacy of their own homes, to do a host of things that used to require social interaction. Combined with the, controversial at best, demands upon so many workers to have direct deposit (as most government entities also now require), bank visits are now optional. Bills can be paid online, and most shopping can be done that way as well. Cell phones can check prices of goods on store shelves miles away. Social interactions can be conducted without ever making eye contact, and business is done without leaving home or hearing another human voice. A growing number of people can actually work from home in this manner also. Its almost possible to live without meeting another human being.

At the same time, the children of each new generation are raised to be less dependent on their parents than the one before. This present-day "Generation. Y" is, at the present, bucking the trend, as many still live with parents well into their 20s and are trending to a more social attitude, but Twitter isolates even as people communicate. The general trend does seem irreversible in our culture. The continued rise in the numbers of single parents and of cohabitation outside of marriage testify to our fear of commitment and desire for privacy. This also shows in the deep loneliness felt by an ever increasing share of our population. Disrespect is also on the rise, as so many of our children now have a Bart Simpson mentality: they are encouraged to disobey rules, and adults in general, reject God, and be their own person. Our deep loneliness only grows.

Humans were created as social creatures. This is made evident in one very effective means of breaking down prisoners, both in jails and prison camps. That is solitary confinement. The more solitary, the more effective this is. In extreme cases of isolation, food is slid under the door or down a chute. Waste products are either left in the cell or slid under a door as well. The prisoner is usually deprived of natural sunlight and darkness. Insanity often results from such treatment. Both North Vietnam and North Korea have used this effectively on many American prisoners of war. In one account, that of POW Eugene Mc Daniel, he says "…I feared isolation more than the possibility of torture."[19]

Over history, there have been many cases of isolation through war, shipwreck, or other disasters. In some cases, people spent as long as decades without the sound of a human voice. Usually, their environments provided enough stimulation to keep these people going. Isolation was also part of the curse on Cain: "My punishment is too great to bear! Behold, Thou hast driven me this day from the face of the ground; and from Thy face I shall be hidden, and I shall be a vagrant and a wonderer on the earth, and it will come about that whoever finds me will kill me" (Genesis 4:13,14). This was a reason why he, with his son Enoch, was the first city builder in the Bible (Genesis 4:17). Enoch, as well, was probably separated from God and his grandparents and felt his father's loneliness. City life, at least, eased that pain.

There have been others who have chosen a life, or an extended period, of enforced solitude. Gautama, the great Buddha, spent a protracted time in isolation with little or no food and no human contact. It was during this time that he had his vision of the devil and his three daughters. At that point, he was near death and so drained of physical and mental strength that he could no longer respond as normal. A person under extreme pain, stress, and privation can come to a point where at least parts of the brain shut down or close off due to trauma or a lack of glucose.

Among those who have gone the route of isolation and asceticism are two in the early Church age, St. Anthony (AD 251-AD 356) and St. Symeon Stylites (AD 390-AD 459). Symeon achieved fame by living thirty-nine years on a small platform on a pillar near Aleppo in Syria and inspired others to follow his model by living on pillars (stele) as well. He was also dead for several days before anyone realized it. He would often keep the same prayer posture for extended periods, but for those who have

---

[19]    Eugene N. McDaniel, Scars And Stripes (A.J. Holman Co., 1975), 58.

been in solitude for long stretches, no matter what else they did without, they will all answer that what they missed most was the sound of a human voice. Even Elijah, one of the greatest loners in history, had his own servant (I Kings 19:3).

"For not one of us lives to himself, and not one dies to himself" (Romans 14:7). While this is primarily a reference to our relationship with Jesus, it also applies to our fellowship with others. We all have a stake in each other's lives. To a point, we all own a piece of each other. We are all in this together, and we all, in one way or another, affect each other. Society is made up of billions of parts, of which each of us is one, despite any efforts we may try to deny this.

Years ago, one of the slogans of the Now Generation reflected on the "maximum individual autonomy" beliefs of the age. Whenever a person was approached about a questionable life choice, their response was, "This is my body, and I am only hurting myself." It always made some of us wonder why they would want to hurt themselves to begin with, but this excuse was used to cover inappropriate behaviors like immorality, marijuana and street drug usage, drunkenness, and others. It also covered the avoidance of positive behavior, such as study, work, or church attendance. Other slogans reflected this also, "Live and let live." "It's my life" or "You're tripping me out," when someone got too close, or involved in directing their life choices. The goal was unlimited personal choice, and they wanted to be neither accountable to, or for, anyone else. The only moral caveat seemed to be, "Don't kill anybody."

This philosophy of maximum individual autonomy needs scrutiny in the light of God's word. This is reflected in one of the very first acts of God. "Then the Lord God said, 'It is not good for the man to dwell alone; I will make him a helper suitable for him'" (Genesis 2:18). God created the higher animals, and then from Adam's rib, Eve. This fellowship circle proved quite adequate until Eve sinned and Adam joined her.

While this particular sin was a statement of independence, ironically, it intensified the need for companionship. There is a loneliness especially felt by those outside of Christ. Women are keener to feel this in a personal way than are men and are more prone to fill this spiritual vacuum in spiritual ways. Throughout history, most spiritists, Wiccans (witches), and for those in fellowship with God, church attendees, have been women. Men feeling this loneliness are inclined to fill it with things, legacies, and monuments or, for those of lower classes, alcohol, sex, sports, muscle, and drugs are employed. There's an old saying, "The rich get richer, and the poor have children." Men feel security in possessions, and even in numbers, despite their loner facades.

As it was said before, Augustine spoke of a God-sized emptiness (vacuum) in our hearts. A variety of idols are used to fill it, and this is often manifested in greed or a lust for wealth. Covetousness takes this a step further into a realm of comparing themselves to each other, and this usually brings hostility into the equation. Either way, Jesus said, "For what is a man profited, if he gains the whole world, and forfeits his soul? Or what shall a man give in exchange for his soul?" (Matthew 16:26). Greed is definitely a form of idolatry (Ephesians 5:5), but idolatry is not limited to greed. There is a host of other things that our modem world offers to titillate us with. For those outside of God, these serve as a replacement. For the Christian, they are a draw, or a subtle pull by things that aren't necessarily bad in themselves. They may even be things that serve a purpose and, in a social setting, provide good. They can become our focus, however, and the most important thing in our lives. Serving in a soup kitchen may be a very worthwhile part of our life, but it should never take God's place in being our life. If we are not careful, our spirit "bone" can die. Just as minerals gradually leech in to turn bone into fossils, the devil will gradually leech in things or activities to replace our devotion to God. If we aren't being constantly renewed in God, we become a spiritual fossil: all form, but no life.

Civic or family activities offer an excellent opportunity for spiritual fossilization and a substitute for Christian fellowship, as well. This gradual process usually begins as a "just this once" argument. Then it becomes "once in a while" and grows from there. There is an old admonition on how a camel gets into its master's tent. It begins with its nose and then comes the head, neck, and finally the whole body. In the process, the tent is often knocked down or torn up. "Once in a while" activities tend to act in the same way. Sports often provide this flesh-placating lure. As much of a sports fan as I am, especially of football, it concerns me that game time in the National Football League (NFL) keeps a lot of people out of church. If the league could somehow either postpone game time, or play them on

Saturdays and broadcast them on Sundays, there wouldn't be this conflict. As it is, over the years, many others have followed their example, as little league, youth football, basketball, hockey, and others have found their way to Sunday and into conflict with church. Christiana are put in a dilemma of either supporting their children's activities or attending worship.

Less frequently, but no less distracting to our walk with the Lord, we can be torn between worship and family reunions and get-togethers. If Christian family members are encouraged to worship, these can be very positive to both the family and the Lord. All too frequently, though, they are not, and activities conflict with worship. Christians may feel that missing worship in order to spend more time with family provides opportunity for them to be a positive influence on the lost in their families. The same argument is used to justify attending Sunday morning sports activities. But how can someone be a witness for Jesus when they are not honoring Him in worship? This also discourages the rest of the Church, both by their example and in their failure to provide fellowship and encouragement to the rest of the body.

This line of reasoning presumes the importance of collective worship, but many Sunday morning golfers or fishermen would answer, "No," to its importance. Frequently they will justify this absence claiming, "I can worship God just as well in a field or golf course as I can at Church." But will they? For a fisherman, this could provide a time to meditate, sing spiritual songs, worship God, pray, and read their Bibles. I actually heard one claim to do this. On the golf course, this would prove a little harder. A double bogey might lead one to mention God's name but not necessarily in a worshipful way.

It is also true that being outside puts one in touch with nature. Golfing, hiking, and otherwise enjoying the outdoors is relaxing to both body and soul, but how much of this time is actually spent in worshipping God? The intent of these outings is for solitude and unwinding from a hard day or week of work. This is therapeutic and good for a person, and it is Biblical. "And the apostles gathered together with Jesus; and they reported to Him all that they had done and taught. And He said to them, 'Come away by yourselves to a lonely place and rest a while'" (Mark 6:30, 31). This may have involved worship, and the disciples had the distinct advantage of being in the very presence of Jesus, but it didn't constitute collective worship itself. To a person in a group or family setting, their activities may involve fellowship, but this rarely substitutes for collective worship, either.

Some will retort that even if they were in Church, it would be for naught, their minds would still be in the field. In Ezekiel 8:7-13, God provided Ezekiel a vision of the thought processes of the priests who were ministering in the Temple. "Go in and see the wicked abominations they are committing here" (Verse 9). We are called to love God with our minds as well as the rest of us. "And you shall love the Lord your God with all of your heart {mind] and with all of your soul and with all of your might" (Deuteronomy 6:5). This excuse only exposes spiritual immaturity and a greater need to get close to God.

For many of these naturalists, nature love can become nature worship. There are many majesties of nature, and these can awe people into a worshipful spirit. Several of our national parks owe their very existence to this beauty as well as a sense of fragility. If glory is given to God for this, then this is good, but frequently, glory is given to nature rather than nature's God. All things aside on the credibility of global warming, one thing is clear, a large segment of the environmental movement worships the environment. This is also true of many naturalists. "And beware, lest you lift up your eyes to Heaven and see the sun and the moon and the stars, all the host of heaven, and be drawn away and worship them and serve them" (Deuteronomy 4:19). Many who claim to be in worship of God in the field are actually worshipping the creation instead.

The real question is how much family, sports, and outdoor enthusiasts desire to serve God. It's possible to worship Jesus in nature, this happens in Christian Bible camps every year, and there are times on vacation it is the only option available. On July 5, 1992, our family was on vacation at the Grand Canyon in Arizona. We weren't aware of any church close enough to go meet with them. To worship, we shared together in a time of songs, prayer, Scripture reading, and the Lord's Supper at the rim of the canyon. From the looks of the people who observed us, it appeared that they had never seen anyone worship God in nature before. While there was opportunity for any to join us, none did.

God intends for His followers to worship both individually and in a collective manner. This was commonly understood in the Old Testament. "I will tell of Thy name to the brethren; in the midst of the assembly I will praise Thee" (Psalm 22:22). The passage, "But an hour is coming, and now is, when the true worshippers shall worship the Father in spirit and truth" (John 4:23) doesn't mean that solo worship can replace collective. We are called to do both: worship God in the field and in the pew. These are not mutually exclusive of each other. "For where two or three have gathered in My name, there I am in their midst" (Matthew 18:20). The purpose of assembly is for mutual encouragement.

During the history of Israel, especially from the Exodus in 1446 BC until the Captivity in 586 BC there is documentation of their involvement in many sins. A catalogue could be made of their idolatry, immorality, murder, and injustices, to name a few, but the very last sin most were guilty of was the forsaking of the public assembly. "Can a virgin forget her ornaments, or a bride her attire? Yet My people have forgotten Me days without number" (Jeremiah 2:32). This verse was written about 610 BC, shortly before the Babylonian invasions and destruction of Jerusalem. This was over a century after Amos wrote, "Enter Bethel and transgress; in Gilgal multiply transgression! Bring your sacrifices every morning, your tithes every three days. Offer a thank offering also from that which is leavened" (Amos 4:4, 5). Here, God condemned false, worldly, contaminated, half-hearted worship, but it took another century plus for them to stop worshipping at all.

Collective worship was honored during the captivity and, except for the short period 168-165 BC during the persecution by Antiochus Theos Epiphanes, it continued into the establishment of the Church. "And on the Sabbath day, we [Paul, Silas, and company] went outside the gate to a riverside, where we were supposing that there would be a place of prayer; and we sat down and began speaking to the women who were assembled" (Acts 16:13). Both the Jews and the Church worshipped collectively, the Christians did so often on both the Sabbath and on Sunday. Many aspects of Jewish synagogue worship were incorporated into the Church as well. These may be some of the traditions Paul mentioned in II Thessalonians 2:15 and elsewhere.

Several ingredients of Christian worship are listed in Acts 2:42: "And they were continually devoting themselves to the apostles' teaching and to fellowship, to the breaking of bread and prayer." Four areas are easy to see: the Apostles' teaching or instruction, which was often inspired;

Communion, or the Lord's Supper; prayer; and fellowship, which takes many forms. What also was involved is *proskarterountes* continuing steadfastness, or fervency, to meet together. In Jerusalem, where the Church began, they met daily (Acts 2:42, 46). Later, emphasis was placed on Sunday worship, or Saturday evening for many Jewish believers, as a Jewish day begins about 6:00 p.m. the prior evening. As is seen in Acts 20:7, collective worship was important enough to keep Paul in Troas.

Other elements are mentioned in the New Testament. In I Corinthians 16:1, 2, financial contributions for the needs of the saints are addressed. Fellowship dinners, or love feasts are included in Jude 12 and inferred in I Corinthians 11:17-34. In I Corinthians 14:15, singing is mentioned. Other aspects that are at least practiced on occasion are foot washing, holy kisses, and public confessions. The public reading of Scripture is spoken of in I Timothy 4:13. To accommodate all Christians, these meetings were often held before dawn or after dark. At first, this was a way of allowing slaves, who worked seven days a week, to attend. Later, amidst persecution, this also provided some protection.

One of the ingredients for collective worship was the public reading of Scripture: "Until I come, give attention to the public reading of Scripture" (I Timothy 4:13). It was a Jewish tradition as well (Luke 4:17). In those days, books were very expensive and a Church did well to possess one copy of the Old Testament and of any New Testament epistles available. People usually memorized the text, having the word hidden in their hearts, both to not sin (Psalm 119:11) and to be ready to give an account of their faith (I Peter 3:15). Today, it can serve as a reminder for why we meet, aid in building unity, and provide a congregational focus for the week to come.

Fellowship provided for the mutual encouragement of the saints. To a persecuted and stressed church, this was often like a drink of cold water on a hot day. One man in Jerusalem had such a reputation for building others up that his name was changed. "And Joseph, a Levite of Cyprian birth, who was also called Barnabas by the apostles which translated means Son of encouragement" (Acts 4:36). The need was clear, Jewish excommunication, often unemployment for the Gentile, and a growing uncertainty of survival in an increasingly hostile world. This mutual encouragement, along with the promise in their message, sustained them in their dark times. With fervent love, prayers, and fellowship, they enjoyed the deliverance of God working among them on many occasions. One of the most famous was Peter's deliverance from prison (Acts 12:6-17).

Today though, the Church has lost her zeal for fellowship. Part of this is a result of our culture of isolationism and the decline of relationships in general. There are too many distractions and a general lack of urgency as to the need of collective worship. Then there is the "instant church" on the radio and TV. In today's world, it is possible to spend hours listening to and watching these preachers. This is not a blanket critique on the electronic ministry. There are those who are in it for the money and self-glory while a great many others truly love Jesus and seek with a whole heart to please Him. They run the gambit, just as preachers in the pulpit do. This critique is on those who avoid church.

In all fairness, there are those who are unable to get out for worship. Some are invalid, or hospitalized, in nursing homes or sick. Some, as firefighters, are on twenty-four-hour shifts and must be at work. There are a number of good electronic preachers to encourage and edify these people, but many believers use these as a substitute for collective worship. It is convenient, puts no carbon dioxide into the air via the automobile, and involves no getting out into the rain, snow, or cold. If the preacher is long-winded, the station automatically cuts him off. While there are appeals for money, no plates are ever passed, and no one's compelled to give. Most importantly, there is no pressure to attend, and there are no dirty looks if one turns off the TV before the show is over. Since no one else sees them, they could just as easily be watching the NFL pregame show, or "Meet The Press," and nobody's the wiser.

In addition to a tendency for spiritual laziness, several important elements of worship are missed. One of these is the collective experience of sharing together in the Lord's Supper, or Communion. "For as often as you eat this bread and drink the cup, you proclaim the Lord's death until He comes" (I Corinthians 11:26). This was written directly for collective worship. Missed is the opportunity to share in the needs of the saints in the local church. Add to this the opportunity to know of any prayer concerns, a sharing in the ministries of the body, or contributing to the service of the Lord. No friendships are built, there is no fellowship or accountability, nor are encouragement and intimacy in the Church. Just as the Holy Spirit didn't appoint any to the ministry of pew sitting, neither did He appoint any to an armchair ministry.

Some will argue that they stay home because there are too many hypocrites in church. When put to the test, though, their definition is lacking. Our failure to obtain sinless perfection, as many of these critics demand, is not, in itself, hypocrisy. The word *hypocrisy* came from the Greek theatre, where a person who put on a mask was play-acting or being a pretender. The term means someone who only outwardly pretends in public without living the life. Yes, there are always some of these in worship, but most of us are more like: "But the tax-gatherer, standing some distance away, was even unwilling to lift his eyes to Heaven, but was beating his breast saying, 'God be merciful to me a sinner'" (Luke 18:13). Christians are those who realize their imperfections and are in faithful repentance, seeking the heart of God, and finding strength in worship.

It is true, though, that to a degree we are all hypocrites. One proof of this is our answer when someone asks us how we are. We answer "fine" or "okay" or something like that. This type of hypocrisy seems to be eternal and cross-cultural. Biblically, there was a Shunammite woman whose son had just died, and when asked how things were, responded to Elijah's servant, "It is well" (II Kings 4:26). To many in the Muslim world, it is almost viewed as unfaithfulness to not answer in this way when they are greeted. So yes, to a point, all of us are hypocrites.

Interestingly enough, those who avoid worship because of the dread of hypocrites, overcome this well in other places. They have no problem going to the mall, with all the hypocrites there, to work, the grocery store, or other public places. To these people, there are just too many of them at church. Once, I responded to a woman who said this: "There's always room for one more." Her reaction reminded me of what a nuclear war might have been like, but the point was made. This is no excuse to miss worship. Jesus said, reflecting on the Sadducees and Pharisees, "Therefore all that they tell you, do and observe, but do not do according to their deeds; for they say things, and do not do them" (Matthew 23:3). To miss worship for this reason is to directly disobey Jesus.

Joint worship with others of the household of faith is critical to our spiritual strength. The constant drumbeat of the world doesn't just occupy our time. It appeals to the flesh, assaults our minds, and corrodes, or rusts, our spiritual receptors. We need to have this rust knocked off. "As iron sharpens iron, so one man sharpens another" (Proverbs 27:17). We all need at least one close spiritual friend to keep us renewed, sharpened, and refreshed in the Lord, and to be accountable, both to and for.

The Greek word "ecclesian" was the term for the common militia, or the full body of citizen soldiers in ancient Greece. This also is the word translated "church," or the called out body of believers. We are a militia or an army. If the US Army were to be dispatched to a world hot spot, the Pentagon building is not magically transported there, soldiers are sent in. In the same way, the Church isn't so much an organization as it is an organism. Buildings and select groups of leaders are not sent to meet needs, we are. Just as an AWOL (absent without leave) soldier is of no value to the mission of the army, so too is an AWOL Christian of no value to the mission of the Church. In reality, they are a detriment. God has assigned each of us a role. "For even as the body is one and yet has many members, and all the members of the body, though they are many, are one body, so also is Christ" (I Corinthians 12:12). An army in battle needs all its parts and so does the Church. If one is missing, it's like spiritual amputation; the body suffers.

Absence also poses danger to us. Of prime concern is our salvation or our relationship with Jesus. Our goal must be to please and obey Him. Devotion to one another is an essential part of this obedience, as is a desire to save the lost. Neglect of this fellowship is selfishness and a means for Satan to rust us out. It also defeats our purpose. An AWOL might just find themselves drafted into the wrong army. At the very least, it opens the door for us to begin seeking the peace and fulfillment we no longer are receiving in the wrong ways. The world is all too ready to pull, twist, and confuse us. Outside of the body, we can easily end up on the wrong side of the road or on the wrong pathway altogether. Listening to all the wrong voices, we are enticed to accept, and even embrace, error. "For the time will come when they will not endure sound doctrine; but wanting to have their ears tickled, they will accumulate for themselves teachers in accordance with their own desires" (II Timothy 4:3). Without a firm foundation in the Lord and His body, we drift.

Seeking selfishly for our own laziness and pathway is not just a cop-out on our own faith and conviction; it is one of the leading causes of denominationalism and sectarianism. Instead of faithful surrender to Jesus, a myriad of religious options tempt our twisted minds and corroded spirits. We listen to voices that do not have our best interests in mind but, instead, appeal to our empty and hungry hearts. At this fork in the road, we have two choices: either forsake the Lord or, in humility, return to the fellowship and allow His word and other believers to re-sharpen and restore us. "Like newborn babies, long for the pure milk of the word, that by it you may grow in respect to salvation" (I Peter 2:2). This is my prayer for us all.

There is one other part of the body, presently unseen, that also has a vested interest in us. "Therefore, since we have such a great cloud of witnesses surrounding us, let us also lay aside every encumbrance, and the sin which so easily entangles us, and let us run with endurance the race that is set before us: (Hebrews 12:1). These departed saints are watching as both fans and as retired veterans, cheering their favorite team. When we let down the body, the rest of the team, we also let them down.

Neglecting the body also lets down the lost. Part of this is by example. If the Church is not important to us, why should it be to them? On Judgment Day, do we want to have to explain how our selfish laziness and desire for our own privacy kept them out of Heaven? There is a saying "Ch_ch is nothing unless u r in it." Our presence in worship may be the most important thing that influences the lost, as a beacon to bring them to the light of Jesus.

# XII

## SEEKING PEACE

*"It is definitely because they have misled My people by saying, 'Peace!' When there is no peace. And when anyone builds a wall, behold, they plaster it over with whitewash."*

—Ezekiel 13:10

Back in March of 1970, the Beatles song "Let it Be" came out. In this song are the words: "When I find myself in times of trouble, Mother Mary comes to me, speaking words of wisdom, 'Let it be.'" This song hits home to all of us in an appeal to our inner nature. All of us suffer trials, and we all seek peace. If a problem or an issue presents itself, and the only potential solution requires a great deal of effort or has a high cost, its much easier to just ignore it and hope it goes away. While this might be an unfair interpretation of the original meaning of the song, this is exactly how many have applied this message to their own lives. Just ignore it, and sooner or later, it will go away.

Trials and tribulations affect us all. There are great inequalities in our world and in the lives of those around us. Some may be a product of the mind of the complainer, but others are real. Solomon spoke to this unfairness in Ecclesiastes 8:14: "There is a futility [injustice] which is done on the earth, that is, there are righteous men to whom it happens according to the deeds of the wicked. On the other hand, there are evil men to whom it happens according to the deeds of the righteous." One inequality is economic, as one percent of the population owns two-thirds of the nation's wealth. On the other hand, single-parent mothers now head well over half of the households now in poverty, according to the "Women's Legal Defense Fund." [20] While we cry "unfair" to the rich, blame must be put on the poor choices that shackle the lower classes in poverty. For those in between, there is an economic vice squeezing out their livelihood, even without the eight to seventeen percent underemployment, depending on who is keeping the statistics. One source is "Gallup Daily U. S. Employment, July 9, 2012 showing this at just over seventeen percent. To this, add the chaos of nature, disease, and an endless stream of international war, famine, and terrorism, to name a few. Meanwhile, civility dies a bit more every day.

But on this note, credit must be given where credit is due. Relief efforts after the Spring 2011 tornados, and especially after the May 22nd one in Joplin, Missouri, raised our spirits. In Logan, Utah, on September 12, 2011, we observed a display of heroism. There, a motorcyclist was trapped under a burning car. More than a dozen heroes emerged, at the risk of their own lives, to lift up the car and pull him to safety. In general, the decline of civics, and our economic and world crises, bring ample trials even without our personal setbacks and problems we face. The question is in how we handle this.

In the 1950's and into the 1960's, a significant number of Americans shared, to some degree, in the "Ozzie and Harriet" mentality. This TV show modeled a perfect family that rarely had to confront any real national or world issues, during at least most of the fourteen years the show was on air. Theirs was a halcyon world, a hypnotic and amnesic state without real crises or worry-induced insomnia. The appeal then, and today among both Christians and non-Christians, is in being able to seal themselves off from reality and live that way. As we have seen, some do this with isolation and others use denial, which explains the appeal of Existentialism and other religions that deny reality, especially evil.

---

[20] Legal Momentum, "Legal Momentum." Last modified March 2012. http://www.legalmomenturn.org/our-work/women-and-poverty/resources—publications/single-mothers-snapshot.pdf

Part of this is a result of a misguided sense of reality. Planet earth is part of an order that has fallen through sin. Our existence is now in a war-zone between good and evil. As a consequence of this fall, all of us will die barring the imminent return of Jesus. "For as in Adam all die, so also in Christ shall all be made alive" (I Corinthians 15:22). Here, we suffer discord and suffering, but in this is also purpose, especially for the Christian. There is a reason for wars, calamities, our trials, and even in our death. This reality doesn't find acceptance in our human nature, which seeks comfort, peace, and security. If Christians find this baffling, it is totally incompatible to the world.

America, to a great degree, just struggles to cope with reality. This is seen in the despair in our land today. Just three decades ago, President Reagan made famous the idea: "It is morning again in America." Although that decade began in economic chaos and uncertainty, we all saw a sunlit destiny within our grasp. We were on the road to rebuilding American greatness. The worldly sought wealth while we, fundamental Christians, dreamed of a moral restoration.

Today, very few have such illusions. Our nation, our destinies in this life, and our world seem to be spinning out of control. On every front are insurmountable challenges and barriers; it's all caving in on us. Our economic crisis is more symptomatic of this new attitude than the cause, and public rage only seems to be rising over everyone's apparent inability to provide solutions. For the unbeliever, there is only so much the mind can take. The movements, whether Tea Party or Occupy Wall Street, both share the same worries about a smaller prosperity for the common person. It seems that so many, including the president, are trying to rationalize irrationalism. "And you shall be driven mad by the sight of what you see" (Deuteronomy 28:34). This madness takes many forms.

One has been the explosive proliferation of chemical addictions in our society. In seeking peace and tranquility of mind, alcohol is the drug of choice for up to twenty million Americans. According to the Center For Disease Control (CDC), this also cost the economy over two hundred twenty billion dollars in 2010, which can only add to our anxiety.[21] To this, add the abundance of illegal street drugs, which their statistics show that in any given "last month" 8.7% of Americans twelve or over have

---

[21] National Journal, October 17, 2011

used at least once. There is also a burgeoning prescription drug addiction, which according to the CDC, resulted in over fifteen thousand deaths per year. Add this to alcohol, illegal drugs, and of course, marijuana, and there are at least forty million cases of serious sickness and death annually in America today. This doesn't account for the fractured lives and families of those they affect.

These things do provide a temporary release from life's anxieties. If they didn't, no one would use them. They do so at a cost, however. They are all, to a degree, addicting, and a return to reality provides the user more problems than they had before. Even some of the healing drugs can prove self-defeating. Valium, for example, treats anxiety, insomnia, alcohol withdrawal, and in the process, causes addiction. Ecstasy, while treating Post Traumatic Stress Disorder, can also be addictive. The batteries of drugs that pacify behavioral disorders in youth also often alter their minds as well, and—surprise—they often addict. All these only offer the user a temporary peace, which, if used as God intended, does serve a purpose, but outside of God, they often only serve as a mask, providing a false covering for a deeper need and at a terrible cost.

Another form of the madness referred to in the Deuteronomy passage is mental illness. This leads many to turn to psychiatric medicine. Much of this is self-inflicted; a result of misguided expectations about life and wrongful life choices, but much of it is not. Millions among us have been traumatized by events beyond their control. An abused or neglected child has done nothing to bring evil upon themselves, but unjustly, they may suffer for life because of it. The Bible does speak to the science of psychotherapy. "Anxiety in the heart of a man weighs him down, but a good word (from the wise) makes it glad" (Proverbs 12:25). The problem arises from the applied humanistic dogma encapsulated in modern psychotherapy. Things of man apart from God will never bring genuine or lasting healing, no matter how well intentioned the doctor.

One definition of insanity is to do the same thing over and over and expect different results. That our nation turned away from God is in itself, an open invitation to insanity. As Deuteronomy says, persistence in that error only adds to it. Our nation has gone beyond that, however, with each passing year and in each generation, we only sink to deeper levels of idolatry and immorality. Our nation's love affair with other religions, especially those of East Asia, only affirms this. Today, up to one in three Americans regularly turn to at least one of these for peace and answers. As previously noted, twenty-five percent use horoscopes alone. Over fourteen percent of Americans, in one poll, now have given up on all organized religion and have embraced one of man's own making, either Agnosticism or Atheism, according to the Pew Forum on Religion And Public Life 2007. Listening to the values and purposes advocated by belief systems outside of Christianity is like madness. The most glaring display of this may be in our growing perversion and attachment to unnatural relationships.

For whatever means Americans seek peace outside of Jesus, the same truth abides. "For My people have committed two evils; they have forsaken Me, the fountain of living waters, to hew out for themselves cisterns, broken cisterns, that can hold no water" (Jeremiah 2:13). By focusing inwardly and not upwardly, as humanism ultimately does, in an attempt to find answers, one will never meet with success. Alcohol, psychotherapy, or other religions can't bring true peace, but there is One that can.

Like the song "Looking for Love (in All The Wrong Places)," so our world is looking for peace the same way. This is a result of man's quest for the wrong kind of peace. This comes from seeking the wrong answers, which comes, in turn, from asking the wrong questions. Jesus promised, "Peace I leave with you; My peace I give to you; not as the world gives, do I give to you. Let not your hearts be troubled, nor let them be fearful" (John 14:27). All too often, the world doesn't understand what it seeks.

In this modern age, most Americans feel that this life and our world are all that is important. Their goal, as a result, is to encapsulate themselves from all risk. With so many advancements in modern technology, they believe that safety and security are fully attainable. We see this played out in government agency safety policies. As one example, in 1966, 50,894 Americans died in automobile accidents, or only about six thousand fewer than died in the whole Vietnam War, according to The National Highway Traffic Safety Administration.[22] That year, Ralph Nadar's *Unsafe At Any Speed*, 1965, was peaking public concern about safety. Calls for government action led to the birth, of the National Highway Traffic Safety Administration (NHTSA). The death rate at that time was 5.497 per hundred million miles traveled. This was down nearly eighty percent from

[22] FARS Encyclopedia, "NHTSA." http://wwwfars.nhtsa.dot.gov/Main/index.aspx.

1921, a rate of 24.085 per hundred million miles, the year records were first kept. By 2009, this rate was down to 33,963, or only 1.16 per hundred million miles traveled. This was a drop of over ninety-five percent per mile in less than a century. Yet the belief of the NHTSA, and many Americans, is that, ultimately, all deaths are preventable. There is no acceptable level of fatalities. If our world continues much longer, a future driver will be required to program into a computer device their intended destination, and using GPS, the car will automatically drive itself there. Of course, for several reasons, leisure driving will be a thing of the past.

This isn't the only life choice being made for us in the interest of our safety and security The choice has already been made to go to a system of electronic money, or e-money. By our delegating our responsibilities and liberties to the government, we are bringing this upon ourselves. In the interest of what is for our own good and to reduce the threat of counterfeiting, someone will soon be able to keep track of every dollar we spend. Since the FBI, Homeland Security, and other agencies can now literally access our accounts at will, a complete personal profile would be easy to compile. The Internet is already open to monitoring, as are cell phones and other communication devices and so many other aspects of our lives. Utility companies monitor both when and how much water, gas, or electricity we use. Again, we're being told that this is for our own good and that it will save money. Satellites can watch us from space, ultimately, for our safety and security, but a slight shift in policy turns monitoring into control. The cameras that Progressive Insurance and other car insurers use give an object lesson on how this will work. Any misstep on our part would be sent to a controlling power and some penalty would be imposed on us. In this process, we give up all freedom and become docile puppets. Does this sound far-fetched? Just consider where we have come in the last forty or so years.

Our society has become obsessed with the concept of requiring licenses, certificates, or degrees to be able to do almost anything. While there are commercial interests, the "power of control" undertones are quite evident. This is the very reason our founders had such an aversion to the requirements that ensnare us today. Add to this the over-complication of cars, appliances, and other devices that prevent consumers from fixing them on their own. Step by step, by abrogating our liberties, we are on our way to being dumbed-down into total dependency. This doesn't even address the declining economic status of a majority of us.

Between a dread of death and a desire for total protection, we seem driven to build a world where no one can get hurt. We want to believe that all bad can be prevented, that the right economic policy can guarantee everyone a job, and proper monitoring can prevent all crime. This almost worked in the Soviet Union, at least on the job front. They had a chronic labor shortage. What these peace seekers won't admit is the cost of their goals.

One problem is, that in a humanist, or materialist setting, liberty, or personal choice, is the opposite of safety and security. In 1789, French revolutionaries sought to build a perfect humanist society on a foundation of liberty, equality, and fraternity (brotherhood).

The first casualty was the third part of this tripartite: fraternity. Between the guillotine and Reign of Terror, estimates are that north of fifty thousand French met death at each other's hands. In today's humanist world, liberty and equality are still opposites, as is worldly peace to the unalienable rights of life, liberty, and the pursuit of happiness, as stated in our Declaration of Independence. When peace and security become our idols and our prime directive, as they are becoming in America today, the human spirit is stifled. Inner turmoil can only increase, and eventually burst forth, to violate the very peace that mandated its suffocation. Man without Jesus won't find peace. "Destruction and misery are in their paths, and the path of peace they have not known" (Romans 3:16, 17).

The bottom line is that the type of peace the world seeks ultimately won't work, even without the problem of evil or sin-induced chaos. Perfect world tranquility, no diseases, earthquakes, or physical death is a contradiction in itself. First of all, they don't know what it is. "They do not know the way of peace, and there is no justice in their tracks; they have made their paths crooked; whoever treads on them does not know peace" (Isaiah 59:8). Also, our selfish desires prevent peace. The presence of sin, by nature itself, is the absence of true peace, and any reliance on us, instead of God, is sin. To be led by our spirit, will, or desire to meet our goals through self-trust has consequences. "What is the source of wars and conflicts among you? Is not the source your pleasures that wage war in your members? You lust and do not have; so you commit murder. And you are envious and cannot obtain; so you fight and quarrel" (James 4:1, 2).

There is also a spiritual war going on around us. Daniel learned this when his prayers didn't get answered in the timely manner he had anticipated. "But the prince of the kingdom of Persia was withstanding me for twenty-one days; then behold Michael, one of the chief princes, came to help me, for I had been left there with the king of Persia" (Daniel 10:13). This constant warfare helps explain the dual ownership claims of God and Satan. It also explains both the need and purpose of prayer. Every time someone listens to the hosts of darkness and sins, more evil is introduced into our world. The first casualty was spiritual death; the second is peace.

Peace can be elusive in the Church as well. Jesus promised, "These things I have spoken to you, that in Me you may have peace. In the world you will have tribulation, but take courage, I have overcome the world" (John 16:33). We want to have it both ways, though. Many churches have bought into the promises of relativism and tolerance. They abandon the set standards of right and wrong that help preserve God's peace in an effort to make peace with the world, yet they still presume to pray to Jesus for His peace. This ultimately is a cop-out on faith and conviction and is a driving force in the splintering of the Church. Instead of faith that demands our surrender to Jesus, they offer people a religious supermarket with the option of how much of the world people want to keep and how much they're willing to give up. People only need to shop around to find one that makes them happy. Thus, we have feel-good religion as churches compete with each other to promise the most peace, love, and blessings with the least conviction, fear of Hell, or call to service. Also lacking is any acknowledgment of a spiritual warfare, which, in our compromised state, imperils our salvation, and a door to peace outside of Jesus is opened.

This gospel has much in common with Daoism; both teach peace by going with the flow and not rocking the boat. While getting along with the world through compromise, or seeking common ground between good and evil, gives a sense of peace, it also assumes that the world won't come along and move the goalposts at a later time, when we are comfortable and vulnerable. It also renders us, at best, lukewarm. "I know your deeds, that you are neither cold nor hot; I would that you were cold or hot. So because you are lukewarm... I will spit you out of My mouth" (Revelation 3:15, 16).

In laying a foundation for false peace, these believers actually bring their own demise. No common ground exists, and any foundation not on Christ is on sand (Matthew 7:26). "Do not be bound together with unbelievers, for what partnership have righteousness and lawlessness, or what fellowship has light with darkness? Or what harmony has Christ with Belial?" (II Corinthians 6:14, 15). In a quest for peaceful coexistence, compromise and tolerance only bring us an enmity with the Prince of Peace.

Peace on the world's terms is allowing evil anywhere to go unchecked. It is like allowing a spoiled brat child to go unchallenged. Compromise and appeasement only encourage more bad behavior and less peace. God ordained government to keep physical peace, if necessary, by using the sword. "Whoever sheds man's blood, by man shall his blood be shed, for in the image of God He made man" (Genesis 9:6). Violence is often needed to confront evil and give peace a chance. Involved in peace, is a fear of what will happen if that peace is violated.

Before we go any further with this, confrontation is not always the best option in dealing with evil. In Matthew 5:39, Jesus taught about turning the other cheek. Paul adds, "But if your enemy is hungry, feed him, and if he is thirsty, give him drink; for by so doing you will heap burning coals upon his head. Do not be overcome with evil, but overcome evil with good" (Romans 12:20, 21). Our kingdom is spiritual, our goal is to win souls to Jesus, and our peace is a spiritual peace. To those who have any concept of right and wrong, a gift of forgiving love, and a kindness borne out of a willing spirit of Holy Spirit strength can melt the hardest of hearts.

There are those in the Church today who believe in total pacifism. They don't serve in the military and won't even defend their own homes or property. Those who are consistent in their view also don't vote. Their calling of peace can be a highly effective witness for the Lord. Sadly, though, there are others who claim pacifism but have no trouble using the courts to sue others, as with the Jehovah's Witnesses, to push their own agenda. All other doctrine aside, this gives God a black eye, but for those who truly believe in pacifism, no other burden should be laid upon them, as they, in their faith, are using their liberty to serve Christ as they see best. "So then each one shall give account of himself to God" (Romans 14:12).

Government is charged to keep social order. "Let every person be in subjection to the governing authorities. For there is no authority except from God, and those which exist are established by God" (Romans 13:1). While God doesn't approve of corruption, egos, or violations of civil liberties, the alternative is anarchy and chaos. Rarely is a government overthrown and a better one rises to take its place. Examples like France, Russia, China, and Iran prove this point. While revolutionary fervor may mellow, and a better system evolves, all of these went through a period of terror and brutal revenge. The rights of all but a chosen few were suppressed. The fall of the Soviet Bloc and the American Revolution were exceptions because the structure of a replacement governmental order was already in place.

When government fails to uphold a basic standard of justice, either for its own people or in dealings with others, war is often the result. There comes a point when anger over injustice leads to a breach of peace by those who feel death is preferable to injustice. "For oppression makes a wise man mad" (Ecclesiastes 7:7). Not all wars begin this way, but in the late 1960s, El Salvadoran citizens, who were legally in Honduras, endured discriminatory injustice including the seizure of land they legally possessed. A border dispute between the two nations was also unresolved, This resulted in a war over a soccer game in 1969.

Some wars are ordained of God. "Now go and strike Amalek and utterly destroy all that he has, and do not spare him" (I Samuel 15:3). Because of their wickedness, God ordered extermination. In Deuteronomy 20:16-18, He ordered the same sentence against the Canaanites that Israel was to dispossess. The removal of sin was, and is, essential for peace to happen.

Some will argue that this was an Old Testament God who was more wrathful than Jesus in the New Testament. What many don't understand is the idolatrous evil of Canaan. Babies were roasted alive on the altars of Baal and Moloch (Milcom). Small children were plastered into walls in the dedication of houses or add on rooms and allowed to scream until they died. Immorality was raised to worship status, treachery, and generic injustice ruled the land. In this destruction, God allowed those who sought Him to be spared, as were Rahab the Harlot and the deceptive Gibeonites. In God's eyes there is such a thing as just purpose or a spiritual opportunity in war.

This appears to be true in the Church age as well. Among the greatest tragedies in European history was the Thirty Years War (1618-1648). Among the casualties was half of the population of Germany. In Bohemia, ethnic cleansing (against Protestants) killed at least eighty percent of the population. Surrounding nations suffered to lesser degrees. The desolation, anarchy, hatred, and wickedness of that war left scars in Europe that have yet to completely heal. Even into the twentieth-century, Germans had misgivings of democracy because of that war and the fractured Germany it created. In his book *Twentieth Century Germany From Bismarck to Brandt*, A.J. Rider states, "It also confirmed the tendency to see absolute government [as] the alternative to a 'Hobbesian state of brutalized anarchy.'"[23] "Hobbesian" refers to Thomas Hobbes (1588-1679), a political philosopher who saw weak leadership as what had led to the brutal murder and anarchy of that war.

Sadly, it was the actions of all the players in Central Europe that made this war an inevitable necessity. The roll call included the Lutherans, Calvinists, the Church of Rome, and less so, foreign powers like France. This was an age where power triumphed over Christian love and acceptance between the various religious factions.

God also never intended that there be world peace or union outside of Him (Genesis 11:4-9). He saw such as a threat to the survival of the light of truth in our fallen order. Nor does He keep bad from happening; He preserves His people and purposes through them. His ways are not our ways. "For as the Heavens are higher than the earth, so are My ways higher than your ways, and My thoughts than your thoughts" (Isaiah 55:9).

The peace of God (Jesus) is not as the world gives. The world seeks international peace, inner peace, and security peace. The world can't understand trials, evil, death, or wars. We, in the Church, don't often either, but Jesus promises us peace in the storms around us. This is what He promised His disciples, as their world was about to unravel with His death. This is a peace first and foremost between God and us. "And when you were dead in your transgressions and the uncirumcision of your flesh, He made you alive together with Him, having forgiven us all our transgressions having cancelled out the certificate of debt... and which was hostile to us; and He has taken it out of the way, having nailed it to the cross" (Colossians 2:13,14). God declared an end to the war that we, by our sins, caused, "Having made peace through the blood of His cross," (Colossians 1:20). This is God's peace, one that can he enjoyed,

---

[23]  A. J. Rider, Twentieth Century Germany From Bismarck To Brandt, (Columbia University Press 1973), p.9.

regardless of our circumstances. God doesn't prevent evil; He triumphs over it. He doesn't always quiet the storms in our lives, rather He quiets us in the storm.

Evil is allowed, often to prove character, to demonstrate the conflict between good and evil and bring us to depend on His power, strength, and grace. When we reach our limits, His power is just beginning, as Paul learned. "Concerning this I entreated the Lord three times that it might depart from me. And He said to me, 'My grace is sufficient for you, for My power is perfected in weakness'" (II Corinthians 12:8, 9). The beacon of faith in God's power both in and through us may be the only light of hope the unbeliever sees. In the evil day (Ephesians 5:16) it affords them salvation they might otherwise never know.

This peace the world doesn't understand, and the false claims of so-called Christian prophets and preachers, have only contributed to this confusion. "And they heal the brokenness of the daughter of My people superficially, saying, 'Peace, peace,' but there is no peace" (Jeremiah 8:11). But God made His peace to abide in our hearts. "And the peace of God which surpasses all comprehension, shall guard your hearts and your minds in Christ Jesus" (Philippians 4:7). His peace is our guarantee of deliverance and eternal life with Him. He has renewed our hearts in this hope, and this is His promise of hope to a lost world. Without this gift from Him, there can be no peace.

# XIII

## GOD OWES ME

*"I will get up and go to my father, and I will say to him, 'Father,
I have sinned against Heaven and in your sight; I am no longer
worthy to be your son; make me as one of your hired men.'"*

—Luke 15:18, 19

America is a nation of rights. We all have them, and even those who find themselves here illegally do as well. The present controversy over the 2010 Arizona immigration law (and now others like Alabama, etc.) is a fear that the implied rights of illegal immigrants are being denied. According to one of our founding documents, the Declaration of Independence, all people are ascribed the unalienable rights of life, liberty, and the pursuit of happiness. The US Constitution has a bill of rights, which has been amended over the years. As Christians, we also have spiritual rights.

In the last half-century or so, the original intent of our national rights has been radically redefined. The key contributor to this is the Supreme Court. Humanism has played a major role as has a drift of thought that began a century ago. Two past justices, Oliver Wendell Holmes Jr., who served from 1902-1932, and Louis Brandeis, from 1916-1939, are credited for using the phrase "Living, breathing, document" in reference to the Constitution. A 1920 decision, "Missouri vs. Holland," showed the concept that it was an evolving document, as a necessity brought about by social change and advancement. Brandeis was also credited with the phrase "The right to privacy." Since 1960 and the activist court era, many rights have been interpolated into the Constitution. A famous one is the blanket Miranda Rights, a list including reading a prisoner his rights, right to silence, council, etc. Also created were the right of all to contraceptives, married or not, to abortion, pornography, and classroom access for pregnant or single mothers among others. The Court threw out past laws and policies, especially of Christian ethics, to interpret these into the Constitution. The right to gay or lesbian marriage is now joining these rights.

Politicians, as well, have at least attempted to add to this list. Most famously, Franklin D. Roosevelt, US President from 1933 until his death in 1945, proposed the Second Bill of Rights during the depth of the Great Depression. The first right he proposed was to a useful and remunerative, or paying, job in the industries, shops, farms, or mines of the nation. In other words, everyone has a right to a job. If none were available, logically, it falls to the government to step in and provide one. The second right dovetailed into this: a worker has the right to earn enough to provide adequate food, clothing, and recreation. It is not defined, however, as to how much is enough, nor is it explained as to where it would come from if the employer couldn't pay what is called a living wage. Once again, government subsidies seem inevitable. These two led to the government works jobs of the 1930's, as the Civilian Conservation Corps (CCC), the WPA, and others. The third is the right of every farmer to raise and sell his products at a return, which will give him and his family a decent living. While the second explains the minimum wage and other subsidies, this third one added price supports and land set aside payments, even for large corporations. He also proposed the right for every business, large and small, to trade in an atmosphere of freedom from unfair competition and domination by monopolies at home and abroad. The fifth was the right of every family to adequate medical care and the opportunity to achieve and enjoy good health. The seventh was the right to a social security safety net. This helps explain why now over eight million working-age Americans are on Social Security disability.

To guarantee the rights of businessmen, the National Recovery Act (NRA), made well over four thousand business practices illegal. They issued another three thousand administrative orders that took nearly ten million pages to print. Under the tailors code, one New Jersey tailor, Jacob Maged, was publicly prosecuted for charging thirty-five cents, not the mandated forty cents, to dry clean suits. Raids were periodically conducted in the garment industry; often inflicting considerable property damage, to enforce the ban on nighttime work. These rights have a price, both in dollars and in liberty. This doesn't even consider the present prohibitive costs of government housing or future obligations to it, health care, or other programs. To fully implement these rights today would require a government-planned economy akin to the one the former Soviet Union had and failed.

The demand for these rights, though never ratified, hasn't gone away. Americans now feel they have a right to food, clothing, housing, utilities, health care, education, transportation, and legal aid. The next one might be a partridge in a pear tree. Others would add Internet service, unlimited sexual promiscuity, entertainment, and on it goes. Another one that periodically comes into public debate is the right to a guaranteed income. This right would give every person a subsidy, or basic standard of living, just for being alive.

The issue of sustainability is never a concern with the educated elite, which brings up an incident that happened in Waterloo, Iowa in early 1968. A University of Northern Iowa debate team came to West Junior High to debate the guaranteed income issue. The debate focused on benefit consolidation, costs, taxes to pay for it, and humanitarianism. When the debate ended, the floor was opened for questions from the audience. One ninth grader posed the question, "If you guarantee an income of five thousand dollars for a family of four, is it possible that people making seven or eight thousand a year might quit their jobs and go fishing all the time?" The debate team, which never even addressed this possibility, admitted it could happen. Then that ninth grader asked one more question: "If so many people quit their jobs, who would produce things, and is it possible that the government couldn't support them all?" This team admitted they couldn't answer. They weren't prepared to deal with this possibility, but if a ninth grader could see through this Ponzi scheme, why can't politicians?

The problem isn't in the math; it's in the attitude. Too many now believe in a basic entitlement simply because they exist, and the government is supposed to give them this. In the welfare states of Europe, the average person feels the same way: someone owes them something, whether it be the government or the rich. Margaret Thatcher, Prime Minister of Great Britain from 1979-1990, said it well, "Socialism works very well until my neighbor runs out of money." However, any politician, here or abroad, who dares to take on this entitlement concept soon finds themselves out of office. This is especially true of any program people have paid into over the years, as with the Medicare and Social Security ones.

Entitlement mentality defies common sense. A couple retiring in 2010 would have provided $109,000 toward the costs of their Medicare benefits, including accrued interest. Over their lifetime, they can expect to receive $343,000 in benefits from the system, as it now stands, according to "The Wall Street journal," but for a politician to even hint at postponing the future Social Security and Medicare age requirements is political suicide.[24] Yet a large majority of these same voters believe the Federal budget needs to be balanced. Maybe they are anticipating a bail out by China, the Martians, or a massive gold deposit being found on government lands. This isn't just an American problem. The still ongoing (and widening) austerity mandates and negotiations concerning Greece continue to be a simmering volcano that sporadically erupts. A severe "eruption" with a Greek default would bring down a large piece of the world banking business. This volcano also applies to the riot-torn nation's choice in government. Another country, France, in 2010 bumped up the retirement age from sixty to sixty-two. This, too, led to protest and political upheaval. The austerity moves in Great Britain were a major factor in the August 2011 riots there. At the same time, as we whine, the rise in food and fuel prices has put hundreds of millions world wide on the verge of starvation. For some, 80 percent of their total income now goes to buy food.

Granted, our American heritage has endowed this nation with certain individual rights. Liberty was the matrix, ore, prime ingredient from which all of them arose. These rights were ordained of divine providence and were purchased with blood by the patriots of many generations. Our freedom

---

[24] "Wall Street Journal," Opinions & Commentary, Feb. 26, 2011 http://online.wsj.com/public/page/news-opinion-commentary.html.

is not free. Physical freedom must be repurchased with each generation, as Thomas Jefferson (1743-1826), our third president once said, "The tree of liberty must be refreshed from time to time by the blood of tyrants and patriots." Nowhere in our founding documents, or implied in freedom's heritage, is the promise of prosperity or of a free ride for anyone without labor. What was promised was an opportunity for each person to chart a destiny for themselves, as God allows.

The nature of rights, themselves, needs clarification. Basically, there are two kinds: class and individual. An example of an individual right is the right to leave home, get into a car we purchased, and drive down the road of our choice. A class right is for each person to have a car, it they can't afford one, they will be given one. While our founding fathers saw the need for some class rights, as the right to life, the emphasis was on individual ones, as in the pursuit of happiness. Some overlap, like the right to bear arms, which may require the financial assistance of others when we are required to perform militia duty.

Entitlements, if they are rights at all, are clearly class rights, while liberty and the pursuit of happiness were individual and protected by the Ninth and Tenth Amendments. The First Amendment offers some overlap; speech, assembly, and the freedom of worship are individual, but press freedom is a class one, requiring group effort and involving the fear of publicity for one who steps outside of socially accepted behavior. The fear of exposure is a restricting force on individual rights. As defined today, the right to live safely is a class right since it limits the individual right of anonymity to preserve the collective right to security. The slogan "Safety First" can easily lead to the voiding of all individual rights.

While some class rights are essential, they can cultivate an entitlement mindset while also destroying individual ones. It's no accident that the ACLU is fixated on class action lawsuits, as are movements like gay rights and those that advocate permissive sexuality. This results in a destruction of the individual rights and free choices of those who don't want what they view as evil imposed upon them. God delights in our good free choices, of soaring spirits, and broad horizons. "Now the Lord is spirit; and where the spirit of the Lord is, there is liberty" (II Corinthians 3:17), and this implies more than spiritual liberty.

Even so, this entitlement mentality has spilled over into our religious expectations, as well. Again, this pre-dates our age. In John 6 is one account of Jesus feeding the five thousand, plus families. Most Jewish people felt that they were special because of their covenantal relationship with God. They were God's chosen people and entitled to all the blessings of God and His kingdom. When the Messiah came, from Jerusalem, He would be king over all the earth, in the power and spirit of David, as seen in the Scriptures. "Thou shall break them [the Gentiles] with a rod of iron, Thou shall shatter them like earthenware" (Psalm 2:9). The Jews envisioned Rome as a vassal to Israel just as Israel was then to Rome. They had visions of payback when God brought this about.

When Jesus came on the scene, He gave spirit to the Jewish masses. The zealots, or the hard-core revolutionaries, saw Him as their ideal leader and wanted to make Him king. "Jesus, therefore, perceiving that they were intending to come and take Him by force, to make Him king, withdrew again to the mountain by Himself alone" (John 6:15). He was not about to allow anyone to hijack His ministry or dictate His policy. His was a ministry of salvation from sin, and this offer was for the people of Israel, as it was with one of His twelve: "And Simon who was called the Zealot," (Luke 6:15). But their shortsighted aims of the flesh ignored the world's need for salvation. Jesus's walk on the water was His way to avoid and defuse a situation threatening insurrection and false hopes.

Not to be outdone, the next day, these Zealots went on a search and rescue mission to find Jesus and stoke their ambitions. Ignoring Jesus's rebuke for their self-serving motives, they had the audacity to demand of Him a miracle to justify believing in Him. This isn't too different from our day: we demand lots of goodies in exchange for our votes or reasons as to why we should attend a particular church. "What do you then do for a sign, that we may see and believe you?" (John 6:30). Jesus responded by offering them better "bread" (Himself) than their ancestors had received in their wilderness trek from Egypt to Palestine. Still, refusing to see beyond their worldly ambition they demanded, "Lord, evermore give us this bread" (John 6:34).

Jesus made one final appeal to broaden their vision to a spiritual focus. He was not offering physical bread but spiritual. All who eat and drink on planet earth will die, whether the bread came from their labors or as a miracle of God, but the bread Jesus offered was the sacrifice of Himself to give them eternal life. Unable to grow up spiritually and look beyond entitlements, they departed without receiving this bread.

This was not Jesus's only encounter with the entitlement mentality. In Luke 17:11-19, He was headed for Jerusalem when ten lepers, nine Jew and one Samaritan, met him. Sharing the same social disease brought them together. This great equalizer had erased all radial or cultural stigmas, and now, collectively, they begged Jesus to heal them. As a sign of commitment, or obedience, to show their faith in Jesus to do so, He sent them to their priests. As they began to go, they were healed. Nine of them felt that they had received what any good Jew in the presence of the Messiah was entitled to and went their way, but the Samaritan turned back to give thanks. In so doing, he received a second blessing, in verse 19, "Your faith has made you well," or rather, saved him. He got the better bread.

God is a gracious God who does bless in material ways. Many times, this is in the form of protection from physical tribulations. "And the blood shall be a sign for you on the houses where you live; and when I see the blood I will pass over you, and no plague shall befall you to destroy you when I strike the land of Egypt" (Exodus 12:13). Some of His blessings are for all, the good and the bad. "For He…sends rain on the righteous and the unrighteous" (Matthew 5:45). God loves not just Christians; He loves us all.

It is clear to see that God has blessed America in a special way. We have been delivered from many of the scourges and tribulations that have affected the rest of the world.

The hand of divine providence has been upon us and, to some degree, all of Western Civilization. One example was the 1227 AD Mongol invasion. They were poised to defeat the Hungarians at Budapest and, from there, springboard into all of Western Europe. At a critical moment, news of Genghis Kahn's death came to the Mongol camp. They left to pick a successor, sparing Europe.

Another blessing can be seen in the fruits of the New World. In the sixteenth-century, the Americas yielded treasures to the rest of the world; the greatest were plants, like the potato and the yam. While the potato was lower in nutrition than the yam, it blessed Europe, feeding millions off land otherwise unfit for other crops. Population growth fueled empires. Meanwhile, China took a liking to the more nutritious yam. Easily erosive hills and mountains were cultivated. As a result, flooding destroyed crops in the lowlands, and Chinese civilization went into a decline.

The sparing of America is obvious in just the course of the two great wars of the twentieth-century. Total deaths from bombs and bullets, concentration camps, and disease, exceeded seventy-five million, with some estimates closer to ninety million worldwide. In this, we not only were spared the worst of it, we actually emerged stronger than we were before.

The problem is that we've come to expect blessings and protection. All too often, we even attribute our success to the American spirit and not the Father of spirits. We view our special status with the L'Oreal mentality: "Because we're worth it." God never intended for His blessings be presumed upon or selfishly hoarded, though, not by us, Abraham, the ancient Israelites, nor any one else. God expects spiritual fruit in return as Jesus did of Israel: "Behold, for three years I have come looking for fruit on this fig tree without finding any. Cut it down! Why does it even use up the ground?" (Luke 13:7). God gave a privileged few special opportunities for the purpose of sharing His goodness with the world, but with this also came a special accounting: "You only have I chosen among all of the families of the earth; therefore I will punish you for all your iniquities" (Amos 3:2). Opportunity brings accountability and a greater punishment for disobedience.

This was true in Jesus's day. "Woe to you Chorazin! Woe to you Bethsaida! For if the miracles had been performed in Tyre and Sidon which occurred in you, they would have repented long ago, sitting in sackcloth and ashes. But it will be more tolerable for Tyre and Sidon in the judgment than for you" (Luke 10:13, 14). The Jews were not only liable to greater spiritual punishment, but they also were made a worldly example of. In AD 70, Titus Maximus captured Jerusalem and Rome did something they had never before done: they destroyed the temple of a deity, in this case, the temple of God. All that the Jews valued perished with their nation, including their genealogy records. No Jew today can prove he is a Jew, though DNA tracking may be able to give this back to them.

The early Church had a tinge of this as well. The first hint of it is found in Acts 6:1: "Now at that time when the disciples were increasing in number, a complaint arose on the part of the Hellenistic Jews against the native Hebrews, because their widows were being overlooked in the daily serving of food" (Acts 6:1). The Hellenists were those who had bought into much of the Greek (Gentile) culture. Many Jewish purists looked down on them as a result, but the problem was solved, and all got along again.

The early Church, however, was content to focus on Jews alone with the Gospel. Jesus's last words were, "And you shall be My witnesses both in Jerusalem and in all Judea and Samaria, and even to the remotest part of the earth" (Acts 1:8). They endured the persecution of the Jewish society as led by the Sanhedrin (High Priest and leaders). As these initial hostilities ebbed and became more of a cold war, the Church began to get comfortable and failed to expand into the Gentile world. Their influence was limited to proselytes such as Nicolas (Acts 6:5). Some argue, maybe rightly, that the Church needed time to establish roots in Jerusalem and the Jewish community, but there was also exclusivism.

When persecution hit, the Church was scattered. After the death of Stephen, and the advent of the murderous Saul of Tarsus, the Samaritans were evangelized (Acts 8:1-25), but she still had a stigma with the Gentiles. "Now the apostles and the brethren who were throughout Judea heard that the Gentiles had also received the word of God. And when Peter came up to Jerusalem, those who were circumcised took issue with him" (Acts 11:1, 2). God had to broaden their vision so they could see their mission. Any entitlement mentality was at least stifled enough to enable an outreach into the Gentile world, but as seen in Acts 15 and Galatians 2, the issue still smoldered in the early Church.

Today's Church still struggles with its own root of prejudice. When the Puritans came to the New World, they sought religious liberty; which they held somewhat exclusively for themselves. Prevailing opinion among many of them was that the American Indian had no soul. This type of narrowness wasn't limited to them or just against the Indian. To most of the Protestant world, those outside of Christian Europe were inferior. The doctrine of Calvinism (John Calvin) did little to dissuade this belief. In a nutshell, the belief was, "If God wants the heathen saved, He'll reveal Himself to them." It wasn't until William Carey (1761-1834) that the Protestants had a reality check and were spurred to mission activity. The great modern age of missions began, but many age-old prejudices remained.

The cost in human souls because of exclusivism, and exclusion, especially European and American, has been heavy. This entitlement mentality affected the Church in South Africa at the same time Mohandas (Mahatma) Gandhi (1869-1948) was there. In 1893 he arrived, and as a normal human being of the flesh, he had prejudices against others, in his case, the native Africans. In time, though, he grew out of this and expressed an interest in Christianity; but the South African Church was segregated with a belief, by the ruling European community, in white supremacy or exclusivism. This led Gandhi to reject Christianity as the religion for all humanity: He returned in 1915 to India, a nonbeliever. While this belief in ethnic superiority is one crippling form of an entitlement mentality, it's not the only one.

Many, in the course of history, have had the idea that God somehow owes us salvation. This may not be something that actually is said, but people's lifestyles betray this. In Augustine's day, the belief was that God's salvation could be presumed upon without any repentance or Christian service. While many saw grace as a credit card, others believed they could live a life of sin until death was near and be saved in a deathbed conversion. This licentious population often postponed baptism until just before death. To them, God didn't care if they selfishly enjoyed all the pleasures of the here and now, they were entitled to salvation. This mentality helped force a change in theology. Since many of these converts could no longer be immersed, baptism by pouring water on them became accepted. This also came from a misinterpretation of the Didache, an uninspired book of teachings. This led both to the sacrament of Last Rites, and later beliefs that baptism was not needed at all.

Today in America, there are those as well who feel forgiveness is somehow owed to them. This isn't just reflected in how they view God; it also applies to their expectations of Christians. No matter how they hurt a fellow believer, they claim the right to be forgiven. Jesus did tell us to forgive each other, and this was a requisite for our own forgiveness, "But if you do not forgive men, then your Father will not forgive your transgressions" (Matthew 6:15). Several years ago, an individual who had wronged me informed me that I was obligated to forgive them even as they continued in that same sin. My response was that their forgiveness in God's sight was just as solid as their repentance.

Forgiveness is not a right. It is a free gift that we can't merit and dare not feel entitled to. "He saved us, not on the basis of deeds which we have done in righteousness, but according to his mercy, by the washing of regeneration and the renewing by the Holy Spirit" (Titus 3:5). Forgiveness depends on sincere heartfelt repentance (Acts 2:38). God doesn't owe, He offers. He sent Jesus, not because He had to but because He wanted to and because He loved us (John 3:16). This is freely offered to all, not just to an entitled class, race, or group. Even our often lack of thankfulness is sin. "For even though they knew God, they did not honor Him as God, or give thanks" (Romans 1:21). The concept of forgiveness as a credit card also brings a person dangerously close to, "For if we go on sinning willfully after receiving the knowledge of the truth, there no longer remains a sacrifice for sins" (Hebrews 10:26).

Another Christian belief is the idea that we are entitled to escape trials and have all our prayers answered as we wish and not necessarily as God wills. God did promise to abide with us, deliver us, and answer our prayers. These are promises from both the Old and New Testaments. Belief in this and in our salvation is our "title deed," or assurance of things hoped for, in Jesus. God doesn't always deliver us from every trial. But He does promise salvation from sin, "But deliver us from evil" (Matthew 6:13). God's purpose isn't necessarily for our comfort but for us to bear fruit. He will not give us a hill we can't climb, and He saves us from being pushed beyond our abilities. "God is faithful, who will not allow you to be tempted beyond what you are able, but with the temptation will provide the way of escape also, that you may be able to endure it" (I Corinthians 10:13).

The collision of an entitlement mindset with spiritual reality has led many in America to lose faith in God. It's not enough that God promised them, "Moreover I will make My dwelling among you, and My soul will not reject you. I will also walk among you and be your God, and you shall be My people" (Leviticus 26:11, 12). This is essentially the same promise repeated by Jesus in John 14:23 and Revelation 3:20. Many feel that they are entitled to physical deliverances from all trials, as well, but our present state is under the curse of Adam's sin. We suffer disease, genetic defects, death, and bad things sometimes do happen to good people, or at least what we want to call good. If for no other reason, this makes us realize how much better Heaven will be than this world is.

In reality, though, we all sin and none of us is really good. We need to remember that salvation is an unmerited gift, "As it is written, 'There is none righteous, not even one'" (Romans 3:10). Verse 23 adds, "For all have sinned and fall short of the glory of God." No one is deserving of good. Granted, small children fall under the umbrella of grace (Matthew 18:14), but they suffer the consequences of the fall too. God allows free will, and choices do have consequences. Jonah had a right to disobey when God told him to go to Nineveh, but God also had the right to deal with him (and us) to get his attention. Sadly, in Jonah's case, it caused damage to a boatload of sailors.

People are inclined to argue that their sins really aren't that bad, and from a worldly perspective, we do tend to get more upset over the sin of murder than the sin of sloth. From a spiritual perspective, however, all sin is sin. "For the wages of sin is death, but the free gift of God is eternal life in Christ Jesus our Lord" (Romans 6:23). All sin breaks fellowship with God. God owes us nothing; we owe Him everything. He offers this fellowship back, and does us good in spite of our evil. Our good could never atone for this evil, but God, in His mercy, forgave it.

As humans, we do have the expectation that if we are doing something for God, good things should happen as a result. This is why Jesus reminded us, "So you too, when you do all the things which you are commanded to do, say, 'We are unworthy slaves; we have done only that which we aught to have done'" (Luke 17:10). We may feel we have made a major sacrifice, but this is just our reasonable service. "And at Lystra there was sitting a certain man, without strength in his feet, lame from his mother's womb, who had never walked... [Paul] said with a loud voice, 'Stand upright on your feet.' And he leaped up and began to walk" (Acts 14:8, 10). Just a few days after this great deed, Paul was dragged outside of that city and stoned. He remembered his great suffering there for the rest of his life (II Timothy 3:11). Even as he awaited martyrdom, this was on his mind. From a human perspective, this made no sense at all.

From a spiritual one, this was one of Paul's finest hours, though he didn't see it at the time. A young man named Timothy was a dweller of that city. When Paul passed through again four or five years later, this man, Timothy, joined him and Silas. He was destined to become a key player in the still-infant Church. If Paul had suffered from an entitlement mentality, he may well have quit before this encounter and, if he were like so many modem Americans, lost his faith in God. Instead, great things were done by a soul totally devoted to Jesus.

# XIV

## I Did it My Way

*"There is a way that seems right to a man, but its way is the way of death."*

—Proverbs 14:12

Most Americans either remember when Frank Sinatra sang this song in 1967 or have heard it since. Over the years, other versions have come out as well; Elvis Presley sang his from Hawaii in 1973; Sid Vicious added a later version, and he wasn't the last. The lyrics have an almost haunting appeal to millions worldwide and also to many professing Christians.

The song's message is clear. It pictures the singer, as he faces death, looking back on the life he has lived. As he reflects, he feels satisfaction in having set his own destiny, living by his own rules, and pleasing himself in all he did. That the song has deliberate spiritual undertones is seen in the last stanza. "For what is man, what has he got? If not himself, than he has naught, to say the things he truly feels and not the words of one who kneels [prays]. The record shows I took the blows and did it my way!"[25] In the singer's mind, he is a triumphant soul prepared to face eternity, and he is content with the selfish choices he has made in charting his own pathway.

---

[25]   "AZ Lyrics." Accessed July 2012. http://wwwazlyrics.com/lyrics/franksinatra/myway.html.

He hasn't served any deity, at least not God, in his quest to become himself. Ego, at least, appears to be on the throne of his life.

There's always been a desire in the human spirit to control one's own destiny and plot one's own course in life. Everyone wants to be his own boss and make it big time. All of us find an appeal in living the high-life with all its glamour and to be accountable for nothing. We would be lying to not admit in our hearts that there is, at least, some appeal in this. King Amaziah of Judah felt that, as the king, he could live this way. When a prophet who told him otherwise confronted him, he responded, "Have we appointed you a royal counselor? Stop! Why should you be struck down?" (II Chronicles 25:16). He had no need to listen to God; he had his own plan.

If one can wing their own way to wealth, pleasure, and fame, for both here and eternity, then there's no need to depend upon God (or a god) to do what they can do for themselves. There's no need to be concerned about any moral code to impede them or rules to circumvent. Nothing can make them feel guilty or unworthy. No deity needs to be honored or appeased. While this falls into the same genre as the Buddhist "Eight Fold Path," its tenets are just the opposite. Instead of seeking purity and honor, this is the way of indulgence, but once man decides that he can save himself, only the conditions are negotiable. To quote an old line: "To thine own self be true." After all, what else matters?

Is it possible for man to invent his own belief systems? The answer, obviously, is yes, with or without including the spirit world. The Bible acknowledges this, "In those days there was no king in Israel; every man did what was right in his own eyes" (judges 17:6). During the three hundred or so years between Joshua's death and the kingship of Saul, the people of Israel were free to chart their destiny. It had always been God's intent for them to enjoy liberty in their service to Him. "And I will walk at liberty, for I seek Thy precepts" (Psalms 119:45). Instead, their freedom was abused, becoming a pretext or opportunity to fulfill evil desires. They were idolatrous, stole from, and lied to each other. They weren't afraid to murder, rape, and practice gross immorality and dispossession. This era was remembered in the reign of Asa: "And in those times there was no peace to him who went out or to him who came in, for many disturbances afflicted all the inhabitants of the lands" (II Chronicles 15:5). This verse summarizes the general chaos in the life of Palestine and explained why they were in poverty.

For society to work, there has to be authority and a set of rules. If people constantly fear that someone will steal their property, they seldom wander too far from home. A disproportionate share of time and energy goes towards security measures or in stealing the other guy's stuff first. Productivity and commerce suffer and even cease. "In the days of Shamgar the son of Anath, in the days of Jael, the highways were deserted, and travelers went by roundabout ways" (Judges 5:6). Not only is this economically devastating, it also creates cynicism, selfish distrust, and hatred of others. A lack of commerce causes starvation and privation as well. While prosperity needs freedom for innovation and advancement, it also needs enforced rules to protect it and maintain social order.

When man chooses to be a law unto himself, this hedge of protection vanishes. First, anarchy reigns supreme and then tyranny takes over, and everything suffers. Contrary to what most of us want to believe, just having an ability to do something doesn't necessarily make it right. This was among the tenets of the Women's Rights Movement: if someone has an ability to do something, why shouldn't they? If this were truth, however, if someone came up with the ability to rob Ft. Knox, would it be right to do so? This is tantamount to arguing that "might makes right," but from a moral perspective, it doesn't. Only a strong moral fiber can preserve good and uphold social advancement. Thus, Peter reminds us, "Act as free men, and do not use your freedom as a covering for evil, but use it as bond slaves of God" (I Peter 2:16).

Secondly, and more foundational to our nature, we can never really serve ourselves. Our power is limited in our choosing which god (or God) we will serve. Jesus tried to get the Jewish leaders to understand this. "Truly, truly I say to you, everyone who commits sin is a slave to sin" (John 8:34). Sin is addicting, and addiction is slavery. Drug addiction is a prime example of this.

Most addiction results from illicit drug use with an intent to get high. For most users, this feeling itself is psychologically addicting, even without its chemical counterpart. Each successive high requires a larger and larger dose. Both the chemical and psychological composition of the mind is altered. While chemical addiction, and even death, can happen the first time, it usually takes several hits to build chemical dependency. Whether or not the drug literally kills the user physically, it diminishes both their health and mental abilities. It also destroys any purpose or values in their lives, robs them of joy, and shatters any family ties the addict may have, and even if that person gets into a rehab program, there will always be a pull to return to that drug in their hearts.

In fairness, unlike our choice to sin, not all drug addiction is voluntary. God did create narcotics, like morphine and opiates to treat severe pain. Many veterans of war have been treated with them, as have cancer and other patients suffering severe and chronic pain. Too long of a usage often addicts these people, and for the rest of their lives, they may have to maintain a set daily dose to prevent a life-threatening withdrawal. Thankfully, there are modern treatments like methadone, which can be used to break dependency, but even to do this, a person must be firmly committed to make it work.

## Sin is addicting

All sin is addicting. The signs might not be as obvious as they are with drugs, but it also alters the workings of our minds and spirits. This addiction is always by choice, and it always leads to spiritual death. Sin does bring temporary pleasure; it is usually fun or fulfilling in some way, or we wouldn't do it. How this becomes slavery is not always self evident; it blinds, and it usually involves a process. A person might feel guilt or sorrow, even vow never to do it again, only to fall prey to it again at a later time of weakness. The sinner may fall victim to a self-destructive remorse, to grieve over the consequences without being willing to give up the sin, as did Judas. "Then when Judas who had betrayed Him, saw that he had been condemned, he felt remorse and returned the thirty pieces of silver to the chief priests and elders" (Matthew 27:3). His remorse led him to suicide.

## Sin Separates Us from God

This spiritual death puts the sinner in homage to the spirits of darkness. "You are of your father the devil, and you want to do the desires of your father" (John 8:44). This is what happened to the first couple, and Jesus told the Jewish leaders that the same was true for them. This helps us to see how sin blinds us, or dumbs us down, spiritually. "But to this day whenever Moses is read, a veil lies over their heart; but whenever a man turns to the Lord, the veil is taken away" (II Corinthians 3:15, 16). Not only does it alter the chemistry and workings of our brains, we are blinded as to whom we are in bondage.

## Sin enslaves, kills, and addicts

Its temporary pleasures fool our minds into thinking it is a good thing, just as the deceptive false independence it produces makes our spirits feel empowered to seek their own pathway to happiness. This also leads to a psychological dependency as our minds associate good feelings with disobedience. And the images implanted in our minds of the carnal or other stimulation really never goes away. A perfect example is pornography, as the images are planted, to some degree forever, in a person's mind. This also functions like a drug high. The intense pleasure brought by sexual stimulation dulls the mind in its effects, and it takes greater and greater stimulation to get the same level of satisfaction. It incites the one involved to include others in their desire for gratification and cheapens their regard for all involved. They become potential objects of gratification that are then viewed as less than humans.

Immorality may be the starting point, but it doesn't end there. Another person usually is used or abused to fulfill the cravings of lust. As greater stimulation is needed, this digresses into sadomasochism, child pornography, homosexual activities, mutilations, and a moral descent into the pits of hell. All are logical conclusions for a person trying to satiate an enslaving lust and relieve a self-gratifying sexual craving. Eventually, any ability to find fulfillment and happiness in a God-ordained marital relationship is lost.

But this is not the only obvious addiction that Satan offers us. Over the last few years, our society has been bombarded with technological toys and has embraced once taboo forms of entertainment, like gambling. Addiction to these things has resulted as well. Paul warned, "Therefore do not let sin reign in your mortal body that you should obey its lusts" (Romans 6:12). If the misuse of anything is sin, and sin destroys us, then this is especially true of things designed as evil, like gambling. "All things are lawful to me, but not all things are profitable. All things are lawful for me, but I will not be mastered by anything" (I Corinthians 6:12).

A person really only has two options, they can chose sin, falsely believing they are serving themselves, or they can serve God and do what truly fulfills them. "But now having been set free from sin and enslaved to God, you derive your benefit, resulting in sanctification, and the outcome, eternal life" (Romans 6:22). God promises to give us true happiness and satisfy us if we let Him. "And I will fill the soul of the priests with abundance. And My people shall be satisfied with My goodness, declares the Lord" (Jeremiah 31:14).

Satan wants us to believe that there is a third option: self. He convinced Eve, in this way, to forsake her liberty in God for the bondage of sin. When we chose God instead, becoming a servant of Christ, we are freed from, and die to, the world of false hopes and failed promises. We're freed from the natural forces (elemental spirits of the universe), spirits, and powers of darkness, which not only brought creation under a curse, but would love nothing better than to destroy us with it. We're warned not to return or resubmit to their lures to return us to slavery. "If you have died with Christ to the elementary principles (spirits) of the world, why, as if you were living in the world do you submit?" (Colossians 2:20).

These elemental spirits of the universe have been variously identified, but generically, they are the force behind any false religious concepts, Judaism included. This takes in all the fallen angels, even those that claim to be neutral. These are the ones Wicca (or the ancient craft of the wise), witches, spiritists, and the like claim their powers from. This is the force Sir Alfred Wallace recognized in his concept of evolution. This is one type of false wisdom in James 3:15: "This wisdom is not that which comes down from above, but is earthly, natural [elemental spirits], devilish." According to Jason Michaels in *The Devil Is Alive And Well And Living In America Today*, Wicca believes the source of good and evil, in harmony with these elemental spirits, lies within each individual.[26] Satan again wants to create an illusion that there's a third pathway, one of self, between the opposites of God and His angels and the hosts of darkness. This attempt is to fool man into believing he can control his own destiny, without being in either camp, like in the song "I Did It My Way," but once again, there is no third way, or "Ego is on the throne." We either chose life in Jesus or death in sin.

---

[26] Jason Michaels, The Devil Is Alive And Well And Living In America Today, (Award Books, 1973), 79.

The Wicca way is no more one of liberty than is the Jewish pursuit of salvation by merit or in keeping the Law of Moses. Their way is a mirror image from darkness, of a demonic standard of merit, substituting for God's law a set of standards as to how and when it is permissible to commit certain sins. A study of their beliefs would reveal this, but this isn't recommended as theirs were the kind of books that were burned in Ephesus (Acts 19:18,19). Of both them and Judaism, Paul writes, "So also we, when we were children [under the Law], were held in bondage under the elemental things of the world" (Galatians 4:3). God sent Jesus to redeem those under the Law; as seen in verses 4 and 5. There's no such thing as a good spiritual death. No matter which of Satan's pathways one chooses, to die on, they still die. What matters is life in Christ.

There's within us all a tendency for selfishness. God created part of this for self-preservation or programmed into us a survival instinct. We wouldn't live long without it. Along with this is our ingrained self-awareness and self-knowledge. Whatever thought patterns one may or may not have prior to birth, we are all born with knowledge of little but ourselves. We are the focus of our own private universe and understand, outside of God's innate knowledge, next to nothing about anything else. Our first contact is with a doctor, midwife, parent, or any other person sharing in our birth. This can only be processed in our brains as to how they relate to us. The lights, sounds, and colors are all new, but again, our focus is on ourselves.

A newborn quickly learns how to get attention by crying. They also learn about Mommy, Daddy, and other family members and of their differences. In time, they begin to think beyond a world of "everyone versus me." Through interaction, babies learn to feel more secure around certain people, especially Mommy, and apprehensive about others outside of familiar circles. A good definition of this kind of self-focus is immaturity, which a child should grow out of as they learn to love. "When I was a child. I used to speak as a child, think as a child, reason as a child; when I became a man, I did away with childish things" (I Corinthians 13:11). The more emotionally mature a person is, the easier the transition is from self-love to God's version of love. The command "You shall love your neighbor as yourself" (Mark 12:31) always begins with these first relationships and so does one's ease in coming to love and trust God.

Selfishness of another kind can short circuit into a perpetual drive to get one's own way. This is the antithesis of the love for others that God calls us to; "[Love] does not seek its own" (I Corinthians 13:5). This results when circles of love or relationships fail to properly develop or a person hasn't learned the joy of making other people happy. Sadly, this fits well in our society. This self-centeredness always wants to put self first: have the best house, job, and lover. This love always demands the biggest piece of the world's pie. The phrase "Look out for number one" reflects this lifestyle, as does the term "self serving." Loyalty, honor, and devotion apply only as long as self first, is honored. Depending on social class or the level of aggressiveness involved, a number of traits or manifestations describe such a person. Among them are: bossy, manipulative, conniving, backstabbing, boastful, envious, suspicious, and almost always, very lonely inside.

Rules apply only as long as they benefit the self-serving aims of this person. If not, they will meticulously search for any possible escape clause. Nabal serves as an example. "Who is David? And who is the son of Jesse? There are many servants today who are each breaking away from their masters. Shall I then take my bread and my water and my meat that I have slaughtered for my shearers, and give it to men whose origin I do not know?" (1 Samuel 25:10,11). Thus, Nabal responded to both the benevolent kindness of David and the Old Testament rules of hospitality. If not for his wife, Abigail, David, as well, would have sinned in response through self-vindication: by killing him.

The selfish seeking for one's own way, or destiny, isn't limited to individuals; it can control whole nations. "And they said to one another, 'Come, let us make bricks and burn them thoroughly.' And they used brick for stone, and they used tar for mortar. And they said, 'Come, let us build for ourselves a city, and a tower whose top will reach into heaven, and let us make for ourselves a name; lest we be scattered abroad over the face of the whole earth' (Genesis 11:3,4). The post-flood world started early to chart a destiny based on the power of man, or humanism. This belief system that claims to be a New Age, modern alternative to Christianity, predates it by at least three millennia. All that is new about selfishness as seen in humanism is the souls it is deceiving.

History is a soap opera of the collective force of self-determination and the selfishness of nations. The words imperialism, colonialism, militarism, manifest destiny, and empire building are just a few that reflect on the ambitions of nations and people groups. Hearts that are far away from God only stoke such ambition. Barbara Tuchman, in *The Proud Tower*, offers a portrait of a world in the generation that led up to World War I: "As faith in God retreated before the advance of science, love of country began to fill the empty spaces of the heart. Nationalism absorbed the strength once belonging to religion."[27] We all know the rest of the story, as two world wars tore apart a world set on romanticism. This belief, "romanticism," saw only a gilded destiny for mankind as a new age of happiness for a new man was right around the corner. In this evolutionistic belief, the very things that promised life and happiness instead brought misery and death.

Today, under the banners of rationalism and relativism, the humanist vision of a glorious future through man's charting his own destiny has joined with the elemental spirits of the universe. The result has proved devastating to the fabric of all we hold dear. One is the destruction of the family through the claimed irrelevance of Biblical morality.

We are taught that since sex is only natural, lust and permissiveness are healthy expressions of our basic instincts, but how they can explain homosexuality as among these natural urges is baffling. Paul gives a better one. "For this reason [rejecting God] God gave them over to degrading passions; for their women exchanged the natural function for that which is unnatural, and in the same way also the men abandoned the natural function of the woman and burned in their desire toward one another" (Romans 1:26,27), but since all desires of the flesh are labeled as natural and normal, all who dare to oppose this new humanist dogma are labeled as controversial, extremist, bigoted, or fanatic.

As history shows, though, theirs has been the way of untold misery and emptiness. The sacrifice of relationships for self destroys our ability to properly relate to one another. Homosexuality is one that shows how this affects the world on a national, as well as a personal level. In 334 BC, Alexander the Great (356-323 BC) set out to conquer the known world with his bisexual army. He masterfully succeeded, but before his dead body was even cold, his empire was already splintered into four parts. Such selfishness gratification only brings division, loneliness, and discord.

[27]  Barbara Tuchman, The Proud Tower, (Bantam Books, The Macmillian Company, 1966), 292.

Christians usually don't abandon themselves to the worldview of "I did it my way," but we do experiment. We tend to be refined sinners. While not abandoning ourselves to the elemental spirits of the universe, we try to be discreet by staying two steps behind the world. One area many have become involved with is the mind-control meditation based on Eastern religious models. There's nothing wrong with meditation in itself, it is an ingredient in prayer, can focus devotion, aid relaxation, and promote mental health, but if we truly wish to benefit ourselves, seek tranquility in the Lord, and ease our minds, prudence in using the right pathway is essential.

The paths of the Eastern religions are definitely not the right ones. Hinayana Buddhism, for example, teaches that the underlying basis of redemption is something each person must work out for themselves. We're each responsible to attain our own salvation or save ourselves. Zen Buddhism's focus is totally inward; truth and fulfillment come through experiences and self-awareness. Hinduism adds to this idea that one can only understand and unite with all creation by knowing themselves. Transcendental Meditation is the pathway to serenity, often through the repetitive chanting of a single phrase or word. Self-awareness comes through self-focus, and this, they claim, assures them they are at least on the pathway to Nirvana. If it isn't essential for God to be involved in achieving fulfillment and salvation, the pathway to finding these outside of Jesus becomes the focus. This helps to explain the popularity of the numerous and varied forms these channels, or means, of meditation are practiced today. This also shows why these alternative ways to tranquility are something a Christian should avoid.

While it is impossible to be genuinely happy outside of Jesus, and people have been trying, without success, to do this for millennia, we keep buying the same old deception. All too often, these pathways have even deceived the elect into believing in "my way," or any other pathway outside of Jesus, to Nirvana, Heaven, Paradise, or whatever else we want to label eternity. Despite Biblical assertions, the empty tomb, and the proofs in history that Jesus is the only way to God, the Church no longer believes this. Even among evangelical Christians, according to a Pew Forum Religion and Public Life poll in 2008, 57 percent won't say absolutely that

Jesus is the only way to Heaven.[28] There is zero hope of ever convincing the world on this issue when the Church herself is not settled.

Christian desire to do it "my way" isn't limited to just questioning as to whether Jesus is the only way. Once this foundational truth goes, the entire Bible is up for revision, but it is the most critical issue. The whole reason it has become a question to begin with is because of our desire to chart our own destiny and still get to Heaven. As previously stated, a major cause of denominationalism lies in our desire to have it both ways. This reflects our self-imposed ignorance of the heart of God and His will for us. This is really not different than the Jewish leadership's rejection, "Those of the Pharisees who were with Him heard these things, and said to Him, 'We are not blind too, are we?' Jesus said to them, 'If you were blind, you would have no sin; but since you say, 'We see', your sin remains'" (John 9:40,41). This willful blindness breaks the heart of God in many ways.

Another casualty of "my way" is unity. "And the glory which Thou hast given Me I have given them; that they may be one, just as we are one; I in them, and Thou in Me that they may be perfected in unity, that this world may know that Thou didst send Me" (John 17:22,23). Until and unless we are willing to totally forsake self and the lie that we can do it our way, we disrespect and disobey the One we claim to be worshipping. At what point salvation is lost through stubborn disobedience is something I pray none of us will ever learn by experience.

Thankfully, God is a merciful god. "Just as a father has compassion on his children, so the Lord has compassion on those who fear Him. For He knows our frame; He is mindful that we are but dust" (Psalms 103:13,14). God has, to a certain degree, demonstrated a willingness to accept us where we are, and if we cry out to Him with a whole heart, He will take us to where we need to be. Jesus lived this mercy as He showed over and over.

One example was in Jericho as He headed to Jerusalem to die. Zaccheus, a rich and hated tax collector lived there. He sought Jesus out of the guilt and emptiness in his heart, which led him to climb a tree. Depending on his age and physical strength, this may have been a real challenge in itself, and a risky one at that. "And when Jesus came to the place, He looked up

---

[28] "Many Americans Say Other Faiths Can Lead to Eternal Life," Pew Forum on Religion & Public Life, http://pewresearch.org/pubs/1062/manyamericans-say-other-faiths-can-lead-to-eternal-life.

and said to him, 'Zaccheus, hurry And Come down, for today I must stay at your house'" (Luke 19:5). He surrendered all to Jesus, giving half of all he had to the poor, and went beyond any legal demands on repayment for any past sin of overcharging in the performance of his job. His showed true repentance and submission to doing it God's way. Jesus responded, "Today salvation has come to this house" (verse 9).

We are to be sternly admonished against deliberately presuming on God's mercy. "Or do you think lightly of the riches of His kindness and forbearance and patience, not knowing that the kindness of God leads you to repentance?" (Romans 2:4). Yet God often takes the messes that man gives Him in hopes of bringing repentance and restoration.

If God does accept some relaxing of the rules on some occasions, it is as He, and not we see fit. If we're truly seeking the heart of God, we'll seek Him in His way as He calls us to do. Two gardens have been foundational to our human condition. The first was the Garden of Eden. With the love, perfection, and order around them, the first couple was also blessed with the very presence of God. They also were given free will and a choice. In Genesis 3:6,7, the choice to sin, was, in essence, "Not Thy will but my, or our, will be done." As a result, the world will never again be the same. Selfishness brought only grief, hostility, emptiness, and both physical and spiritual death.

The second garden was the rougher, stony, steeply hilled one of Gethsemane. In a world darkened by discord, injustice, hate, and sin, Jesus too, had a choice. He asked God about any possible plan-B, other than the one of suffering and humiliating death. "My Father, if it is possible, let this cup pass from Me" (Matthew 26:39). In this critical hour, He put all aside and, rather than "my way," responded to God, "Yet not as I will, but as Thou wilt" (verse 39). While the first garden was beautiful, it brought death. The second was scarred by man's sin, but it brought life. Our salvation is in submitting to God's way.

Theologians over the years have debated why God planned for the human race as He did. There can be no question that He knew sin was going to happen. In Revelation 13:8, the original language reads, "...The Lamb who has been slain from the foundation of the world." Why would God allow the fall, and ordain so much suffering, sin, and death? First of all, God had already faced one rebellion, that of Satan and all the hosts of darkness. Heaven was tainted and corrupted by sin. Revelation 21:1 shows this purged out by the renewing, or creation, of a new one. God didn't want another rebellion, this first one had to break His heart as well as destroy His home.

God created a universe for man, and gave him choices: either God's way or "my way." He warned Adam, "From any tree of the garden you may eat freely, but from the Tree of the Knowledge of Good and Evil you shall not eat, for in the day that you eat from it you shall surly die" (Genesis 2:16,17). The second ties into this, we have a choice to return. God didn't want to force us to worship; He wanted us to choose Him. Life here is a testing ground, not an end unto itself, and God's yearning is for us to come to love Him. Human history is a chronicle of God's calling to our hearts.

There is one more reason for God having allowed the fall. If Adam and Eve had never sinned, and stayed in the garden, they would never have known the fullness of God's love, blessing, and power. They would never have really known to what depths that love would go or the greatness of His mercy and forgiveness (John 3:16). Character is never proved when things are going good; it's when there are trials and difficulties in life that we are shown what we are really made of and who God really is. "He made Him who knew no sin to be sin" (II Corinthians 5:21). God loves us so much that He gave us all He had to give. All He asks of us is for us to choose His way over our way. Our eternity depends on how we answer Him.

# XV

## GOD WILL MAKE AN EXCEPTION FOR ME

*"Therefore you are without excuse, every man of you who passes judgment, for in that you judge another, you condemn yourself, for you who judge practice the same things."*

—Romans 2:1

There are several things about our modem entertainment culture that are obvious, especially with TV, movies, and the lifestyles of celebrities. The most easily observed, of course, is the moral cesspool that so much of it portrays. Another is the constant drumbeat of humanistic beliefs and values. If nothing else, there is endless base language, immoral situations, attacks on conservative values, and the swipes taken at Christians and their God. There is another value that is a bit subtler, as well, except in the tabloid accounts of celebrity lifestyles. Popular people often feel that rules apply to every one but them. They are an exception. In movies or TV, the hero (especially) can flaunt rules at will. TV private eyes, lawyers, and police are among the worst. Their activities frequently skirt the law and, at the least, are down right unethical. How many laws are violated in a single high-speed chase? But the hero never gets in trouble for it.

This seeps into society at large. Ever watch kids play while mimicking their favorite movie star, program, or movie? I remember when I was young; the 1960s TV show "Combat" was one of my favorites. In one episode, Sgt. "Chip" Sanders, while in battle, lit a cigarette and flipped the burning match to the ground. The next day, I played army men with friends. I had a candy cigarette in my mouth and tried the same stunt. Not only did my cigarette not light, my neighbor let me know, in no uncertain terms, what he thought of my flipping a burning match in his yard. He also upbraided me for having matches at my age to begin with.

It's not so amusing to see adults act the same way. Try driving down a road where you have the right of way. Even if your police department is on the ball, there will still probably be at least one occasion where some one pulls out in front of you, slides up through a stop sign to your street, or fails to stop at all. If there is a line at a convenience store that can be circumvented, there's always one person who will try to sneak past everyone else. The same actions apply to merge lanes or left and right turn lanes on streets and highways, there's always someone who thinks they're special.

This is nothing new or limited to our culture. One of the mission stations of the Norwegian Lutheran Church in the early nineteenth-century found an intriguing challenge in working among the Zulus they sought to evangelize. For decades, there were few legitimate converts. The Zulu leadership discovered, as the Frankish and German chieftains had a millennia and a half before, that Christianity changed lives. It led to divided loyalties for a Christian between Jesus and their chief. In 1873, then Chief Cetchwayo outlawed baptism for all his warriors on the pain of death. One of them, Maqhamuseh Khanlye, a warrior in his sixties, wanted to convert. The missionaries told him that the only way to be a Christian was to be baptized; there was no compromise. Over several years, he argued that a special exemption be made for him. Since salvation was by faith, and he believed in Jesus, he should be accepted as a Christian, and in so doing, he could circumvent the edict and be one without fear of death.

White Europeans aren't the only ones having problems with equality. The human race has more in common with itself than any of us wants to admit. We all want rules that are just for ourselves, we all look down on at least some of those not in our racial or cultural group. Even within our groups, we want to have an exception clause just for us; the more money or power we have, the more we expect this. Like the old credit card logo, "Class has privileges."

Power and popularity also are a motivation for exception clause religion. W. C. Fields (1879-1946) was by any modern standard a highly successful actor and comedian. In an eight-year period just before World War II, he starred in eight major movies. He also lived life his way and made no effort to hide this. On his deathbed, he requested that a Bible be brought to him. He believed that for a man as popular and successful as he was, there had to be an escape clause in there somewhere. Another man who felt power had its privileges was, take your pick, Saul, David, Solomon, and many other kings, Jewish or not. At least this was one sin that didn't affect the Greeks as badly as it did the Jews.

Saul is the first on our list. "So Saul said, 'Bring to me the burnt offering and the peace offering.' And he offered the burnt offering. And it came about that as soon as he had finished offering the burnt offering, that behold Samuel came; and Saul went out to meet him and greet him" (I Samuel 13:9,10). Saul was troubled because Samuel, the priest, wasn't there by the appointed time, and his army was deserting. Since he was king over the army and people of God, executive privilege must apply. He applied situation ethics by intruding into the priesthood and, by rights, deserved death (Numbers 18:7). But being an expert in the blame game, he tried to pass it off on Samuel for being late.

David's sins, or at least some of them, were, in his opinion, covered by executive privileges. Later in life, he succumbed to the sin of taking a census of his potential army: all the male population old enough to fight in battle (II Samuel 24:1-9). He realized his sin, maybe he read Deuteronomy 17:14-20, and saw that his trust wasn't in God but in his army. His heart turned, and he accepted that with special privilege comes a special accounting and responsibility. "Then David spoke to the Lord when he saw the angel who was striking down the people, and said, 'Behold, it is I who have sinned, and it is I who have done wrong; but these sheep, what have they done? Please let Thy hand be against me and my father's house" (I Samuel 24:17).

Then there was Solomon. The command of Deuteronomy 17:14-20, which God gave to Israel and her kings, is the closest thing to a Constitutional Monarchy to be found in the Old Testament era. God prohibited the king from building a large standing army, chariot, or cavalry force. He also wasn't to amass a huge fortune or make a legacy of personal wealth, neither was he to have a huge harem and especially not one of foreign, idolatrous women. This most critical prohibition wasn't just for the king; it was for all Israel. Solomon confessed, in Ecclesiastes 2:10, "And all that my eyes desired I did not refuse them. I did not withhold my heart from any pleasure." His army included fourteen hundred chariots and twelve thousand horsemen. During one year alone in his reign, he received for himself 929,000 (by one measure of the talent) ounces of gold plus silver, gems, and other wealth. Beginning with his marriage alliance and the taking of Pharaoh's daughter, a number of foreign, idolatrous wives turned his heart away from God. His total harem was seven hundred wives and three hundred concubines. Many Bible scholars question whether he ever fully returned to the Lord.

Today, many people have come up with their own exception clauses to escape judgment. One scheme is based on the sheer weight of numbers involved. With all the tens of billions of people since Adam and Eve, the numbers are indeed immense. Some feel that there is no way God could possibly keep track of them all, and they will sneak in. In 1983, one man I witnessed to actually was so brash as to claim he would get into heaven that way. This, too, isn't a novel concept.

In Isaiah 29:15, it says, "Woe to those who deeply hide their plans from the Lord, and whose deeds are done in a dark place, and they say, 'Who sees us?' or 'Who knows us?'" Now, a person might be able to hide something from a friend, or even from a spouse, one might even fool their mother, but no one will hide from God. "Even the darkness is not dark to Thee" (Psalms 139:12). Before someone thinks they can hide from God, they should consider this fact: God created all the stars, billions of them in each of billions of galaxies. The number could well exceed ten sextillion, or one followed by twenty-two zeros. Yet "He gives names to all of them" (Psalms 147:4). This amounts to about ten billion stars for every person who has ever lived. God will have no problem keeping track of us.

The Chinese philosopher Confucius (551-479 BC) is credited with another argument for a special exception clause to escape accountability for one's actions. He asserted that a person is only guilty if they are caught. Remember the business ethic "Don't get caught?" This was quite similar to ancient Sparta where deception, thievery, and rape were actually encouraged, so long as the offender didn't get caught, as a means of building character in a man. Being special was measured by how much they could get away with. This actually put them well on the way to becoming a hero. This belief has found a large following among humanists and, unfortunately, has even made its way into the Church, but again, this ancient, humanist accepted belief is totally untrue.

"For the eyes of the Lord move to and fro throughout the earth" (II Chronicles 16:9). Again, God reminds us of His omnipresence. "For My eyes are on all their ways; they are not hidden from My face" (Jeremiah 16:17). God knows all; hiding didn't work for Adam and Eve, even though they assumed no one was watching, and neither has anyone else ever gotten special treatment from trying to hide from God. We become guilty, not because we are caught, but because sin is written on our hearts. It is kind of like Edgar Allen Poe's *The Telltale Heart*, our guilt will always give us away, and sin kills. "The person who sins will die" (Ezekiel 18:20). There's no heroism in sin and no escape because our deeds are hidden. There is only the reality of guilt and accountability.

Among Christians, there's often a hope beyond reality for God's unconditional compassion and for a special escape clause. As, Origen proposed, they hope that God won't allow any of His creation to perish. First Timothy 2:4 says: "Who (God) desires all men to be saved and to come to the knowledge of the truth." This word "desires" is the strongest in the Greek language for will or intent. It's also true that God has stacked the deck in our favor. He meets us where we are to take us to where we need to be, as Jesus did with Peter after His own death, burial, and resurrection.

During the night of His betrayal, Peter, in his own strength, almost vowed to die with Jesus. "But Peter kept saying insistently, 'Even if I have to die with you I will not deny You" (Mark 14:31). He strove to live up to those words, even cutting off the High Priest's slave, Malchus' ear (John 18:10). But a few hours later, still in his own strength, he denied Jesus three times before the cock crowed twice (Mark 14:30). "But he began to curse and swear, 'I do not know this man you are talking about'" (Mark 14:71). He was a broken man.

Over the next six weeks, Jesus engaged in a rebuilding project. This culminated in an encounter by the Sea of Galilee. Recorded in John 21:1-14, Jesus began by replicating a miracle He had done when He first called

Peter to His group three and a half years earlier. Jesus touched a chord in Peter's heart in this. As they were eating, Jesus built upon it.

"'Simon, son of John, do you love [agape] Me more than these?' He [Peter] said to Him, 'Yes Lord, You know that I love [phileo] you'" (verse 15). Jesus used the word for a totally self-sacrificing love. Peter wasn't sure of himself; having failed so miserably in his own strength. He told Jesus that he loved Him as a dear friend. He could, at that moment, promise no more. Jesus repeated the same question in verse 16, and Peter answers as he had before. But the third time Jesus asked, "Simon, son of John do you love [phileo] Me?" (verse 17). In Jesus's third request of Peter, He meets him where he is. Jesus cut a special grace for him right out of the heart of God.

Years ago, in a supervisory training program, the instructor reminded us of an old pat response bosses usually gave to employee requests for special favors. The worker would be told, "I [boss] don't treat anyone special." We were challenged to take a new attitude of: "I treat everyone special." The point was to impress upon the employee their worth, that they were important to the company. This is a good analogy of God's love for us and His desire that none be lost. "What man among you, if he has one hundred sheep and has lost one of them, does not leave the ninety-nine in the open pasture and go after the one which is lost until he finds it?" (Luke 15:4). We are special to God; more than just an employee in His kingdom, we are His special family and creation.

God loves each of us in a unique and special way. There is a hint of this in Revelation 2:17, "I will give him a white stone, and a new name written on that stone which no one knows but he who receives it." In the Jewish world, there was a special significance involved in naming a child. Much of this is lost in our culture, but among other things, it was a statement of uniqueness in the eyes of the parents. So also is God's love for every one of us, saved or unsaved. "As I live! Declares the Lord God, 'I take no pleasure in the death of the wicked, but rather that the wicked turn from his way and live'" (Ezekiel 33:11). God has gone far beyond doing all that is needful to provide for our salvation; this includes His redemptive grace and forgiveness, "Which He lavished upon us" (Ephesians 1:8). His love and specialness isn't always shown in ways we want Him to, though. God always loves, but He doesn't always save in ways we think He should.

First of all, the fires of hell are eternal. "And the devil who deceived them was thrown into the lake of fire and brimstone, where the beast and the false prophet are also; and they were tormented day and night for ever and ever" (Revelation 20:10). God didn't intend for any human being to perish, but neither does He force salvation on us contrary to our wills, if we refuse to serve and obey Him. "Then He will also say to those on his left, 'Depart from Me, accursed ones into the eternal fire which has been prepared for the devil and his angels" (Matthew 25:41). No matter what Origen wanted, God said the fire is eternal. Part of this fire will be the regret that the lost feel for having rejected God.

This doesn't in the least diminish the special love God has for each of us, though. He even allowed His own Son to experience hell in our place. "And about the ninth hour Jesus cried out with a loud voice, saying, 'Eli Eli lama sabachthani?' that is, 'My God My God why hast Thou forsaken Me?'" (Matthew 27:46). God turned His back on His very own Son to save us from death, but if there were no consequence for doing evil, there would be no reason to seek His grace. Because there is a consequence, God can save us from it.

"I am the Good Shepherd; the Good Shepherd lays down His life for the sheep" (John10:11). When we abide with Him, we remain part of His fold. God's special love shows in His bringing back the stray to that fold. When a shepherd had a sheep with a particular problem of remaining in the fold, he'd break one of its legs. He then would carry it around his neck, taking it off only to graze and for water. This special treatment may not seem so special, but in this way, the sheep bonded with the shepherd.

In the book of Hosea, God pictured His love in another illustration. "The Lord said to Hosea, 'Go take to yourself a wife of harlotry, and have children of harlotry; for the land commits flagrant harlotry, forsaking the Lord'" (Hosea 1:2). God later told him to hedge up Gomer, his wayward wife (Hosea 2:6), in hopes of instilling a bonding between her and her husband. So God appealed to Samaria in the same fashion, by separating her from the sinful nations around her.

In the case of Saul (Paul), God used this same love to bring him closer to His heart. After his conversion, Paul spent three years in the wilderness with God (Galatians 1:17,18). This was for divine inspiration, as well, as Jesus was revealed over this time. This filling with Jesus helped pull him away from the attachments of his past life with all its temptations to compromise or reject the Lord. His extraordinary ministry owes itself; to a large degree, to this deep bonding.

When the average person thinks about being treated in a special way, this isn't what comes to mind. Instead, most of us are looking for a special sign, blessing, or a personal miracle. Rarely does God work in this way, to a large degree, because of our nature. If God gave each of us ten million dollars upon our conversion, might we not be tempted to focus on the gift more than the giver? And could this gift be viewed more as an entitlement than a call to service? Who would want to leave that kind of money behind to go serve in Somalia? The Rich Young Ruler answered this one for us: next to nobody. The real gift is salvation itself, but this isn't to say we should never pray for material blessings or physical deliverance. We just need to keep it in perspective of the real gift.

Often, special favor or deliverance is requested as part of the conversion process. This is for no other reason than the reality that, quite often, we feel no particular need for the Lord when all is going well. Foxhole conversions fit this pattern. A soldier in a serious situation will make a covenant, or commitment, to God in exchange for physical deliverance.

Foxhole commitments don't always result in deliverance from death. Sometimes it is a calling to a personal sacrifice to save others. "And Samson said, 'Let me die with the Philistines!' And he bent with all his might so that the house fell on the lords and all the people who were in it" (Judges 16:30). While many today might associate his role with that of a suicide bomber, in his faith to God, he was an Old Testament hero whose name is listed in the roll call of the righteous (Hebrews 11:32-34), None the less, the actions of modern suicide bombers led to several accounts of God's deliverance on September 11, 2001.

On that day, many received a special deliverance, in some cases, almost miraculously. In a number of cases, people who worked in the offices of the World Trade Center were prevented, in one way or another, from getting to their jobs that day. There have been several amazing testimonials. Others have literally incredible stories of being saved from the buildings, themselves. The dual accounts of two police officers, John McLoughlin and William Jimeno, trapped in freight elevators for thirteen and twenty-two hours respectively are almost miraculous. Their stories made it into the movie "World Trade Center," 2006, by Oliver Stone.

There's a saying that there is no such thing as a foxhole atheist. Whether or not this is true, there is something about a crisis or a calamity, whether self inflicted or not, that leads at least most of us to pray. The prayer is often like this. "God, if you get me out of this intact I will _____ (fill in the blank) in return for You." Very often, this prayer goes up when a person meets the consequences of a bad life decision. It may be a teenage girl or young woman who has allowed her morals to slip. She bargains with God to avoid an unwanted pregnancy. Sometimes the answer isn't what they want it to be. It would be safe to assume that at least Bathsheba, and probably David, offered such a prayer after David's indiscretion. When God said, "No," David opted for plan-B and answered it his way. In so doing, he missed an opportunity to receive a special blessing in God's working through his sin.

God isn't obligated to deliver us from the consequences of our sins. If He were, then all fear of them; either physically or spiritually, would vanish. If our actions got us into trouble, all we would have to do is hit a reset button and go on. Adam and Eve would have appreciated this. So would Moses, "'Listen now, you rebels; shall we bring forth water for you out of this rock?' Then Moses lifted up his hand and struck the rock twice with his rod; and water came forth abundantly, and the congregation and their beasts drank" (Numbers 20:11,12). If Moses had been given this second chance, the odds are he would have obeyed God that time and told the rock, instead of smiting it, given God the glory, and entered the Promised Land, but what would he have learned?

If all it took when we got into a jam were to push a reset button, would we grow? How long would it be before some aggressive opportunist rationalized through it all and figured out, via the reset button, just how close they could come to the consequences of sin and not get caught, or how much consequence they were willing to accept in exchange for as much of the world as possible? Scripture tells us that God isn't a respecter of persons (shows no favoritism), as is seen in Acts 10:34 and Ephesians 6:9. If He gave some this privilege, He would have to do it for all. Imagine the mess created if everyone were forever punching these buttons. Instead, God's special treatment allows us to grow through a sin or crisis. If the girl with this unplanned pregnancy repents and obeys God, who knows what her child's future might be? Seeing God's love reflected in their mother, the child might grow up to be a missionary.

Or what about a person who, while in a drunken state, takes a one ton bullet out on the road and crashes it into a family in another vehicle? In our hearts, all of us might long for a reset button, especially in the face of the shattered future of an innocent child. First of all, however, choices have consequences, and sin causes death. If all choices that caused this could be reset, what fear would there be in bad choices? Secondly, if the drunk faces up to the realities of their deeds, they can find a meaning and purpose in life they otherwise wouldn't know, even if it's from a prison cell for the rest of their lives. A reset button could never give this or the character that comes from it.

It's often through self-inflicted tragedy that we grow and come to fully understand God's love for us and of His offer of saving grace. Only when we realize how bad we are and the damage sin causes that we really understand how good God is. When we see ourselves for what we really are, we stop employing the victim mentality and take responsibility. We stop crying for others to sympathize in our weaknesses, understand, and help us. Instead, when we accept what God can do for us, we begin to look for ways to sympathize with, understand, and help others.

Still, if a survey were taken of Christians, we all pray for special treatment and for miracles or blessings for either our loved ones or ourselves. Maybe we haven't really come to understand what God has done for us. Once again, this isn't to say we shouldn't pray for His blessing. To the contrary, He wants us to cry to Him, and Him alone, for deliverance. "Preserve me, O God, for I take refuge in Thee. I said to the Lord, 'Thou are my Lord; I have no good besides Thee'" (Psalms 16:1,2). He promises for our needs to be met, and He wills for our genuine happiness, both physically and spiritually. He also wants us to fully mature and be equipped for the work of His service. As humans, though, we see happiness in a different dimension and seek something special, just for us. This is an equal opportunity desire not limited to Christians. Muslims are the same way; they put great faith in dreams and feel that a special revelation is needed before they make a major decision. What we tend to forget though, is that the same Jesus who miraculously gave sight to the blind (John 9:1-11) also made seeing eyes blind (Acts 13:8-11). Be careful what you pray for; when you get it, the answer might not be what you were expecting.

God doesn't just want for us to be blessed, He wants us also to be a blessing. There is definitely a comfort and warm assurance that comes from receiving a personal blessing from God. There's also a warm comfort that comes in sharing it with others. This often provides an opportunity for witness. One of the greatest of these was the Gadarene demoniac. "Go home to your people and report to them what great things the Lord has done for you, and how He has mercy on you" (Mark 5:19). There comes a fulfillment to our purpose of being and a feeling of value that comes by being of service to someone else. Are we more inclined to pray, "Bless me," or, "Make me a blessing"? When God made a special exception for Paul, he was "A chosen instrument of Mine, to bear My name before the Gentiles and kings" (Acts 9:15). Special treatment, privilege, or exceptions carries with it, as well, a special responsibility and accounting.

Maqhamaseh Khanlye", the Zulu warrior who sought that special deal, continued in his own personal struggle. For the years between 1873 and 1877, he would enter a religious class only to drop out again. Finally, he stopped his struggle with Jesus and the missionaries and committed to be baptized and follow Jesus. On March 9, 1877, Chief Cetchwayo had him martyred. As a, then, seventy-year-old man, his value to anyone seemed very limited, but in his death, it was priceless. The door to the Zulu people that seemed forever locked was opened, and the conversion of the whole nation followed. While much of it remains marginal, estimates today show that nearly eighty percent of the Zulu are Christian. God gave Maqhamusela a special blessing and blessed others through him.

In our dealing with God, sometimes we forget just who is in charge. We are the servant, or the inferior, and He is the Creator, or the superior. He sets the rules standards, the order of our lives, and what the conditions and exceptions will be. If He chooses to bargain with us, it is on His terms. In Genesis 18 is the account of Abraham and his conversation with three heavenly visitors. In this encounter, they share with him God's intent to destroy Sodom (and Gomorrah) for their wickedness. Abraham asks, "Wilt Thou indeed sweep away the righteous with the wicked?" (verse 23). God chose to bargain with him, but in his bargaining with God, Abraham didn't ask blessing for himself, he was pleading for another or, in this case, his nephew Lot. In return, God came to this promise of mercy, "I will not destroy it on account of the ten" (verse 32). In his plea, Abraham appeals to the nature of God and touches

His heart. For this, and for his faith, he is repeatedly called the friend of God (II Chronicles 20:7, James 2:23, and others). This was in part a fulfillment of God's promise to Abraham years before: "And in you all the families of the earth shall be blessed" (Genesis 12:3).

In the September 11, 2001 terrorist attacks, God blessed some and treated them special by preserving their lives. For others, His special treatment was not in what He did for them but in what He did through them. In their faithful actions, He gave to us a testimony of His love, deliverance, and grace. Theirs was the calling to be that example through courage and sacrifice. United Flight 93 left Newark, New Jersey that fateful morning and was bound for San Francisco International Airport. There were forty-four on-board, four of them were terrorists. In the early stages of the flight, these men seized control of the plane and turned it around. Its new destination was, in all likelihood, either the Capitol Building or the White House in Washington D.C.

By using their cell phones, the other passengers learned that hijacked planes had already been deliberately crashed into the World Trade Center and the Pentagon. Todd Beamer, a Christian, rallied the other passengers, and with the words, "Are you ready? Let's roll," they attacked the terrorists and attempted to storm the pilot's cabin. The terrorists crashed the plane just outside of Shanksville, Pennsylvania, killing all aboard. In the process, many others, and in all probability, numerous national leaders were spared death. For reasons unknown, their plane was chosen but they rose to be the special blessing they were called to be. They left their legacy in the history of our nation.

God may make an exception for us, but if He gives special privilege, makes exceptions, or if He gives someone a special calling, it's to serve His purpose in saving the world. His blessing isn't intended to feather our nests but to further His kingdom. As an admonition, there is one noteworthy case in Scripture where God makes an exception for a person's own benefit. In this case, it was a king. "In those days Hezekiah became mortally ill; and he prayed to the Lord, and the Lord spoke to him and gave him a sign" (II Chronicles 32:24). God granted him an extension of life, but this led to one of the worst kings in Judah's history: Manasseh. Granting this selfish desire led to a curse on many others. As the saying goes, be careful what you pray for.

# XVI

## WHY ME?

*"But Moses said to God, who am I that I should go to Pharaoh,*
*and that I should bring the sons of Israel out of Egypt?"*

—Exodus 3:11

God's calling isn't always met with joy by the one who is being called. Moses shows us a perfect example of this. He was obviously in a groove with where he was in life, or if nothing else, his familiarity with it was far more comfortable with the status quo at his age than to charge off into the great unknown. He had spent approximately the last thirty-nine years of his life in a majestic desert, free from the pressures of city life, herding sheep for his father in law, Jethro (Ruel). He was married to Zipporah and had a son, Gershom. His longings for an unfulfilled destination did show, though, as the name Gershom meant "sojourner." He may have felt distant from God, but his status in that simple society, a loving family, and maybe even servants, was not one he now wanted to give up. He was in a well-established comfort zone.

Moses was also a man with a past. His first roughly forty years of life were spent in a palace, probably in the court of Pharaoh Amenhotep I who reigned from 1524-1503 BC. Queen Hatshepsut (1491-1479 BC) was likely his adoptive mother, and he may well have been heir to the throne, but even in a life of worldly blessing, he was aware of God's presence and his kinship with the Hebrews. "By faith, Moses, when he had grown up, refused to be called the sun of Pharaoh's daughter, choosing rather to endure ill treatment with the people of God than to enjoy the passing pleasures of sin" (Hebrews 11:24,25). We do not know of all the potential political intrigues and undertones, but what we know about Moses was his compassion for his people. Seeing one being abused by an Egyptian overlord, he rose to their defense and killed the Egyptian. As a reward for his righteous zeal he was ratted out by one of his own people to the Egyptians (Exodus 2:14,15). This probably cut him deeper than any whip ever could. All alliances, friendships, or career possibilities were now history, evaporating like water in the desert sun. He was forced to run for his life. Any faith he had in the promise of God to deliver His people was dashed. Now, when God called him to this service, he responded, "God, you want me to deliver Israel?"(Exodus 3:11).

As humans, we have the ability to rise to the highest plane of commitment and zeal for a cause. If our hearts are in it, and the adrenaline is flowing, we will do whatever it takes to see that cause through and, depending on what it is, to die for it if necessary. We may presume that if our cause is just, God and other people will join into it and bring forth the victory, but in our own spirit, without the proper discipline, discretion, and direction that only God provides, we may be acting prematurely or improperly. When things don't happen as planned, or the consequences of our actions result in a severe threat to our well being, it is easy to become disillusioned and give up. Sometimes we even give up on God. This could well have happened to Moses. In his response was a measure of bitterness and despair. Many have lost their faith, or become atheists, over such things.

There have been others who have showed reluctance to the calling of God. Among them was Gideon. The Midianites and Amalekites, desert nomads, had overrun the land of Israel for seven years. In a previous confrontation with these invaders, his brothers died while trying to protect their homes and families. Gideon's community had also suffered greatly, and he had lost any hope he had in God to deliver them. Now, he hid from everyone. This is shown in his actions, but his family was still, to some degree, respected in his community, maybe in part because they had sacrificed in blood for their people, and partly, because they were rich enough to have servants.

The Midianite invasion was the result of sin on the part of Israel. "I am the Lord your God; you shall not fear the gods of the Amorites, in whose land you live. But you have not obeyed Me" (Judges 6:10). Based on Gideon's response to the angel, he gives the appearance of having never heard this message or about this prophet. From his perspective, God had abandoned them, and he now was afraid to trust.

When the angel appeared to him at Ophrah, both his doubts and bitterness poured out. "0 my lord, if the Lord is with us, why then has all this happened to us?" (Judges 6:13). He had to overcome his bitterness, some of which was directed at God. Once again, he had suffered a personal loss, or defeat, while engaged in a perceived rightful cause. The loss of loved ones had seemed senseless, the feeling of abandonment and defeat, and fear for his own safety in a critical hour, have been the reasons why many turned away from God over the millennia. We humans have trouble with any tragedy, often even the ones that are self inflicted consequences of our sin. This is even truer in the case of those like Gideon. They had held true to God in an age of idolatry, and now seemed to be suffering the consequences of someone else's sins. At least today we can comfort ourselves in the knowledge that this is what Jesus did for us; He took the curse of our sins, and at least it is a little easier to bear up for Him when we are following His example. Gideon didn't have this, yet he was able to look beyond his anger and follow God in faithfulness. This he did, even though he was timid and repeatedly needed reassurance. God used him to bring deliverance to his nation and also blessed him with riches. In this case, he received about eighteen hundred ounces of gold as spoil and eternal life.

His ministry as a general was short term, though under his oversight the land had rest for forty years. He was given an opportunity to compromise and extend his ministry beyond God's calling. The people wanted a king, and that would be a heady opportunity for most of us, but his desire was to serve God and was not for his own glory. "I will not rule over you, nor shall my son rule over you; the Lord will rule over you" (Judges 8:23). Sometimes a minister finds success and popularity exhilarating and addicting and does not know when to quit. Gideon didn't have that problem.

Another reluctant follower was Jonah. Unlike Moses and Gideon, he was a prophet during a boom time in his people's history. Under the kingship of Jeroboam II (789-750 BC, plus or minus) Samaria bloomed both in wealth and in territory. Jonah himself was a devoutly patriotic man who wanted this to go on forever. If a song like, "God bless Samaria, land that I love," had been written, he was the kind of person who would have made it famous. He also was keenly aware of the rising power of Assyria (Nineveh). While Assyria had crushed Syria to allow Samaria opportunity to rise to begin with, she was also a grave threat, much like my generation once viewed the Soviet Union.

If Jonah knew of his contemporaries, the prophets Amos and Hosea, it didn't seem to matter. These two spoke of the impending doom of Samaria because of her idolatry, oppression of the poor, and other sins. On the other hand, this may have been a factor in his actions. He may have hoped to somehow alter destiny or to change the course of history by his actions, much as we might feel if we knew of an impending fall of our own nation.

When God called him to go to Nineveh, the capital of Assyria, his rationalizing probably went into overdrive. He knew the nature of God. "For I knew that Thou art a gracious and compassionate God, slow to anger and abundant in loving kindness, and one who relents concerning calamity" (Jonah 4:2). He wanted the hated Assyrians to be destroyed, not spared through their repentance. With a blind eye to his own people's sin, he fled west towards Tarshish, the closest to an exact opposite direction that he could find. When God finally got his attention, and his obedience, He redirected him to a city ready to listen. After three days in a whale belly, sprayed with diluted stomach acid, or hydrochloric acid that functions much like bleach, he was probably a ghostly white. The city repented, and God relented. This made Jonah angry, and in his distress, he cried out for death. Evidently, his wish was soon granted, as there was in Nineveh "Nebi Yunas," or the "Tomb of Jonah," along the Tigris River, near the city wall. Much is open to speculation, but if Jonah had come to love his calling more than his patriotic vision, there is no telling what God's mercies might have accomplished among them. Jesus alluded to this, "The men of Nineveh shall stand up with this generation at the judgment and condemn it because they repented at the preaching of Jonah" (Matthew 12:41).

Following God's calling is not always at the top of our wish lists. Now, if God promised an easy and successful mission in whatever way we were called, and it fit with what we want to do, that might be different, but God's will doesn't always mesh with our personal desires. Like Moses, we all have our comfort zones, and these can be very hard to grow out of. We view His ways through our immature and worldly eyes. While we may look with admiration on those who have followed, we aren't ready to let go of what we want in life when His calling comes our way. We are babes in Christ and still in the flesh. "And I, brethren, could not speak to you as spiritual men, but as to men of flesh, as to babes in Christ" (I Corinthians 3:1).

Some Christians seem to "luck out" and get what are viewed as the easy ministries. They might be a preacher in a growing church with a spiritual board, or theirs could be a calling to a social gospel concern, as in a food kitchen of a relief service to needy people around us, where the rewards of service are seen almost every day. God may allow us to spend most of our lives within our comfort zone, but this is not a given. One thing is for sure, we are never called to live a worldly lifestyle and by worldly standards. Ours is a calling to minister in some way to the saints, and to save the lost. In order to do this, we must leave behind our love for the world and commit wholly to Jesus. God may call us to a mission that meets sinners right where they are. This only underlines our need to leave the world behind us. Sin is always a temptation anyway, but if we still crave the things of worldly fulfillment, it is all the more difficult to untangle others when we inwardly crave to be entwined with them. Without a heart totally set on Jesus, we can easily get sucked in or, at least, prove less than effective in leading them out of sin.

This may be the very ministry God has in mind for some among us. There's great need for those willing to be used of God to help heal broken lives. There are countless worn out prostitutes, druggies, and ex-cons who desperately need some one to care and show them that God loves them. Then there is the mushrooming gay community, the atheists, college elite, abortionists, and environmental activists. We all sometimes forget that just because these people are in an adversarial relationship with us, they still have spiritual needs. Jesus saw people as having greater value than political positions or scruples. "And this woman, a daughter of Abraham as she is, whom Satan has bound for eighteen years, should she not have been released from this bond on the Sabbath Day?" (Luke 13:16). Again, this emphasizes our need for moral maturity; we cannot lead if we, ourselves, are compromised. It's the way of the world that we are leading these out of, and we have God's promise to sustain us. In whatever He calls us to, He is there both ahead of us and within us.

The conversion of Rahab, the prostitute, exemplifies this. "For we have heard how the Lord dried up the water of the Red Sea before you when you came out of Egypt... And when we heard it, our hearts melted and no courage remained in any man any longer because of you; for the Lord your God, He is God in Heaven above and on earth beneath" (Joshua 2:10,11). Rahab was no street prostitute, as we think of today; she was highly esteemed in the Canaanite religion, possibly a high level priestess of Ashtoreth, identified with the planet Venus. Even the king of the city would have respected her. She lived an upper-class life. This is hardly one that we, in our own understanding, would consider a prime candidate for conversion, but God knew different when He sent in the two spies. God never leaves us to go it alone. Even if no one else is called to join us, He always is (Matthew 28:20).

Although He goes ahead of us, He may not be calling us to what we would consider a successful ministry. Sometimes, what we have spent years laboring and praying for only seems to fall apart. Things are not always linear, or upwardly headed, as Isaiah found out. Upon experiencing God's calling, he felt fear and yet expectation, and exhilaration mingled with unworthiness. "Woe is me! For I am ruined [undone]; because I am a man of unclean lips" (Isaiah 6:5). Yet when God put out His challenge, Isaiah answered, "Here am I, send me" (Isaiah 6:8). It was at this point that God gave him the bottom line. "Go, and tell this people: Keep on listening, and do not perceive; keep on looking, but do not understand" (Isaiah 6:9). As for a promising ministry, he was told in verse 11 of Isaiah, "Until cities are devastated and without inhabitant."

In the year of the death of a somewhat God-fearing, but also proud and presumptuous, Uzziah, Isaiah began his ministry. Uzziah's son Jotham, in his reign, attempted to restore righteousness, but he was not totally successful. "Only the high places were not taken away" (II Kings 15:35). After a sixteen-year reign, his evil son Ahaz took over and almost destroyed the kingdom. He abandoned himself first to idolatry and all manner of evil, then he engaged in foolish warfare with Samaria, Edom, and Philistia, made a faithless and costly alliance with Assyria, and turned even more to idolatry as his world crumbled around him. Then came Hezekiah and a spiritual reprieve as he sought God from the heart for most of his reign. This revival and rededication even included many of the Samarians in a joyous Passover celebration (II Chronicles 30:1-27). During his reign, a brutal Assyrian invasion took place that was only ended by divine intervention through a plague, which killed 185,000 soldiers in one night.

This spiritual high was followed by an even deeper low. This moral and spiritual descent into darkness was led by king Manasseh. For half a century, Isaiah had preached, prophesied, and ministered to an on again off again people, but the trend was down as the nation's soul drifted ever farther from God. This king was so vile that he actually erected idols in the very Temple of God (II Chronicles 33:4,5). Isaiah had lived to see the prophesy of God come true, not just in his life but in his death as well. According to tradition, he was martyred under Manasseh by being sawn in two while attempting to hide in a tree.

One can only wonder what it must have felt like each day as he watched evil unfold and ultimately consume his homeland. Did he ever ask of God, "Why me"? He could only grieve as his congregation continued to decline, at least in spirit. Isaiah 17:10 hints at the possibility that some forsook God-worship all together in their abandonment into idolatry, but most held a form of devotion even as they dropped out in spirit. The modern American has nothing on the ancient Jewish nation when it comes to playing church. Their worship centers, as often are ours, were also beset with false prophets and faithless leadership. There were a few high points, like when God's faithful came from Samaria to celebrate the Passover in worship and reconnect with their Judean brothers. But then there was Hezekiah's pride that threatened the kingdom and the evil Manasseh. With each setback, each defeat, he became ever more aware of the coming doom of Judah and of God's impending spiritual judgment. It ceased being an "if," and more and more was a "when." He proved to be an inspiration for those of later ages, however, including ours, today.

In America, this transition has been most evident since about 1960. It was observed years ago, that the great dividing line fell within the 1965-1968 time frame. In 1960, it was fashionable to go to church, but by 1970, it was more fashionable to not.

In 1960, both American political parties, from their leaders on down, sought the direction of God, and at that time, it seemed the Democrats were the closer of the two. Today, only one, the Republicans, do so marginally, and many of them see Christianity as more of an impediment, or even an embarrassment, than an asset to the party. Pleasing God now ranks lower than balanced budget amendments, tax policy, and domestic energy production. From time to time, issues that do touch His heart come up in a positive way, but this is more often novelty than policy. We have fallen a long way since the 1892 declaration that we were a Christian nation in "Church of the Holy Trinity vs. United States."[29]

The growing discord against Christians by our culture has not resulted in great revival, much less even a genuine soul searching by most Christians, to the issues we face. To the contrary, Church membership continues to slide, as does Christian conviction to the Master. At the same time, alternative religious beliefs are exploding. Today, only seventy-six to seventy-eight percent of Americans even identify themselves with Christianity. According to the "American Church Research Project," in 2010, only seventeen percent of us attended church on any given Sunday. Another survey was even more distressing. Only nine percent of us feel that God is the most important thing in our lives. For many of today's preachers sent to battle this apostasy, the question has often been asked, "Why me?"

What none of us can see, however, is the end result of our ministries. We don't know how many people are yet to be saved because of the conviction of an embattled preacher or from the witness of Joe or Jane Christian. Neither did Isaiah. He, like us, couldn't know the effects of his faith on later kings, on Jewish exiles during the Babylonian captivity, or on someone else.

If God allows time to continue, we who are alive now don't know how many future Americans, including our own offspring, will be Christians because of our faithfulness today. How many others in the Third World will be in heaven because we refused to give up, even if we felt defeated in our lifetimes? None of us can see the future or what effect our own personal faithfulness may have. To whatever ministry God has called you to, accept His calling and be faithful. In this God's purposes are fulfilled. "So shall My word be which goes forth from My mouth; it shall not return

---

[29] Dee Wampler, The Myth Of The Separation Between Church And State (Wine Press Publishing, 2002), 83.

to Me empty, but accomplishing whatever I desire, and without succeeding in the matter for which I sent it" (Isaiah 55:11).

There is a feeling of unworthiness that we all have when we are called to Christian service. I feel it right now as I am writing. This is not unique to us; in the Scriptures there are many others who expressed this at the point of their calling. If we don't feel it to some degree, no matter what God calls us to, then we really aren't ready to trust in Him, nor are we able to serve with our whole hearts. When Jesus called Peter, He performed a miracle by causing him and his brother Andrew, and also James and John, to catch a great shoal of fish. Peter was awed in the presence of God and responded accordingly. "Depart from me, for I am a sinful man, O Lord" (Luke 5:8). Standing in the very company of God, with His light upon him, Peter could only see his own spiritual frailty. As we look at Peter, he was hardly the sinful soul that so often comes to mind with sailors. He was no moral reprobate, and neither were the others in his circle. In fact, their spiritual integrity might have served as the glue that kept them together, At least several of them were followers of John the Baptist (John 1:40).

No matter how well anyone feels they've lived their lives, the light of God's glory exposes flaws and weaknesses they never before knew existed. God's word functions in the same way. "For the word of God is living and active and sharper than any two edged sword, and piercing as far as the division of soul and spirit, of both joints and marrow, and able to judge the thoughts and intentions of the heart" (Hebrews 4:12). For we who are of less moral character than Peter, realizing just how far short we've fallen, makes this even more daunting, but this is just the heart, and servant spirit, that Jesus wants.

Unfortunately, many will react to this light in other ways. Adam was all too quick to play the victim card, hiding from God and shifting the blame to someone else for his own failure. Much of the Jewish leadership tried to discredit Jesus in some way. They tried to create a Mexican standoff; where both parties had something to lose and labored to get some "dirt" on Jesus in hopes of keeping their "game" going. This was obvious in the challenges they made to His actions and teaching, but when all else failed, they decided to destroy Him in an effort to make their sin vanish. Others have tried to hide in a crowd or mock and deny reality, and there are those who feel their own goodness is enough to mostly merit their way. After all, shouldn't there be a special credit for those who don't need as great of an investment of God's grace as others?

In Luke 7:36-50, Jesus and his disciples were invited to the home of Simon the Pharisee. He was a man who wanted to follow Jesus and had every reason to believe that his life of disciplined righteousness put him well ahead of most others on that road. While he appeared ready to accept his imperfections, he saw his service more as a contract, than of surrender to Jesus. During the meal, a sinful woman entered, washed Jesus's feet with her tears and wiped them with her hair. Simon was horrified by what he saw. Jesus responded with a parable about two debtors, one owing ten times what the other did; in this case, Simon and the sinful woman. When both were forgiven, Jesus asked which loved more. Simon rightly answered: it was the one who was forgiven the most. Jesus responded, "For this reason I say to you, her sins, which are many, are forgiven, for (thus) she loved much; but he who is forgiven little loves little" (Luke 7:47). Jesus was not advocating sin, but He was addressing a logical conclusion. Those who realize just how much Jesus has forgiven them are very often the most powerful witnesses.

This is exactly where the Gadarene demoniac we talked about before was. He obeyed Jesus's command to tell his family and friends what God had done for him. Later, when Jesus returned to the region (Matthew 15:32-39), He fed a crowd of four thousand plus families. More than anything else, this man's witness caused this crowd. These are the kind of servants God delights in. It is not a sin to feel unworthy, instead, this should make us realize that it is God who forgives, equips, transforms, and empowers us.

In God we are winners, His is the winning team no matter what, even if our field, as Isaiah's did, only seems to offer more and more defeat. "But in all these things we overwhelmingly conquer through Him who loved us" (Romans 8:37). God provides us His strength so we will never have to face it alone, nor should we even try to. We are not contractual equals with God, we are His servants: He is our righteousness and strength. When Mary was called to be the mother of God, her trust was in God, and thus, she replied to Gabriel: "Behold, (I am) the bond-slave of the Lord" (Luke 1:38). She had little idea of all the trials and pain that came with her calling, though she likely sensed the first one coming. This pregnancy almost cost her a marriage until the Lord intervened. She probably had no clue that her son would one day die on a cross for the sins of mankind.

Although, months later, she did hear the words of Simeon, "And a sword will pierce even your own soul" (Luke 2:35), the full effects may not have registered. Just as God promises to us, she was borne in His strength.

The weeping prophet, Jeremiah, was at times totally overcome by the weight of his ministry. The predicted decline and darkness that began with Isaiah met its finale with Jeremiah. He often spoke his mind to God about it. This passage is one: "O Lord, Thou hast deceived me, and I was deceived; Thou hast overcome me and prevailed. I have become a laughing stock all the day long; everyone mocks me" (Jeremiah 20:7). On more than one occasion, he vents, God rebukes, he repents, and his ministry continues. To his sorrow, though, his ministry continues through the ultimate destruction of Judah and Jerusalem and the Jewish deportation to Babylon. He surely cried out, "Why me Lord?"

God has extended His calling to every personality type, as well. Elijah was a man with very few personal relationships. He was a "loner." He also was true to God in all of his callings. On Mount Carmel, he, by the hand of God, wrought a great victory over the false prophets and prophetesses of Baal and Asherah. He even had all the false prophets put to death by the very people whom they had deceived. Elijah, in his own mind, surely envisioned, right then and there, a national revival, beginning with the royal couple, Ahab and Jezebel. What happened next blew him away. Jezebel responded, "So may the gods do to me, and even more, if I do not make your life as the life of one of them [dead prophets] by tomorrow about this time" (I Kings 19:2). This also broke his spirit. For all the personal trauma the socially connected Jeremiah had endured, these words alone were enough to undo the lone wolf, Elijah. This totally unexpected defeat, and in short order, Post Traumatic Stress Disorder undid him. After he fled in fear, and wallowed in his brokenness at Mount Horeb (Sinai), God began the work of his healing.

If we are faithful, God will never cast us off. We are an asset, not a commodity, even in our infirmity and old age. God promises never to forsake those who are His. He didn't give up on Elijah, either, but commissioned him (I Kings 19:15-18). "Go return on your way to the wilderness of Damascus" (verse 15). God sent him this direction for his own mental health and feeling of safety. While he could never again be as fruitful as he once was, God still held him in His hand and His heart. God is the same today as He was then and does not love His children any less.

Some Christians today try to hide behind past injuries or claim inability to be of service out of feelings of personal inadequacy. In this, they are either forgetting, or denying the source of their strength. Moses did the same. In his initial response to God, He asked, "Who am I?" or "Why me?" God assured him, as He does us, of His presence. In fairness to Moses, we, today, have the benefit of the complete Bible. Moses had very little. It's doubtful in his flight that he took any written record the Israelites may have had of God's message up to that point. While his knowledge of God was limited, God chose him to fulfill His mission anyway. Knowledge is an essential part of a Christian's faith and witness (Ephesians 6:13-17), but faithful obedience is our most essential attribute.

Moses did ask one question in Exodus 3:13 we all should ask, as we spoke of earlier. "Who, God, are You?" (Exodus 3:13). There are many voices in this world. Most claim to represent God, and of these, a number of them do. Others outwardly appear, or make claims of being grounded in the truth, but are not. We need to establish, more than anything else in this present life, that we are serving God, and He is the one calling us to discipleship. One way to determine this is through earnest and fervent prayer. Listening to the Holy Spirit by searching the Scriptures to see if our calling lines up with His word is a must. God also has put a measure of this in our hearts, "But you have the anointing from the Holy One (Holy Spirit), and you all know (all things)" (I John 2:20). This is not listening to our heart; it is listening to God's. Ask, as well, the advice of at least one mature Christian who can be trusted for objective guidance. If God's heart is sought, He will be faithful. He will open any door He wills us to go through and will equip us for every good work. He will also overcome any scars or hang ups, weaknesses to follow the flesh, or sins to make us more fruitful, if we let Him.

Moses also wisely asked in Exodus 4:1, "What if they do not believe me?" Once again, God equipped Moses with all that he would need. He would have to contend with those who were spiritually empowered by the forces of darkness. Second Timothy 3:8 gives us the names of two of them, James and Jambres, who were able to duplicate several of the miracles that God worked through Moses. God's power to save is always greater than Satan's to deceive and destroy. "This is the finger of God" (Exodus 8:19), these men came to acknowledge. The Christian message is also backed by power and irrefutable proofs, as seen earlier. Our calling is made secure and our mission sure.

God answered Moses's fourth objection about his feelings of inability just as he will ours. He made us how He willed. We are His; He will enable and equip us to do His work. In Moses's case, He gave him a partner, Aaron. He also did this for Paul; this was something he needed as well (II Corinthians 2:12,13). God will, as He has promised, meet any need we have in effectively serving Jesus. He will not forsake us.

Moses' final objection is the one that usually holds us back as well, "Please, Lord, send the message by whomever [not me] Thou wilt" (Exodus 4:13). This made God angry. I remember a minister from my youth, Earl McCrea. He had a saying: "If we are not faithful, God will raise up someone who will be, but it won't be to our benefit." One of God's expectations for His people has always been that they be a light to the nations (Isaiah 42:1,6,7). When they refused, God raised up the nations and brought them to His people. Naaman, the Syrian general, Nebuchadnezzar and the Babylonians, Shalmaneser and the Assyrians, the Barbarians, and the Vikings all come to mind, and He also brought Antiochus Theos Epiphanes, whose very name claims to be God made manifest. In none of these cases was it pleasant for God's people. In fact, Antiochus desecrated their very Temple in 167 BC and tried to destroy them.

History records the ensuing Maccabean Revolt, which succeeded in defeating the far superior armies of Antiochus through divine deliverance. At this time also, a purifying fire swept through Palestine, bringing to a luke-warm Jewish people the fire of conviction and back to God with their hearts. What most historians overlook is how this affected the Greek world. Will Grant stated that "The Greeks were surprised to find the strength of the old faith; not for centuries had they seen such loyalty to an idea."[30] Not only did it create a reverent respect in many in that day, two centuries later, when the Gospel of Jesus entered their domains, a fear of God had preceded it.

If God intends to use us, and we remain faithful, He will find a way to reveal His glory. He will bring people into our world or move us to them. There is an old saying, "If the mountain won't come to Mohammad, Mohammad must go to the mountain," but as God brings this about in our lives, the question remains, what will our response be? Will we attempt to hide from God? Will we try to compromise in an effort to fit in and avoid

---

[30]  Will Durant, The Life of Greece, (New York City: Simon and Schuster, 1939), 583.

controversy? Will we dread being called fanatics or mentally ill more than we fear God? Will we "cop out," by claiming that no one can possibly know the truth or maybe Jesus is only one way of many? Do we fear family or friend, job, or the government, or do we love both them and God enough to shine for Him anyway?

Dietrich Bonhoeffer (1906-1945) was a leading German theologian and, in 1931, was a lecturer in Berlin. After the Nazis took power in Germany, March 5, 1933, he found himself quite unpopular with the government and left Germany for London, England. While his theology might be questioned, he was a faithful voice against the evils of Nazism. He was soon brought to realize his inability to influence Germany from abroad and returned in 1934. There, he helped to establish the Confessing Church. He also took leadership in an illegal seminary in Finkenwalde. In 1939, he left to visit America, but again, could not ignore God's calling him back to Germany, once more, to lead the spiritual opposition to Nazism.

In 1938, Hitler made an oath of allegiance the law in Germany. Bonhoeffer opposed it. Now an official law-breaker, he worked against the mistreatment of the Jews and other persecuted groups. He also opposed any spirit of compromise from within the church community in Germany with the Nazis. He was arrested in April of 1943 by the dreaded Gestapo, German secret police, and put into a concentration camp where he endured much abuse. Faithful to the end, the Nazis martyred him on April 9, 1945 at Buchenwald.

"And others experienced mockings and scourgings, yes, also chains and imprisonment. They were stoned, they were sawn in two, they were tempted, they were put to death with the sword; they went about in sheepskins, in goatskins, being destitute, afflicted, ill treated, men of whom the world was not worthy" (Hebrews 11:36-38). God is calling today to us, His Church, "I want you!" Are we willing to hear His call? Will we honor His Lordship and witness to His glory, even if it costs us all things here? Why me? Because He calls us. Are we willing to say with all of our hearts, "I surrender all?" This is the most important question we will ever be called upon to answer.

www.ingramcontent.com/pod-product-compliance
Lightning Source LLC
Chambersburg PA
CBHW022050020426
42335CB00012B/630